CHARLEVOIX

TWO CENTURIES AT
MURRAY BAY

CHARLEVOIX

TWO CENTURIES AT
MURRAY BAY

PHILIPPE DUBÉ

in collaboration with the photographer
Jacques Blouin

Preface by
Timothy Porteous

Translated by
Tony Martin-Sperry

McGill-Queen's University Press
Kingston & Montreal • London • Buffalo

© McGill-Queen's University Press 1990
ISBN 0-7735-0726-4
Legal deposit first quarter 1990
Bibliothèque nationale du Québec

Printed in Canada on acid-free paper

This book is a translation of *Deux cent ans de villégiature dans Charlevoix :
L'Histoire du pays visité*, © Les Presses de l'Université Laval 1986. Translation
and publication have been assisted by grants from the Canada Council.

Canadian Cataloguing in Publication Data

Dubé, Philippe, 1949-
    Summer resort life
    Translation of: Deux cent ans de villégiature dans
    Charlevoix.
    Bibliography: p.
    ISBN 0-7735-0726-4
    1. Summer resorts — Quebec (Province) — Charlevoix
    Region — History — 19th century.   2. Charlevoix Region
    (Quebec) — History.   3. Architecture, Domestic — Quebec
    (Province) — Charlevoix Region.   I. Blouin, Jacques
    II. Title.
    FC2945.C45D8213 1989   971.4'4903   C89-090214-3
    F1054.C445D8213 1989

Designed by Dan O'Leary

Jacket illustration

"Murray Bay," by Charles Jones Way,
Musée régional Laure-Conan
(La Malbaie), on permanent loan from
The Historical Society of Lake St Louis

A LITTLE volume about
La Malbaie that needed
writing, a little volume on
rose-tinted silk paper, where
the smell of seaweed lies
mingled with the perfume of
heliotrope — one of those little
volumes that are found in
scented boudoirs, or that girls
carry with them when they
walk along the seashore,
the long shadows of their
eyelashes fluttering in time
with the swaying of the
young tree branches or the
sleepy harmonies of the rising
wave.

Arthur Buies,
Chroniques canadiennes,
humeurs et caprices

Contents

Preface

I WELCOME THE ENGLISH EDITION of Philippe Dubé's fascinating history of Murray Bay. Since its first publication in French, it has been one of my favourite books. As one who spent many happy summers of childhood and adolescence in Charlevoix, it offers me the twin pleasures of nostalgia and discovery.

M. Dubé has adopted a novel approach. "I chose to concentrate on the tourist. No longer was my gaze to be directed at the customary object of ethnography; the local, abandoning his passive role as the object of attention, would now be studying the outsider."

It is a bit disconcerting, at first, to discover that one has become an object of scholarly research, like a Bronze Age Minoan or a head-hunter from Papua New Guinea. It may be partly a question of terminology. In his original text the author writes of *villégiateurs*, an elegant term for which there is no exact equivalent in English. "Tourist" or "visitor" sound too transient; "stranger" or "outsider" too detached. *Résidents d'été*, often foreshortened to *rés d'été*, was what we called ourselves, and we carried the title with pride and affection.

So many aspects of this beautiful and beloved region are described in these pages. A single paragraph or photograph can call up an almost endless string of memories. Photograph no. 95, for instance, shows Leo Romanelli and his band posing rather awkwardly beside the pool at the Manoir Richelieu. Seated in the foreground I recognize the beauteous Madeleine Garneau and Sue Dunton, modelling the latest in provocative one-piece swimsuits. (In those days "Bikini" was an unknown atoll in the South Pacific, and there were signs on the main street of Pointe-au-Pic which warned: DEFENSE DE CIRCULER EN SHORTS.) Just looking at the photo brings back those sun-baked mornings of my teens with the band playing "I'll be seeing you in all those old, familiar places" or "I'll get by as long as I have you." Those songs, those swim-suits ... that was the stuff of adolescent fantasy in the 40s! Meanwhile, my trusty CCM bike was waiting to carry me along the dusty Boulevard to a lunch of smelts freshly caught off the wharf, and blueberries freshly picked in the hills ...

Readers already familiar with Murray Bay and those discovering it for the first time will find a treasury of information on the history of the region, the hotels, the Saguenay steamships, and the great families which gave the resort its unique character. But pride of place is rightly given to architecture, the "mother of the arts," and to the "villas on the cliff," those outstanding survivors of the golden era.

Not the least of this book's virtues is to document the career of Charles Warren, from the Minturn house in 1895 to the Dawes house in 1925, and to establish his pre-eminence as a builder of summer homes. Before this book was published I doubt if many people, even among those fortunate enough to have lived in his houses, were aware of the full extent of his remarkable achievements.

The work of other architects, both Canadian and American, is also carefully analysed in a text enriched with personal anecdotes. Who would have guessed that the stately *Mur Blanc* was created from a sketch which William Adams Delano included in a bread-and-butter letter?

A whole spectrum of architectural influences – beaux-arts, colonial, French, Flemish, Dutch, even Japanese – are identified and evaluated. Despite such eclecticism, the overriding impression of those who have frequented these houses is of their harmonious relationship to their surroundings and to each other, a harmony arising from the common use of local materials and craftsmanship, and the shared tastes and values of the builders and occupants.

The exploration of these shared values gives an extra dimension to Philippe Dubé's work. "The self awareness of a region is formed in part by the visitor from outside," he writes, and the reverse is also true. Coming to Murray Bay from our very different worlds, the *rés d'été* were profoundly and permanently affected by the experience. To cite but one example, the folk songs of Québec became our own most familiar and most cherished songs.

No evening gathering, indoors or outdoors, was complete without traditional music. Sometimes the singing was led by three generations of the Villeneuve family, sometimes by the erudite and entertaining "Hozzy" Taft, who was equally at home in the repertoires of French Canada and the American West. *A la claire fontaine* is one of the oldest and loveliest of these songs. Its chorus, addressed to a long-lost mistress, may serve to express the passionate attachment of the summer residents to their seasonal home, a sentiment so vividly evoked by this delightful book.

> *Il y a longtemps que je t'aime,*
> *jamais je ne t'oublierai.*

Timothy Porteous
November, 1989

Acknowledgments

It is difficult to mention all those who have contributed directly or indirectly to the unveiling of this page of history. There is a long list of public organizations — libraries, archives, and museums — that have made the work possible; but my warmest thanks go to those who have shown interest in and enthusiasm for the subject.

I am indebted to a certain number of people who have directly assisted me in the organization and interpretation of material and in preparing the final version. The idea of researching summer-resort life in Charlevoix came from François Tremblay, ex-director of the Musée régional Laure-Conan at La Malbaie. In putting the finishing touches to the text, Lise Bellavance was a great help; without her, this task would not have been so rewarding. Nor must I forget to mention the warm support of Jean-Claude Dupont and the well-advised direction of Luc Noppen during the research stage at Université Laval. As for the architectural sketches, Jean-Claude Carbonneau, Pierre Delisle, Alexis Morgan, and Simon Drolet have produced flawless and accurate drawings. Madame Naphile Girard, my landlady at Pointe-au-Pic, used her natural eloquence to describe certain aspects of the history of the region's inhabitants. I should also like to mention the affectionate support of Fabienne Fournier, my wife, throughout this lengthy task, for which I shall always be grateful.

I must not overlook those who were interested in the history of Charlevoix before me and who made their manuscripts available to me: Esther W. Kerry, Helen Macmillan, Katherine Mackenzie, Erskine Buchanan, Brian Buchanan, Thomas Hoopes, Roger Lemoine, Patrick Morgan, Louis R. Pelletier, and Murray Warren. Without their cooperation, I could never have covered such a vast field of study. I would also like to mention the generous contribution of Francis H. Cabot, who brought not only his knowledge of language but his intelligent sensibility to his revisions of the English version of the text. Finally, I would like to thank collectively all those named below, who gave technical assistance or simply lent me their family records, of which I hope I have made good use. May this book serve as a record of my very sincere gratitude.

Mr and Mrs A.S. Adair
Mme Danielle Amyot
Mme Louis-Joseph Adjutor Amyot
M. Simon Archambault
Mrs C.H.A. Armstrong
Mr and Mrs Christopher Armstrong
Mme Adjutor Asselin
M. le Sénateur et Mme Martial Asselin
Mrs Barbara Atkinson
M. Percy Auger
Mrs Elizabeth Bacque
Mr and Mrs Warren Baker
Mrs A. Sharples Baldwin
Canon and Mrs F. Sydney Bancroft
Mr and Mrs Harding F. Bancroft
Mme Marie-Andrée Bastien
Mr and Mrs J. Wallace Beaton
M. et Mme Claude P. Beaubien
Mme Danielle Belley
Mme Louise F. Belley
M. et Mme Richard Belley
Mr and Mrs Gordon Bensley
M. et Mme Jean Bergeron
M. Nazaire Bergeron
Mrs Richard E. Berlin
Mme Ginette Bernatchez
M. Jean-Claude Bernier
M. Jean-Paul Bernier
M. Paul Bernier
M. et Mme J.H.R. Bertrand
M. et Mme Wilbrod Bhérer
Mme Lisa Binsse
M. et Mme Jean-Paul Biron
M. Michel Biron
Miss Eileen Bishop
M. et Mme W.A. Blackburn
Mr John D. Blackwell
Mr Patrick Blake
Mr John Bland
M. et Mme Jules Blouin
Me Raymond Boily
M. Louis Bolduc
Mr Bruce Bolton
M. Clément-Joseph Bouchard
Mme Hermine Bouchard
Mme Johanne Bouchard
M. Laurent Bouchard
M. Alain Boucher
Mme Hendrika Boucher
Mme Diane Boulianne
M. Ronald Bourgeois
Mr and Mrs John G. Bourne
M. et Mme Pierre Boutin

M. Roger Brière
Mme Charlotte Brisson
Mr Ian E. Buchanan
M. Luc Bureau
Mrs Donald F. Bush
Mr and Mrs Francis H. Cabot
M. et Mme E. Caire
Mrs Christina Cameron
Mme Fernande K. Cantero
Mme Thérèse Casgrain
M. Victor Cayer
Mrs Elisabeth Chamard
Mr John Chamard
Mrs Peggie Chamard
Mr and Mrs William M. Chamard
Mme Christiane Charette
M. René Chartrand
M. et Mme Jean Chenevert
Mme Marthe Chercuitte
Mrs Zena Cherry
Miss Frances S. Childs
Mr and Mrs Brock F. Clarke
Mme Nathalie Clerk
Dr and Mrs A.M. Cloutier
Rev. and Mrs Tennesse Cogan
Mr John N. Cole
M. Bruno Côté
M. Bernard Couet
M. Luc Courchesne
Mme Yvette Cousineau
M. Paul Couturier
Miss Louise Crane
Mrs Luella Creighton
Mrs A.F. Culver
Mr Robert H. Cundill
Mrs Katharine G. Currier
M. Pierre Danjou
M. Réal Danjou
M. J. Darbelnet
M. Roger D'Astous
Mrs A.S. Dawes
Mme Thérèse Gouin Décarie
Mme Zita De Koninck
Mr and Mrs John B. Dempsey II
M. J.-Raymond Denault
M. et Mme Paul Desmarais
M. Paul Desmarais jr.
M. et Mme Paul Desmeules
M. Léopold Désy
M. et Mme Pierre Désy
M. Robert Noël De Tilly
Mme Jacqueline Dion
M. et Mme Thomas Donohue

Mr and Mrs Bud Donovan
Mme Doreen Warren Doucet
M. Michel Doyon
Mme Jeannine Dubé
Dr et Mme V.A. Dubé
Mme Corinne Du Berger
M. Jean Duberger
M. et Mme Julien Dufour
M. et Mme Henri-Paul Dufour
M. et Mme Rémy Dufour
Mr Alastair Duncan
Dr Jean-Luc Dupuis
M. et Mme Marcel Dupuis
M. et Mme Joachim Duque
Mr and Mrs F. Victor Elkin
Mr Hamilton Fish 3rd
Mme Lucie Forget
M. Benoît G. Fortier, ptre
Mme Margot Fortier
M. et Mme Georges Fournier
M. et Mme Roger Fournier
M. Alain Franck
Mme Colette Fraser
M. et Mme Roland Gagné
Mme Claire Wells Gagnon
M. Jean Gagnon
M. Melvin Gallant
Col. Strome Galloway
Mme Line Gaudreault
Mme Manon Gaudreault
Mme Thérèse Gaudry
Miss Frances H. Gault
Mr and Mrs Leslie H. Gault
Mme Raymonde Gauthier
M. Yvan Gauthier
M. et Mme André Gervais
Mme Alphonse Giguère
Mme Lorenzo Gilbert
Mr and Mrs A.R. Gillespie
M. Maurice Girard, ptre
Mme Pauline E. Goosens
Mr Conrad Graham
Mrs John Graham
Mrs Christine Grant
Mrs Betty Guernsey
Mrs Nora Haig
Mrs Richard W. Hale
Mrs Donald T. Hall
Mr and Mrs Virginius C. Hall jr.
M. Germain Halley
Mr Lawrence A. Halsey
M. Jean Hamelin
Col. J. Ralph Harper

Mrs E.C. Harrington
Mr Robert M. Harrold
M. et Mme Bertrand Harvey
M. et Mme Guy Harvey
Mme J.-Édouard Harvey
M. et Mme Lucien Harvey
Mrs Mary M. Harvey
Mme Pierrette N. Harvey
Dr and Mme Gilles Hébert
Mme Sylvie Hébert
Mr and Mrs Ian Y. Henderson
M. Gilles Héon
Mrs Carlos Hepp
Mr Charles Hill
Mr Robert G. Hill
Mr and Mrs David M. Hoopes
Mr and Mrs Thomas C. Hoopes
Mr and Mrs E.P. Hudek
Mr and Mrs Frank J. Humphrey
Mr Peter B. Humphrey
Mrs Sarah Humphrey
Mrs Holland Hunter
M. Paul Hunter
Mme Véronique Hippolyte
M. René Jean
Mr and Mrs William J. Jovanovitch
Mme Patricia Kennedy
Miss Sybil Kennedy
Mr Richard D. Kernan
Miss Eileen F. Kerr
Mr Colin W. Kerry
Mr Leonard L. Knott
Mr and Mrs George A. Kyle
Mme Josée Labossière
M. Pierre Lahoud
M. Jean C. Lallemant
Mr and Mrs J. Lambros
M. Yvan Lamonde
Mr and Mrs Theodore Lande
M. Pierre Landry
M. Marc Laplante
M. David Lapointe
M. et Mme Jean Lapointe
M. Georges Gauthier Larouche
Mme Ginette Lavoie
M. et Mme Fernand Lebeau
M. Marc Lebel
M. Jean-Pierre Leblanc
Mme Denise Leclerc
Mrs A.W. Lederer
Mme J.-Thérèse Legendre
M. Robert Lemire
M. Claude Lemoine

M. Georges-P. Léonidoff
M. et Mme Guy Lépine
M. Pierre Lépine
Mme Berthe Lesage
M. et Mme Charles Letarte
Mr Jeff Limerick
Mme Sharon Little
Mr and Mrs John J. Livingood
Mme Thérèse Fraser Lizotte
Capt. G.D. Lodge
Rev. and Mrs Donald B. Mackay
Mrs Margery Mackenzie
Mr and Mrs Philip Mackenzie
Mrs Charles W. Macmullen
Mr Kenneth R. Macpherson
Mr and Mrs George A. Main
M. Philippe Maltais
Mrs Helen Taft Manning
M. Raymond Marcoux
M. et Mme Paul-Louis Martin
Mrs Lucy B. Martyn
M. Claude Masson
Mme Jeanine Masson
Mrs Margaret McBurney
Mrs Raymond McGrath
Mr and Mrs John McGreevy
Mrs Edwin McMillan
Mr Newton P.S. Merrill
Mrs Pamela J. Miller
Mrs Robert B. Minturn
Mr Herbert Mitchell
Mrs J. Kearsley Mitchell
M. Guy St-A. Mongenais
M. Raymond Montpetit
M. André Morency
Mrs Maud Morgan
Dr and Mrs Sean B. Murphy
Mrs Sally McGuire Muspratt
Mme Claire Nadeau
Mrs W.B. Nash
Mrs Mary B. Naylor
Mrs A.E. Neergard
Me Roger Néron
Mrs Clinton Neville
Mrs Diana T. Nicholson
M. Jean-Marc Nicole
Mme Colette O'Donnell
Mme Joanne O'Donnell
Mr and Mrs F.R.L. Osborne
Mr Winchester Page
Mme Lucien Parent
Miss Janet Parks
Mr and Mrs Alex K. Paterson

Mrs Hartland M. Paterson
Dr et Mme Laurent Patry
Mr and Mrs Gibson H. Peck
M. et Mme Louis R. Pelletier
M. et Mme Burroughs Pelletier
Mr Charles Phillips
M. Jacques Plante
Mr Timothy Porteous
Mme Elaine Post
M. Claude Poulin
Mr and Mrs Irwin A. Powell
Mme France Gagnon-Pratte
M. Jean Primeau, ptre
M. et Mme Louis Riverin
Mr James Hampden Robb
Mr and Mrs P.H. Robb
M. Roger Roche
M. et Mme Charles-Eugène Rochette
Mme Isabelle Rochette
Mme Aline Rolland
M. et Mme Lucien G. Rolland
Mme Madeleine Rolland
Mme Jacqueline B. Ross
Mme Ruth H. Ross
Maj.-Gen. Roger Rowley
Mme Jacqueline Roy
Mr and Mrs Fortune Peter Ryan
Rev. Lyle Sams
M. Napoléon Savard
Mr and Mrs Reeve Schley III
M. Robert-Guy Scully
Mr Vincent J. Scully
M. Patrick Séguin
M. et Mme Pierre Sévigny
Miss Wendy Shadwell
Mrs C.N. Shanley
Mr and Mrs A.C. Shennett
M. Jean Simard
Mme Paul M.A. Simard
Dr and Mrs Hervey I. Sloane
M. Marcel Soucy
Dr. Max Stern
Mr and Mrs David M. Stewart
Mr Lynn Stewart
Mr Charles P. Taft
Mr and Mrs Horace Taft
Mr Lloyd B. Taft
Mme Louise Piller-Tahy
M. et Mme René Therrien
M. Claude Thibault
M. Laurent Thibault
Mrs Jessie Thomas
Rev. Leo Timmins

Mrs Graham F. Towers
Mme Angéline T. Tremblay
M. et Mme Antonio Tremblay
M. Ferdinand Tremblay
M. et Mme Gabriel Tremblay
Dr et Mme Georges-William Tremblay
M. et Mme Gérard Tremblay
M. et Mme Gualbert Tremblay
M. Henri Tremblay
M. et Mme Jean Tremblay
M. Réjean Tremblay
M. Yvan Tremblay
Mr Stanley G. Triggs
M. et Mme M.L. Turcotte
M. et Mme Jean Valade
M. et Mme Guy Van Duyse
Mme Luce Vermette
M. et Mme Alfred Villeneuve
Mme Aliette Villeneuve
M. et Mme Ernest Villeneuve
M. et Mme Jacques Villeneuve

Mme Lucie Villeneuve
Mme Sylvie Forcier Villeneuve
M. et Mme Auguste Vincent
Me Benoît Warren
Mrs Catherine Warren
Me Gilles Warren
Mme Henriette Warren
M. et Mme Jean De Roussel Warren
Dr et Mme John Warren
M. Laurent Warren
M. et Mme Louis Warren
M. et Mme Pierre Warren
M. et Mme Roger Warren
M. et Mme Walter Warren
Mme Madeleine Wheare
Mr George H. Wilkie
Mr Richard G. Wilson
Miss Marian Wright
Mrs Nancy Wright
M. et Mme William G. Yonkers

Introduction

CHARLEVOIX sits on the north shore of the St Lawrence River in a fertile valley first colonized by the merchants of Québec. Its early development under the French régime was sporadic, but in due course the commercial climate improved. In 1762 Messrs John Nairne and Malcolm Fraser, officers of the Regiment of Fraser Highlanders, began work on their respective properties of Murray Bay[1] and Mount Murray, granted by Governor James Murray. In their time the area was already renowned for its scenery and picturesque way of life, and visitors would come from countries as far off as Scotland to stay for several months. Ever since, Charlevoix has fascinated travellers and charmed summer vacationers searching for peace and quiet. The locals, for their part, have welcomed outsiders. For over two centuries, then, Charlevoix has been a meeting place for the rural culture of the French and the urban culture that is by tradition in Canada predominantly Anglo-Saxon. It is the cultural activity of tourism in Charlevoix that I will survey here,[2] from an ethno-historic perspective so that readers can best understand the remarkable story of this region.

For some two centuries Charlevoix has been idealized by its admirers, who have referred to it as the Eden of America, the Newport[3] of Canada, and more recently the Switzerland of Québec. There are certain aspects of its history that I should explain, though they may be familiar, for they are continually posing new questions to the attentive observer.

A study such as this must be well researched.[4] As the bibliography shows, there are many sources of information on the La Malbaie–Murray Bay area available to the public in Canada and the United States: manuscripts, printed works, illustrations, films, and photographs. I consulted a considerable number of documents: travel narratives, personal memoirs, brochures, and tourist books. As for primary sources, I paid particular attention to notarized deeds, property registrations, municipal, provincial, and federal archives, and private documents such as correspondence, family records, and guestbooks, which add a personal touch. Newspapers and magazines, guidebooks and yearbooks, helped me recreate the social context of each period covered and to observe several generations of vacationers from the vantage point of the press.[5] Most of these documents belong to collections in record offices, such as the Cabot, Blackburn, and Roland Gagné bequests to the Musée régional Laure-Conan, the Blake bequest to the archives of Ontario, the Wallace and Wrong bequests to the University of Toronto, and the Sedgwick bequest to the Massachusetts Historical Society of Boston. The collections come from families that have played a part in the development of Charlevoix as a summer resort. I also made personal inquiries, and these led to a wealth of invaluable oral information about the families of early summer residents. Finally, there are many illustrated documents. These trace the evolution of Charlevoix from rural countryside to a vacation spot for the privileged. For their valuable documentary content, I selected photographs, drawings, and maps that call to mind various aspects of summer vacationing from 1787 to the present. In all, there are more than fifteen hundred photographs, including some hundred postcards dating back to 1867, and nearly five hundred recent colour slides of the villas of Pointe-au-Pic and Cap-à-l'Aigle. Seventeen architectural plans and drawings provide technical and aesthetic information. Paintings, water-colours, and prints — mainly nineteen century — enrich the visual documentation, while geographical maps going back to 1794 permit us to date the stages of Charlevoix's development.

In general, the works inspired by Charlevoix cover regional and architectural history, economics, politics, ethnography, and geography. There is a marked absence of studies on tourism in the region, which is only of interest to a few geographers these days, despite many effusive comments on its potential as a tourist haven.[6]

Perhaps Québec historians have been put off by the seasonal nature of resort life, or by the visitors themselves, mostly foreigners, whose discreet comings and goings have failed to arouse their curiosity. In my research into the history of Charlevoix, I started with the work of George M. Wrong, professor of history at the University of Toronto, who brought to light the first century of the seigneury of Murray Bay under the evocative title *A Canadian Manor and Its Seigneurs: The Story of a Hundred Years, 1761–1861*. Professor Wrong spent more than twenty years vacationing at Murray Bay around the turn of the century. In his opinion, the arrival of Scottish seigneurs posed no real problems — despite the fact that one of the first, Colonel John Nairne, had plans to impose the language and religion of the conquerors on local land-owners. However, he soon came to understand how unreal this plan was when the Highlanders who had come with him began adopting French ways, chiefly as a result of marrying local women. The last chapter of Professor Wrong's book, "The Coming of the Pleasure Seekers," is useful for our own purposes, dealing as it does with the resort aspect of life in Murray Bay. The locals were interested in the visitors that came to the area and seemed anxious to interact with them. Yet he finds the *rapprochement* of the two peoples disquieting, a menace to the peace of traditional society in Charlevoix:

We who are among them in the summer are citizens of another and unknown world. New York and Chicago, Boston and Washington, Toronto and Montreal, are to us realities with one or other of which, in some way, each of us is linked. To this simple people they are all merely that outer world whence come their fleeting visitors of summer, as out of the unknown come the migrant birds to pause and rest awhile. We bring with us substantial benefits: but it is not clear that our moral influence is good.[7]

Adding to the picture of the old seigneurial families at La Malbaie is Burt Brown Barker's *The McLoughlin Empire and Its Rulers*.[8] This gives valuable though strictly descriptive information on the Fraser family, who shared with the Nairnes all the joys and the sorrows of this enchanting place. Elsewhere, Canon F.-X. Eugène Frenette, a native of La Malbaie, has produced a collection of articles written for history buffs under the modest title *Notes historiques sur la paroisse Saint-Étienne de La Malbaie*.[9] The collection is purely anecdotal; Roger Lemoine, professor of literature at the University of Ottawa, sketches in nine pages the chronology of events round which is woven the story of La Malbaie's tercentenary — without concealing, thank heavens, his love for his native town and its inhabitants.[10] In addition to these four works, there is one that has been of great help to me: France Gagnon-Pratte's *L'architecture et la nature à Québec au dix-neuvième siècle: les villas*. This study deals with the birth of resort living, when secondary residences began to appear outside the fortified walls of the town of Québec. Mme Gagnon-Pratte links the introduction of villas in the region of Québec to the romantic movement of the early nineteenth century, which favoured the return of close contact between one's habitat and nature: "Villas sprang from the wish to re-establish contact and balance between Architecture and Nature."[11] Her study retraces the origins of the very idea of summer resort life and explains how resorts, gradually losing sight of these origins, gave birth to the era of modern tourism.

My major preoccupation throughout this investigation has been to understand the personality, or rather the regional identity, of Charlevoix. As we will see, this has been shaped by the inhabitants' consciousness of their history. But first it seems essential to assess the progress made in my research. At the start, my aim was to use imagery to catch the local person as mythicized by the outsider. But influenced by research carried out at the Musée régional Laure-Conan at La Malbaie, I chose rather to concentrate on the tourist. Instead of hanging on his shoulder and noting the way he viewed the traditional Canadian, I took this stranger as my target and observed him as the principal actor in an activity, tourism, which had long been part of the life of Murray Bay. No longer was my gaze to be directed at the customary object of ethnography; the local, abandoning his passive role as the object of attention, would now be studying the outsider.

Such an approach may seem odd for someone researching a regional identity; but I believe it opens up some new perspectives on our cultural history. The first part of this book, by chronological compilation of travel reports, shows how the outsider sees the region. Travel notes and impressions are proof of the time-honoured practice of ethnography, often describing in detail the traditional society that clung stubbornly to this area in downstream Québec. The second part deals with an occupation quite new to North America—namely, summer resort life. Under its influence the work ethic relaxed and holidays became a social necessity. The third part tackles the architecture of summer resorts as evidence in space of this new life-style. It is essentially modern construction, reflecting the relationship the architect sought to establish with nature in such features as the panorama. Finally, we will see what sort of image emerges of Charlevoix after two hundred years of history. The study of the constant flow of visitors will paint a portrait of an area with a distinct regional consciousness.

After I had studied the history of summer resort life at Charlevoix and collated my research in a casual sketch for the traveling exhibition titled *Deux cents ans de villégiature dans Charlevoix/Summer Resort Life: Two Centuries at Murray Bay*, it seemed essential to study the subject in more depth with the help of historical ethnology, that is, developing a picture of everyday life through an all-inclusive presentation of summer holidays in Charlevoix.[12] This study is based on an empirical method in which numerous descriptions are supplemented by historical documents. My approach had to be one of synthesis, in order to capture the various aspects of an elusive reality. Historical ethnology was a useful tool for investigating the phenomenon of resort life at Charlevoix: history allowed me to determine its extent, ethnology to measure its depth.

Advances in historical ethnology, which is interested principally in traditional culture, have given the social historian an invaluable tool for studying rural society. But because ethnology is still young, some uncertainties of definition and method are unavoidable. In Québec, the first task of this discipline was to study traditional society from several points of view—literary and linguistic, geographical and historical. Thus, from the very start, it had the look of a "crossroads discipline."[13] However, a science must be defined not merely by the material it studies—in this case, popular arts and traditions—but also by the way in which it treats that material. Ethnology stresses direct contact with reality, by experience in the field, as the best approach to its material. It touches on folklore and "archeo-civilization,"[14] which study the traces of traditional culture in a socially advanced society; but some writers, such as Jean Poirier, have come to define it as the study of socially restricted groups: villages, parishes, associations, families, and so forth.[15]

Without labouring the point, my interest was to find out how ethnology could help me in this study. As mentioned above, this work called at the start for experience in the field—that is, direct observation, interviews, investigation, collection of documents and firsthand evidence, objects, photographs, films, and sound recordings. Next came the task of pulling

1 *The Old Bread Oven, Murray Bay, lower St Lawrence* A nice example of the sort of postcard in circulation in the 1930s, which idealized the life of the habitant. The old man with the wooden leg is taking a few moments' rest in front of a bread oven, chewing a blade of grass. This is the habitant glorified, the way the outsider liked to see him, inoffensive and somehow reassuring.

the material into shape, classifying it, and describing it. This type of approach is the appropriate one for ethnography, an eminently concrete discipline in direct contact with social reality. It is as difficult to trace a clear-cut frontier between ethnography and ethnology as to trace one between ethnology and history. Starting with data from ancient documents, historical ethnology uses thematic logic to reconstruct into a chronological whole all the information it has on a given group, or a particular aspect of its culture, observed in the field. This was what led me to go beyond my first approach and use the memoirs of the earliest families in Charlevoix, both summer residents and local inhabitants: these concrete documents gave me a feel for the period. And the interviews offered me a sort of portrait of the time with many details about the tastes and behaviour of those early summer residents.

My research focused especially on the bourgeoisie coming to the countryside from the towns and bringing with them the values of industrial society. However, my attempt to understand this "civilization," as is our wont in ethnology, was only a partial success.[16] Does this imply that the means of investigation available to ethnology are insufficient for the study of a dominant society? Dare one risk the conclusion that ethnology is the science *par excellence* of the dominated, as opposed to certain social sciences that are identified with power? I did not go so far as that; but all the same I felt I had to abandon an overly rigorous examination of habits and customs to which my normal working practice confined me.

Thus it was that I came to broaden my study of the region. The seasonal visits of hundreds of families to Murray Bay have literally transformed the neighbourhood. I still find it surprising that for more than a century the area was the meeting place for the leading families of northeastern North America — the Blakes, the Cabots, the Tafts, the Fitzpatricks, the Taschereaus, the Gouins — and that, contrary to expectation, this fact should have remained unknown. And yet this past, not so very distant, still lives in the architecture and in the memory of the good folk of Charlevoix. And so I will begin this study by referring to the model of the descriptive monograph. Ethnology's emphasis on immediate experience of the world is on a par with a particular type of looking and listening: it calls for understanding rather than explanation.[17] Hence I will attempt to tell the story of everyday life in Charlevoix.

I have not yet mentioned the interesting effect that the mixing of cultures had. By helping people understand each other, summer resort life smoothed out some of their differences. It put hasty generalizations to the test, the thereby developed a sense of openness and tolerance. Some people, like an assistant parish priest in 1910, concluded that experience of the outside world was harmful:

> The people of La Malbaie are slowly being induced to imitate their visitors, tourists who come from all parts of Canada and even the United States. Please God let them resist! La Malbaie is beautiful, and will remain so as

long as it itself remains the fine parish of peace and tranquillity, where truly Canadian families live, wearing Canadian costume, speaking the pure language of the country, and keeping the faith and observances of our blessed religion.[18]

Others regarded mixing as individual and collective enrichment. One thing is certain, Charlevoix has so charmed its visitors that they are unanimous in their praise. In this study I have tried to go beyond common opinion, as others have done before me. James Macpherson Lemoine, nineteenth-century man of science and letters, used a touch of irony and fantasy when he sought to pierce the veil of mystery surrounding Charlevoix:

> As long as the season lasts, the "foreigners" seem almost to have taken La Malbaie over, to the exclusion of the "locals." In the next century, the tourists will talk of the former inhabitants, the descendants of the Fraser Highlanders, as an extinct race; and scholars will perhaps try to trace their complex genealogy, lost in the mists of time, back to the Picts or the Lapplanders. There will be only one throw-back which will flourish long-lived till the end of time: the tribe of carters, a race corrupted by its extortions and its Homeric thirst for spirits. Who knows but what some scholar in the next century, in summer residence at La Malbaie, may not try to apply Darwin's "Theory of Species" to them; and give a scientific explanation for an old tradition, which has it that the first carter of the North Shore was the offspring of a Lapp woman and a porpoise in the time of Erik the Red, a monarch of renown among that clan?[19]

Despite the forebodings of this worthy scholar, long contact with the outside world has not resulted in the extinction of the race, as was feared; and against all expectation, the meeting between cultures has helped form the personality of Charlevoix. A great number of the local inhabitants have had their vision of the world enlarged by contact with visitors; nor must it be underestimated what they, in their turn, have given the summer residents. Their influence has been deep and long-lasting and goes further than merely having instilled in these latter a sense of well-being and *joie de vivre*. Think of the effect Charlevoix's culture has had on Canadian cuisine, architecture, the visual arts, literature—and, of course, ethnology. More-over, traditional ethnography, which came to the assistance of Quebecers in a recent "crisis of identity," was found, astonishingly, to have its roots in visitors' sketch-books and in diaries kept by the never-ending stream of travellers on the north shore of the St Lawrence.

This discipline grew as the people of New France played an increasing part in the major events of America's early days. As I tell the story of summer residence in Charlevoix, I try to show that the self-awareness of a region is formed in part by the visitor from outside. Wise folk of Charlevoix should be on the lookout for the pitfalls inherent in such a phenomenon. It is up to them, if they wish to avoid playing the moribund role of "quaint folk," to create a personality that knowledge of their history will supply to them. Otherwise, their identity will have no meaning,[20] and will neither inspire continuity nor ensure permanence.

CHARLEVOIX

A COUNTRY

2 *Philippe Gaultier de Comporté at Malbaie, New France, 1672* "Grand provost of our seigneurs, the marshals of France, in this land," Gaultier de Comporté was by all accounts the chief seigneur in La Malbaie. Forty-six seigneuries were granted in 1672, in accordance with Administrator Talon's plans for the reorganization of the colony's development.

The Land of Landscapes

T HE SCENERY OF CHARLEVOIX, from Cape Tourmente to Tadoussac, has no equal. It brings together the wonderful Laurentian Mountains, all bowed with age, and the beautiful St Lawrence which, below Québec, becomes salty and takes on the face of the sea — majestic as it rises, stately as it falls in rhythm with the tides.

THE DISCOVERERS

Each of the first Europeans to sail to the foot of the Laurentians made some admiring remark about them. First came Jacques Cartier, who explored the St Lawrence valley on his second voyage in search of a road to the silk and spices of the Orient. His descriptions upon discovering the Saguenay River were general, but they became more specific as he continued his voyage and encountered one surprise after another. Here is his succinct narrative of Friday, 3 September 1535:

> Next morning, we made sail and got under way to move on; and we became aware of a kind of fish, which no man can remember having seen or heard of before. The said fish are as big as cod, without any fin, and their head and body are made near enough after the fashion of a greyhound, as white as snow, without any blemish; and there are a very great number of them in the said river, which live between the sea and the fresh water. The people of the country call them "adhothuys" and they told us they were very good to eat; and they also informed us there were none in the said river, nor anywhere in the land, save only in that place.[1]

The place mentioned by our explorer, where these "fish" — now known as beluga whales — were to be found, is none other than the waters that lap the steep bank of Charlevoix. At this point in the great river, fishing for belugas was an important activity on both banks. Some three-quarters of a century later, when France was resolved to take possession of a new territory in the king's name, Champlain sailed upstream and passed Tadoussac. He described the countryside as follows: "From there, we reached another cape which we named Cap à l'Aigle, distant 8 leagues from Cap Dauphin.[†] Between the two lies a large cove, at the bottom of which is a little stream which dries up at low tide; we called it "the flat river," or *malle baye*."[††][2]

Needless to say, the geography of this region did not offer the welcoming natural harbours sailors were anxiously seeking. Unable to anchor at La Malbaie, the father of New France gave it the name that best described it. Thus the region first became known by its physical features.

THE SEIGNEURY OF LA MALBAYE[3]

At the start, New France developed in spurts, for reinforcements to swell the ranks of pioneers came only slowly. The colonist who came from the Perche, the Vendée, or Normandy undertook a merciless struggle to establish a way of life modeled in many respects on the one he had followed in his homeland. While Amerinds lived close to nature, the newly arrived Europeans wore themselves out trying to take root on a continent they found hostile at the outset.

Among their number was Jean Bourdon, surveyor-general of New France. In 1653, as a reward for services rendered, Governor Jean de Lauson granted him a property in the name of the Company of a Hundred Associates, founded in April 1627 by Cardinal Richelieu. The estate, which consisted of "a stretch of land on the great St Lawrence river from Cap-aux-Oies to a point ten arpents below the river of La Malbaye, for a depth of four leagues inland,"[4] became known as the seigneury of La Malbaye.

Appointed the king's procurator-general in the Council of State, and holding several other posts, Bourdon neglected the estate and failed to settle colonists there for agricultural development. The king therefore resumed his rights over it, and it was not until 1672 that Administrator Talon granted it to Philippe Gaultier de Comporté.[5] Originally from the neighbourhood of Poitiers, de Comporté had arrived in Québec in 1665, at the age of twenty-four, with the firm intention of settling there. He succeeded very well; when he married Marie Bazire, shortly after being granted the seigneury of La Malbaie, he already held another seigneury on the south shore—a magnificent mansion on rue Nôtre-Dame in Québec City—and a shop, which seemed to bring in a good income. Eleven children were born of this marriage, none of whom lived in the seigneury. In 1687 de Comporté found himself short of equipment for working his distant property, and sold two-thirds of it to François Hazeur and the latter's father-in-law, Pierre Soumande.[6] A few months later he died unexpectedly; consequently, the provost of Québec awarded the final third of the property to the two majority owners, after distraint of the deceased's holdings.

---

†The league measures 4.99 kilometres.

††*Malle baye* here means *mauvaise baie* ("bad bay") in accordance with the meaning of *malle* at the time. Champlain did not like the shallow anchorage at La Malbaie.

After 1688, then, Hazeur and Soumande, both Québec merchants, shared ownership of the seigneury. The new proprietors found a thick forest on it with such a variety of trees that they were prompted to export wood to France, in partnership with Jean Grignon, a merchant in La Rochelle. In fact, French ports counted on the resources of the new colony to provide them with materials necessary for naval construction, especially masts; and thus La Malbaie became the main centre of the lumber industry in Canada. Unfortunately, inadequate transport and poor economic conditions made it difficult to establish a profitable export business. From 1692, the seigneury showed such heavy losses that the two businessmen had to abandon the lumber industry and turn to other ventures, such as beluga fishing off Rivière-Ouelle and Kamouraska, and fur trading at Tadoussac, which would earn them more immediate profits.

François Hazeur had become one of the most enterprising merchants of his day when he died in Québec in 1708, and was greatly missed by his fellow citizens. None of his heirs was interested in taking over the seigneury, which was probably not very profitable. Its upkeep continued to be handled by tenant farmers, as evidenced by a contract signed between the seigneur and his sharecropper Jean-Baptiste Côté, who was to have "the care and

3 *Map of The Estate in Canada, dedicated to the dauphin* This hand-drawn document, done by the Jesuit Pierre-Michel Laure at Chicoutimi on 23 August 1751, was both an explorer's map and a plan of the lines of communication, showing the watercourses and the portages that lay between various posts.

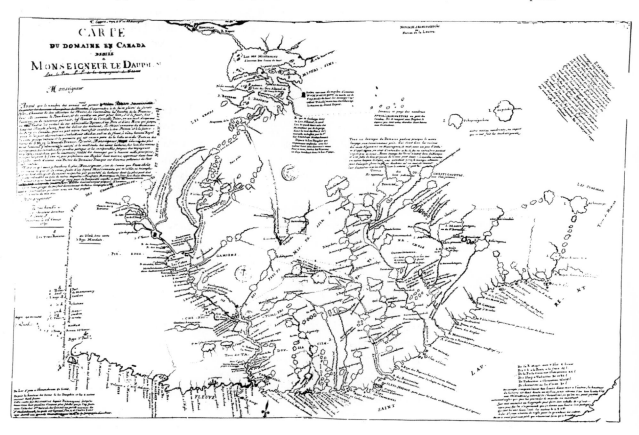

conduct of all works which the said Sieur Hazeur may judge appropriate
to be done, such as the sawmills, clearing and cultivation of land, care of
animals, and all other works of any sort whatsoever, and also fishing for
salmon for the use and service of the household of the said Sieur Hazeur
in the said location of La Malbaye."[7]

Thierry, François Hazeur's eldest son, and his brother Pierre, both
canons, finally sold the estate and outbuildings to the king in 1724.[8] Before
proceeding with the purchase, Administrator Bégon, acting in the king's
name, ordered an inventory of the land, buildings, barns, stables, gardens,
corn mill, and sawmill.[9] La Malbaie later became part of the great Western
Estate, also known as the King's Estate, reserved exclusively for fur trading.

A FARM ON THE WESTERN ESTATE

From 1724 on, La Malbaie provided meat and grain to the trading posts
of the Western Estate. François-Étienne Cugnet, administrator of the
estate, saw that it was sufficiently prosperous as a farm to provision the
more northerly posts of Tadoussac, Îlets-Jérémie, Rivière-Moisie, Chicoutimi, and Métabetchouan.[10] Colonization of this immense territory was
forbidden, and the state made sure that the fur trade would prosper there.
The natives—the Montagnais, the Papinachois, and the Mistassins—
seemed like savages to whites; but this did not stop the apostolic zeal of
missionaries such as the Jesuits.[11] La Malbaie, as the provisioning centre,
saw many of these messengers of providence pass through. Among them
was Father Laure, one of those devout missionaries who devoted the last
eighteen years of his short life to the spiritual succour of the isolated natives.
Despite the rigours of the climate, his frequent travels across the Western
Estate enabled him to produce, in 1731, one of the first cartographic surveys
establishing its boundaries. His map contained numerous notes on the
people he had visited and descriptions of places he had passed through as
far north as Labrador and as far east as Sept-Îles.

In 1731, Louis Aubert de la Chesnaye, son of the richest merchant of
New France and captain of the governor's guard, was charged with setting
the boundaries of the Western Estate. He gave a very precise description
of the place in his journal:

> On Saturday 9 [June] and Sunday 10 after having said prayers together, and
> not being able to hear Mass, we visited La Malbaie. We went as far as Pointe-
> au-Pic, where I found fifty-odd arpents of new land under crops; the land
> was rich, and well drained. There were eight arpents newly fenced this year,
> and plenty of unused stakes available to fence almost as much again; there
> were a hundred and thirty-four minots of wheat, twenty-seven minots of
> peas, and ten minots of oats. All the grains looked very healthy ...
>
> Since there are no canoes on the River Maillou, our visit to Pointe-
> au-Pic had to be all on land; the elevated ground seemed to us much better
> than the low, because the low ground was too cold ...
>
> There are fifty-eight or fifty-nine arpents of land under crops; another

seventy-four arpents of grasslands could be sown, thirty arpents of old land, and sixty arpents of standing woodland; there are only about twenty or so arpents which lie alongside the house and in several odd spots. The quality of the soil is sandy, but it is good underneath. The timber consists mainly of aspen, birch, poplar, and alder.

There is a pine plantation up the river, about a league and a half from the house. As to the animals at the said seigneury of La Malbaie: there are two horses in fair enough condition, two fine mares, a yearling colt, twenty-five cows, fifteen heavy ploughing oxen, eight of this year's calves, eighteen pigs, and forty-five sheep. More animals could be raised if the supply of fodder were increased; there are eight or nine bales of hay remaining from the past winter. The roads from La Malbaie to Baie-St-Paul will be built to facilitate the transport of the horned beasts that could be raised here.

There is a little chapel; the house in which Sieur de la Roche lives is old, but will last some time yet if a few minor repairs are carried out, such as patching the eaves with a few tiles. There is a new house without fireplace, which is used to store grain; it is built on a most convenient piece of raised ground. There is a barn, half of which is new; it is in a very poor position, on low, damp ground. There is a newly built stable which lies on sufficiently high ground; this is used to house the working oxen and the calves. There is an old stable, which is used to house the cows; this will soon need repairing and enlarging. There is a new sheepfold, and the stable for the horses is new. There is an old shell of a building, which is used to store fodder; there is an old bakehouse, part of which serves as a forge. All the buildings on this property are built of wood, in layers.[12]

After reading a description so rich in detail, I was interested in finding out what it had been like to live on this farm. According to an inventory made by the royal notary Pinguet de Vaucour and dated 5 June 1733, La Malbaie comprised two houses and two mills, a flour mill and a sawmill.[13] Eight people, six men and two women, saw to the work of the farm. Later others joined them—or so at least it is suggested by an order from Administrator Hocquart permitting Pierre Denis to set up his tar furnaces on the king's land in 1736.[14] Apart from a few such operations, this isolated property was hardly used, only developed to meet the food requirements of trading posts. Despite this, François-Étienne Cugnet carried out his duties well as the estate's agent, for the Jesuit Claude-Godefroy Coquart, in a private report prepared for Administrator Bigot in 1750, refers to it as "the finest farm in the country."[15]

So fine, in fact, that the missionary was surprised much of the estate should be left unfarmed: "more of it could have been stripped out than has been; but since they only wanted enough tilled to feed the farmer and his hands, they have left the most beautiful land in the world to lie fallow or under standing timber."[16] According to Coquart, the intention of the authorities was perfectly clear: they wanted to limit the growth of La Malbaie so as not to attract Amerinds, who were seeking a larger trading market. They could not, however, abandon the original purpose of this farm, which was to provide the outposts of the Western Estate with food. They forbade all trading, which crippled the development of a region rich in resources. By this time, two farms had been established in the area: the newer one on the east side of the Malbaie River, Comporté Farm, the older one on the west side, La Malbaie. With pragmatic self-assurance, Father Coquart suggested that salmon, which was plentiful in the river, be exploited as one of the trading company's resources, and that the tar industry be encouraged through the issue of permits. In addition, La Malbaie's services were profitably developed by an excellent sharecropper called Joseph Dufour, of whom the missionary said, "One could not find a better farmer."[17] In short, Dufour ran the farm as though it were his own; even better, he had a peculiar talent for turning everything to profit.

The seigneury of La Malbaie, then, never made the progress one would have expected. It was restricted to serving the mercantile interests of its succession of owners, none of whom ever got established there. Unlike many other seigneuries, La Malbaie was thwarted in its development because of a remote location and difficulty of access. Moreover, the men who farmed it were too frequently replaced, and therefore too often negligent. But the greatest problem lay with incompetent authorities, who held that a colony only exists to serve the needs of a metropolis. The fragile dream of New France gradually grew blurred, and its pioneers, cut off too long from the motherland, clung desperately to the banks of the St. Lawrence. However, the seigneury of La Malbaie, which had grown so slowly at the start, suddenly found itself favoured by a combination of circumstances that led to the arrival of new seigneurs from Scotland.

A Mixture of France and Scotland

THE ARRIVAL OF A REGIMENT FROM SCOTLAND, the Seventy-eighth Fraser Highlanders, was a surprise to more than one French Canadian. Up until that time the Scots had been known above all as faithful allies of France, and here they were, joining the British troops of Wolfe. What was going on? No one could have predicted that the Highlanders, humiliated and despoiled of all their possessions after the defeat at Culloden in 1746, would answer Simon Fraser's call only ten years later for a battalion of infantry to fight alongside the English, who were determined to conquer New France.

4 *Colonel Fraser, master of Lovat* As commanding officer, he raised the Seventy-eighth Fraser Highlanders, who would lend a helping hand to England at Louisbourg in 1758 and, a year later, at Québec.

The short — but no less glorious — history of this regiment provides some sort of explanation. The notable Fraser family who made their mark on our country's history were the descendants, oddly enough, of an old Norman family who left France in the thirteenth century and settled in the north of Scotland, in Inverness. Family legend has it that the name Frasière was bestowed by Charles III, king of France, on Julius de Berry, who served him some exquisite strawberries. The family coat of arms is embellished with strawberry flowers and carries the French motto *Je Suis Prest*. The descendants of these Frasers will always be ready to take up arms in defence of the clan, of Scotland, and of Scotland's allies.

Simon Fraser, master of Lovat, loyal to the Stuart dynasty, led three hundred Highlanders in the Jacobite uprising at Culloden in 1745–46. Some ten years later, by a curious concatenation of circumstances, he was charged with raising his own regiment of infantry and appointed commanding officer. One thousand four hundred and sixty Highlanders answered his call; they embarked for New France in May 1757, clad in their regimental uniform of bonnet, kilt, tartan, and sporran.[†] Raised for the sole purpose of serving England's cause in North America, the Seventy-eighth Fraser Highlanders had on hand several officers who not only came from long-standing military families but also had taken part in several

†Part of British military uniform worn on the front of the kilt and used as a purse for the soldier's money and small personal effects.

campaigns in Europe, notably in Holland. Fraser himself was highly respected, held in awe by those "savages from Scotland," the gallant Highlanders. The Highlanders were in great demand for any operation making use of shock troops, so fierce were they in battle.

On 18 September 1759, Fraser's soldiers were present when the surrender of Québec was negotiated by De Ramesay, himself a Frenchman of Scottish stock. For three years after the fall of Québec and Montréal, they served as garrison troops, always ready to be called whenever their services might be required. Stationed in a country whose winter was more severe than in their own native land, the soldiers suffered. Sisters in the Ursuline convent school took pity on the men with the "short skirts" and knitted long woollen stockings to protect them from chilblains.

In 1763, when the Treaty of Paris put an end to the Seven Years' War that had racked France and England, several regiments were scheduled for demobilization. After November of that year, each officer or soldier became entitled to a grant of land apportioned according to his army rank. The king of England issued a proclamation authorizing governors to grant five thousand acres to a senior officer, three thousand to a captain, two thousand to a subaltern, and fifty to a private soldier. Some of these men expressed their desire to settle in the country, as had personnel from the Regiment de Carignan-Sallières a hundred years earlier. They were more than simple farmers: in addition to developing the colony's agriculture, they guaranteed the existence of a valuable reserve of fighting men should hostilities break out again. Thus was established across the colony a network of reliable settlers faithful to the crown. Some of the first Scottish colonists were demobilized Highlanders.

Among them were Captain John Nairne and Ensign† Malcolm Fraser, promoted to lieutenant in 1758; they had chosen immediately to settle in

5 *"View of the Taking of Québec, September 13, 1759"* Under the command of General Wolfe, some 4,800 soldiers, among them many Highlanders, made ready to storm the cliff around four o'clock in the morning. At ten, after a fight of less than half an hour, Canada's future had been radically altered.

†Officer charged with seeing that the flag of his regiment is kept flying.

Canada, thus becoming the nucleus of the colony's first Scottish community. General James Murray granted the former seigneury of La Malbaie to these two young officers. The first grant, in fief and seigneury, was made to Captain Nairne; this, Murray's Bay, extended from Cap-aux-Oies to the Malbaie River, and three thousand acres of it belonged to Nairne alone. A second grant, in fief and seigneury, running east from the Malbaie River to the Black River, was made to Malcolm Fraser; he called it Mount Murray, in honour of the first British governor of Québec. As an officer, Fraser became the owner of two thousand acres of land within the seigneury he was to administer. The Scottish seigneurs, with a handful of demobilized soldiers who came to rejoin their former comrades in arms, associated with the French peasants who had already settled there. Together, they were to give a unique character to the region.

6 *A view of the cathedral, Jesuits College, and Recollect Friars Church, taken from the gate of the governor's house* After the conquest, this sort of military parade formed part of the regular exercises of British troops. This print by Richard Short shows Québec in the eighteenth century, devastated by the bombardments of British naval forces.

THE SEIGNEUR OF MURRAY'S BAY

John Nairne was born into a distinguished Scottish family, a large part of which was condemned to live in exile in Sens, France, because for several generations they had supported the Stuarts. From the age of seventeen — probably to reconcile himself with his own people — John had campaigned in Holland with the Scots Brigade. After nine years of foreign service, he was promoted to lieutenant in a new regiment raised in Scotland, the Seventy-eighth Fraser Highlanders, which embarked for New France in

1757.† Hostilities ceased in 1763; and as soon as his regiment was demobilized, Nairne, aged thirty-one, retired from the army on half pay, receiving for his loyal services the grant that he called Murray's Bay.[19] (It was referred to as Murray's Bay in the patent of grant, but the *s* was soon abandoned in ordinary correspondence.) No doubt the place reminded him of the gorges and glens of his native Scotland; perhaps this was what attracted him to the land of mountains and sea in the new world. From then on, he devoted himself to the development of his seigneury. In a letter to a family friend, he recalled his earliest days: "I came here first in 1761 with the Soldiers and procured some Canadien Servants. One small house contained us all for several years and [we] were separated from every other people for about eighteen miles without any road ... "[20]

7 *Detail from the print by Richard Short, published in London in 1761* Shown here are two Fraser Highlanders of the Seventy-eighth, the only regiment that came from Scotland to support Wolfe's army at Québec. Their uniform can be distinguished from that of the English troops by the kilt, known as the *filibeg* in Gaelic.

8 *Captain John Nairne at Murray Bay, 1761* This was how Jefferys imagined Captain John Nairne unloading arms for the Fraser Highlanders at La Malbaie with five of his companions in arms. Nairne was thirty-one when he decided to live permanently in his seigneury at Murray Bay.

The tasks facing the seigneur remained to all intents and purposes the same as those that had faced the old French seigneurs. Nairne's first responsibility was to settle copyholders in his seigneury to clear and cultivate the land as best they could. Having spent a vast amount of money buying equipment and livestock already on the farm, he had to act quickly to recover his investment. His sole income came from local farmers who brought their grain to be ground in his mill. When he received the three thousand acres to which his captain's rank entitled him, he was already full of plans for the estate. During the first five years of hard labour, he got his seigneury organized, saw to the construction of his future manor house, and started negotiations to open a road — which, much to his disappointment, came to nothing. In 1766, he went to Scotland to settle some family business; and while he was there he married Christiana Emery, who came

---

†He became captain of the Seventy-eighth Highlanders on 24 April 1761.

from a good family in Edinburgh. After a year abroad, he returned to his seigneury with his young wife. Six years later they had four children; an epidemic carried three of them off suddenly. This void was quickly filled by the birth of five more children, two sons and three daughters.

The Nairnes were often visited by friends from Québec, Montréal, and even far-off Scotland. Alexander Gilchrist was one; in the spring of 1774 he came from Edinburgh on business and took the opportunity to pay a visit to his old friend John, who was now a seigneur in Canada. Back in Scotland, he described his host's estate with a touch of nostalgia: "The fishing on that part of the river [Malbaie] is alone worth crossing the Atlantic; ... of one thing you may be certain, that there is no place upon equal terms, and even less than that, ... [where] I would so willingly and happily pass life as in your neighbourhood ... "[21] And in a later letter he praised the place as ideal for holidays: "If I have the pleasure of seeing your sisters, I'll represent MalBay as the counterpart of Paradise before the fall ..."[22]

As the years went by John Nairne found his seigneury more and more peaceful and comfortable. Now in his forties, he led a happy life surrounded by an affectionate family. Unfortunately, his tranquility was not to last. In 1775 the American Revolution broke out and was soon threatening Québec. The empire called on veterans of the Scottish regiment who had remained in Canada to fight off the insurgents. During July and August Governor Guy Carleton expressly asked John Nairne to raise a militia of farmers from his seigneury and those of Baie-St-Paul and Beaupré. These troops were to reinforce the Eighty-fourth Royal Highland Emigrants, a regiment commanded by Colonel Allan MacLean. But recruitment was not as successful as anticipated. Farmers along the banks of the St Lawrence, barely recovered from the disruptions of the British conquest, remembered the ravages of the British Gorham and refused to fight a war under the British flag. As for Nairne, he committed himself to it courageously, if not happily. Thanks to his skill and experience, he distinguished himself in a skirmish with some American rebels, despite the thick December snow covering rue du Sault-au-Matelot to the foot of La Montagne in Québec City.

Several years later, Nairne — now a major, and completely trusted by Governor Haldimand — agreed to the construction of a penitentiary on his estate for prisoners of war.[†] Being held ninety miles from Québec, it was thought, would deter would-be escapees. It was agreed that three barrack huts would be built by the prisoners, and that Sergeant James Thompson, superintendant of military works in Québec, would be responsible for overseeing construction. In May 1780, as his diary records, Thompson

9 *Sergeant James Thompson (1732–1831)* James Thompson enrolled in the ranks of the Fraser Highlanders at the age of twenty-five. When his regiment was disbanded, he became inspector of the fortification works at Québec. In 1780 he was responsible for the construction of detention barracks at La Malbaie to hold captured American rebels. After some of these prisoners escaped, an officer and eight men of the Anhalt Zerbst Regiment were posted to guard the rest. Despite the fact that their services were available for only a short time, some of these mercenaries from Germany were captivated by the area. As proof, a man named Buhrer, a relative of one of the soldiers, settled down at La Malbaie and became the first of the large family of Bhérers.

---

†He was appointed captain of the First Battalion of the Eighty-fourth Royal Highland Emigrants on 14 June 1775, and two years later, in recognition of his acts of gallantry, he was promoted to major. At the end of the war he was a lieutenant-colonel. Later he became colonel of the Baie-St-Paul militia, a post he retained till the end of his life.

began his inspection of the terrain to decide where the future prison should be located:

> A Description of which merits an abler hand. In coming abreast of the Bay Major Nairn's house is the first object that presents itself and makes a very respectable appearance, being about 50 feet long, two Rooms in depth and two stories high, the Joiners work done by English hands, beautifully situated on a rising ground, the River St. Lawrence at high water, washing the bottom of a steep Precepis in front of it; on the west shoulder of the Bay and a few cottages; along the east should[r] runes the River Mal Bay about 250 yards wide, copiously stocked with variety of Fish particularly Salmond & Trout esteemed the best in the Province ... [23]

During construction, the prisoners took advantage of their jailors' trust and escaped on flatboats in the direction of Kamouraska. Although recaptured at once, they were not returned to Murray Bay. The construction of

10 *John Nairne (1731–1802)* This picture, which hung for many years on the wall of the manor at Murray Bay, is unique; it is in fact the only Canadian portrait painted by the great Scottish master Sir Henry Raeburn.

11 *Christine Nairne (1774–1817)* Christine was popular in Québec society; her father referred to her as a "fashionable lady."

12 *Thomas Nairne (1787–1813)* Tom, John Nairne's second son, inherited the seigneury of Murray Bay a few years before his death, in 1813, on the battlefield of Chrysler's Farm, south of Cornwall in Ontario.

the barracks was interrupted, the whole idea of a prisoner-of-war camp at Murray Bay gradually abandoned.

Released from his military duties at the end of the war, John Nairne retired from the army. During the long winters that ensued, he maintained a regular correspondence from the seigneury. The portrait emerging from his letters is that of an austere and methodical man. He sent each of his children to be educated in Edinburgh, where they boarded with his sister Magdalene. And when the eldest, John, began to show himself a little too free and easy, his authoritarian father did not hesitate to remind him that "all our family have ever been temperate, not even the Debauchery of Smoking tobacco a nasty Dutch Damned Custom, a forerunner of Idleness and Drunkenness, therefore, Jack, my Lad, let me hear no more of your handling your Pipe, but handle well your fuzee, your sword, your pen and your books."[24]

He also expended a lot of energy to get a Protestant pastor to La Malbaie. The Catholic Church, he believed, kept its faithful ignorant and submissive. Despite repeated attempts his efforts were unsuccessful; the number of local farmers was not even sufficient to justify the presence of a Catholic priest. Besides, the children of his old comrades in arms — the Blackburns, MacLarens, MacNicols, and others — now spoke French, which they had learned at their mothers' knees. But Scotland was still the mother country in Nairne's eyes, a living heritage he was bent on perpetuating in his country of adoption.

At Murray Bay the manor house was the centre of activity. For several years, while Thomas, the second son, and Mary (nicknamed Polly) were at school in Edinburgh, their parents had only two children with them, Christine and Magdalene. The former was nicknamed Rusty on account of her red hair; according to a portrait sketched by her father, she was a "lady of fashion," a society girl whose company was sought by the whole of Québec. Her sister Madie was the opposite. As eldest of the family, she

13/14 *Imports from Scotland* This arm-chair and piece of silverware were in the Nairne manor when Marius Barbeau, accompanied by Jean Palardy, was making his ethnographic surveys in the Charlevoix area.

15/16 *Nairne's seigneurial property, about 1925* The manor was a large building, shaped like a U. The sides were covered in weather-boarding. To the right stood the pigeon-house, topped by a pinnacle turret in the Scottish style—also found on the Nairnes' ancestral home near Stanley in Scotland; it was used to store grain. These two buildings were demolished in March 1960, in accordance with a clause in the contract of sale.

was attached to life at the manor house. There was nowhere she wanted to be other than Murray Bay—especially after the family suffered two severe blows with the deaths of the youngest, Anne, and the eldest of the boys, John.[†] As time passed, the manor house became a comfortable home, furnished and decorated with items from Scotland. Over the years the colonel made many improvements to the estate, keeping a large part of the reclaimed land for himself. Under his direction Hugh Blackburn, his faithful comrade in arms, and John Hewett, his business agent, ran all three farms. As for Madame Nairne, she looked after the general administration of the seigneury, the upkeep of the gardens in particular.

The home's exact date of construction is uncertain. Two plans of the property were made by Surveyor-General John Collins in 1764; in each case, sketches were included of the manor house.[25] Elsewhere, documents show that construction was completed in 1780. With the exception of the foundations and the two fireplaces, the seigneur's residence was all wood. The front of the house commanded an extensive view of the river. On the ground floor, a huge library in local cedar and a large, well-lit drawing-room gave onto the garden; on the other side of the central entry, in perfect symmetry, was the dining-room, with the kitchens in the other wing. All floors and ceilings were pine. The staircase, of solid oak, led to an upper floor that had nine bedrooms. The property also had a two-storey barn where the seigneur stored his grain. A belfry crowned the roof, in the Scottish manner; on this stood an iron weathercock, topped with a carved wooden cock.

With a house like that, it is easy to understand why the summer season brought a long string of visitors. The Honorable G. Taschereau and Messrs Masson and Usburn often came from Québec to fish for salmon and talk with the seigneur. Christine had her friend Cecilia, the daughter of Judge Bowen, and Mlle Mabane—her hosts in Québec during the winter—for an enjoyable summer stay. And Colonel Nairne recommended the place to his friend Richard Dobie of Montréal for its beneficial qualities:

> I have heard that drinking, and bathing, in sea water is very strengthening, and salutary, in such cases, and perhaps might be effectual towards removing your ailment. Of all places, I really believe if possible, to recover strength and health it is here at Murray Bay, formerly Malbay; ... you shall drink the best of wheys and breath the purest sea air in the world and, although luxurys and delicases will be wanting, our friendship and the best things the place can afford to you, I know, will make ample amends. Col. M. Fraser's House and mine are situated on opposite sides of the Bay about half a mile asunder, so you may visit the one or the other as best you can amuse yourself ... [26]

John Nairne spent the greater part of his life at Murray Bay. As an old man, he found it harder to withstand the cold of winter. He died at the

---

[†]Anne died of tuberculosis at the age of twelve, while a student at Edinburgh. Three years later, the young lieutenant John died at the age of twenty-one from an illness contracted during his military service in India.

age of seventy-one, satisfied that he had done his best to increase the population of the region he loved for its imposing river, its bluish mountains and its bay, which seemed to welcome visitors with widespread arms.

17 *Plan for cultivating the farm at Murray Bay beginning in 1787* This was the plan for working Seigneur Nairne's farm between 1787 and 1795, together with distribution of land under cultivation. Each parcel bore a French name and was to be used for producing fodder, for crops, or for grazing.

THE SEIGNEUR OF MOUNT MURRAY

Malcolm Fraser was not only John Nairne's neighbour but also his best friend. Many events had forged unbreakable bonds between the two seigneurs from Scotland. After Colonel Nairne's death, his old regimental comrade Fraser became the counsellor and protector of the Nairne family. Although fatherless, Fraser had received a good education. He knew Gaelic, English, French, and a fair bit of Latin. Without any real military experience, but because he belonged to the Fraser clan, he became an ensign in the Seventy-eighth Fraser Highlanders at the age of twenty-four. He first met John Nairne in 1757, when the regiment left Scotland. After arriving in New France, they campaigned at Louisburg, and a year later at Québec. According to the invaluable diary he kept, Fraser was wounded for the first time on the Plains of Abraham during the siege of Québec, and then, more seriously, in the spring of 1760 at the battle of Ste-Foy. Soon recovered, he rejoined his battalion at Beaumont, near Québec, where he was said to have shown great generosity towards local people who had lost everything. This inevitably brought him closer to the settlers; probably as a result, he fell in love with Marie Allaire, a young Canadian woman with whom he had six children. Even before his regiment was demobilized, General Murray made him the grant of two thousand acres of land, free of seigneurial tenure, together with the vast estate in fief and seigneury called Mount Murray.[29]

Whereas John Nairne, when he left the army, devoted himself to his seigneury, Malcolm Fraser took an active part in the military affairs of the new English colony as army paymaster. At the age of forty-two, he was promoted to captain in the Royal Highland Emigrants. He was commander of the guard at Québec during the American Revolution. When the city was invaded on the evening of the 31 December 1775, he distinguished himself by giving the alarm that revolutionary troops were about to attack. After the war, Fraser returned to a more peaceful life, dividing his time between the army and his seigneury at Mount Murray. When James Thompson arrived in 1780 to build the prison barracks on Colonel Nairne's estate, he remarked:

> This river seperates the Seigniory of Major Nairn from that of Captain Malcolm Fraser's, both of them late of the 78th Regiment. The latter has a most Elegant farm and a Genteel farm house Barn and stables, with a good stock of Catle, which I am Told has been kept out all the last winter till the month of March, a very singular circumstance in this Climate. The farmer pays only Twenty pounds currency per annum, but is obliged to sell his Butter to the seignior at six pence if demanded; tho' this is the only Farm yet settled on the land.[30]

18 *Simon Fraser (1769–1844)* Simon, the third son of Malcolm Fraser and Marie Allaire, was a surgeon with a practice at Terrebonne when he acquired the seigneury of Contrecoeur. This oil portrait hung for many years in Fraser Manor at Rivière-du-Loup.

Although the owner of a smoothly run farm, Malcolm Fraser had no taste for isolation and so turned to several outside ventures. In 1782 he formed an association with Henry Caldwell to take timber from the forests of St-André and Kamouraska.[†] It seems that until then he had not lived in the seigneury with his first wife, Marie Allaire, and that their children had quickly scattered across the country; their eldest son, Alexander, had been in the service of the North-West Company for more than ten years before deciding to buy the seigneury of Rivière-du-Loup from Henry Caldwell. With the acquisition of this new estate on the south shore of the St Lawrence, Malcolm crossed the river often and even spent several winters with his eldest son. During this time the youngest, Simon, was in Scotland studying medicine at Edinburgh University. He was said to be very much like his father—not only in looks but also in his free-thinking ideas.

---

†Because of numerous commercial activities that often took him to the other bank, Fraser and Nairne had agreed on a code of signals using fire; one fire meant all was well, two meant trouble.

19 *Fraser Manor at Mount Murray*
The house in which Malcolm Fraser lived until his death in 1815 no longer stands. On 7 July 1827, the first stone of Fraser Manor was laid in the presence of Seigneur William Fraser, Malcolm's eldest son. Planned by William's father-in-law, Jean-Baptiste Duberger, it was built by the master mason Pierre Giroix. It was a three-storey house in ashlar, with a four-sided mansard roof and tall, wide chimney-stacks set at each end. The manor at Mount Murray, by now the property of the Cabot family, was destroyed by fire on 7 June 1975.

Since his military duties and business affairs had kept Fraser traveling a great deal, he came to appreciate the simple life at Mount Murray and began to pay more attention to it. In 1773 he built his own sawmill on the Malbaie River, which brought in attractive profits almost immediately. He lived a more settled life with his second wife, Marguerite Ducros, by whom he had three children: Anne, the eldest, and two sons, William and John Malcolm, who became the heirs of Mount Murray.

Besides having charge of a young family, Seigneur Fraser was godfather to Thomas, the second son of John Nairne. It is hardly surprising to find him strongly disapproving of Thomas's adoption of a military career, for he was the only male heir to the seigneury of Murray Bay. Despite Fraser's lectures his godson joined the Tenth Infantry Regiment, stationed at Gibraltar, at the time Napoleon Bonaparte was devastating Europe with his campaigns. The young lieutenant grew bored so far from the battlefield and asked for a change of posting to Canada; this he got immediately, for fresh hostilities had just broken out with the United States. He took leave and spent some time at the seigneury, where he enjoyed the fishing, hunting, and sailing. His stay hardly allowed him to delve deeply into the affairs of the estate, however; his mother looked after everything with considerable success, and he felt rather useless. Thus he was pleased to join the Forty-ninth Regiment in the border region of Upper Canada, the most active part of the front.

On the death of his father, Thomas Nairne had become the sole heir to Murray Bay; the destiny of the estate now depended on him. Malcolm Fraser had well understood that the heir must be protected—in spite of himself—against the dangers of war, but it was already too late. Near the end of hostilities, after a hard-fought battle on land and water, the young seigneur, twenty-six years old, died at the Battle of Chrysler's Farm, struck in the head by a musket bullet. In 1813, when the campaign was over and the enemy had withdrawn, the residents of Murray Bay were grief-stricken. Fraser too was overcome by the tragic news; his spirits flagged. Two years later he died, at the age of eighty-two. His son William, by this time a doctor and married to Mathilde Duberger, became the new seigneur of Mount Murray. He was succeeded by John Malcolm in 1832.

Malcolm Fraser, having spent thirty-five years of his active life with the British army, had not been as devoted to his seigneury as Nairne. He traveled from one end of his territory to the other without any definite plan of colonization or development. He was a debonair individual, slightly nomadic, and gave every indication of being a man of instinct—quite the opposite of the serious-minded Nairne. Indeed, Nairne was a landed proprietor in the old Scottish style who regretted that he had not established a colony in the image of his fatherland. However, if circumstances caused them to depart from their initial plans, the two seigneurs were nevertheless satisfied to have contributed to the growth of a region whose geographic isolation made it difficult to develop. This progress could not have been made without the hard labour of the original colonists, who cleared and cultivated the land after the manner of their French ancestors, in a spirit of hope.

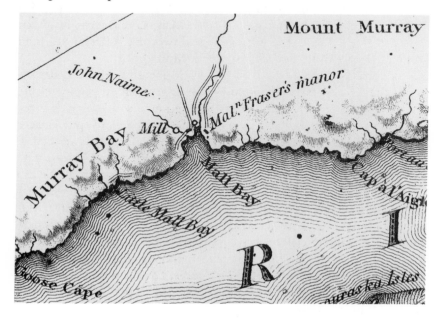

20 *Murray Bay and Mount Murray* Detail from a map of the province of Lower Canada, in 1803, showing the modest beginnings of colonization in La Malbaie and its environs.

Charlevoix

THE FIRST TASK OF THE SEIGNEUR was always to populate his estate by attracting settlers. John Nairne had done this successfully and quickly, reaching twenty new grants per year, which ultimately produced a parish of more than five hundred inhabitants. Such rapid growth was a source of pride to the man who had worked so hard for it:

> According to your desire [I] shall say something of this place. I am flattered by your making that request where the activity of my life these thirty-eight years has been employed. Observing the number of habitations and fertile fields which have been formed during that time I can not help rejoicing a little with the idea of having been instrumental in so useful an alteration. All round the Bay from the sea side the thick woods are now opened and cleared away, the ground inclosed and brought under cultivation (the River St. Lawrence lone we call the sea, its waters being salt and about twenty miles broad). Also for some miles along the banks of a small river which empties itself into the Bay people are now settled on (what we call) lots of land. I have granted away 110 lots numbered for paying rent, each lot consisting generally of 120 acres.[31]

In addition to several Highlanders, some pioneers from the Île-aux-Coudres and Baie-St-Paul received grants of land enabling them to settle in La Malbaie and its environs. They put plenty of hard work into "creating land," as John Nairne called it, although theirs was rudimentary agriculture and this first stage of development made it hard to produce more than the minimum for survival. The colonists kept busy in the fields trying to scrape up enough sustenance for their large families. When agriculture could not meet those needs, the spoils of hunting and fishing helped immensely.

The first grants of land were made along the Mailloux River, then along the Malbaie River, whose fertile banks soon transformed the valley of St-Étienne. The plots ran forty arpents back into the woods and had a frontage of three arpents along the bank so that each concession had access to the water. The houses were strung like beads along the rivers, later along the big river itself.

The feudal system, in the European sense of the term, never really existed here except in name. Each colonist became the absolute holder of the land granted him by the seigneur, in exchange for a small land tax payable in cash or in farm products. Apart from the seigneur there were no large landowners; they all had more or less the same holding. For this reason, most families belonged to the same social class and cultivated their land without outside assistance, except at harvest time. All members of a family devoted themselves almost exclusively to working the farm.

The common method of agricultural development follows a two-year cycle: a crop of cereal, generally corn, is grown on land that is left fallow the following year. An observer from France, Isidore Lebrun, commented during a trip that "Lower Canada still practises the old French method; one year it leaves its fields as pasturage, the following year it sows them with cereal."[32] This method, in use in New France from the earliest days, was a legacy of the Middle Ages. Monsieur Gauldrée-Boilleau, French consul-general in New York, had this to say during a sociological survey at St-Irénée: "The procedures which they [the Canadians of Charlevoix] follow are no different from those their forefathers used two centuries ago: since they own vast stretches of land, they are quite content to let half their holding lie fallow each year while they cultivate the other half."[33]

Any society, however small, whose sole industry is agriculture, soon discovers the limits of its development. Beluga fishing helped the inhabitants of Charlevoix diversify their economy; they exported the oil and skin of this mammal, which allowed them to live almost entirely off their own resources. A family bought very little; the husband was at one and the same time farmer, carpenter, cabinet-maker, blacksmith, and shoemaker, the wife, weaver and seamstress. They were independent, self-sufficient people, proud of their heritage as French peasants, as Isidore Lebrun noted: "The low prices of English merchandise brought about no changes in everyday working dress: there was invariably the grey coat in locally-made cloth, loose-fitting and no lower than the knees, the straw hat in summer, in winter the red woollen tuque or the fur hat. The women were clothed like the peasant women in France: a dark-coloured skirt, a short cloth cape, shoes like men's."[34] The greater their pride in being self-sufficient, the more attached they became to this traditional way of life.

After New France surrendered to England, the fur trade gradually gave way to trade in timber and cereals. Despite its antiquated farming methods, La Malbaie began to profit from a growing market in the town of Québec and by the beginning of the nineteenth century had become prosperous. There was plenty of land to be cleared, and though the population rate was increasing, there was no shortage of space in the seigneury. To ensure further colonization, access roads had to be built. These would speed up trade with the town, whose direct access to the waterway offered a convenient outlet for local products.

The market for agricultural surplus brought certain changes of habit—

for example, the consumption of imported products such as textiles, beverages, and molasses. The farmer's table now offered a more varied menu, which included potatoes and peas. In spite of this, the idea of an independent existence remained firmly anchored and traditional agriculture was still practised. This was in fact fortunate, for Lower Canada gradually lost the British agriculture market because of a sudden drop in demand. The farmer, isolated on his farm, with his family forming his whole universe, developed a somewhat static vision of the world and remained at the mercy of the forces of nature.

The Valley of St Étienne

21 *The valley of St Étienne* The lands granted to the colonists, which spread on either side of the Malbaie River, would alter the valley of St Étienne considerably. This view shows how far land clearing had progressed at the start of the nineteenth century.

The farms lay in rows, on rectangular strips of land facing the Malbaie and St Lawrence rivers. Two water-mills ground the grain, while other mills were used to saw wood, as much for local use as for the shrunken market outside. As Lieutenant-Colonel Joseph Bouchette remarked during his first exploratory voyage in 1815 as surveyor-general of Lower Canada:

> These two seigneuries are separated from each other by the River Malbaye, and contain only a very small proportion of cultivated land, in comparison with their dimensions. In both of them, the surface is generally mountainous, but in certain places the soil is fairly good; every sort of timber for construction is plentiful and of excellent quality, especially pine. The best cultivated areas are those which extend along each side of the River Malbaye for about six miles; a fairly good road runs right through these settlements to the ends, and there are several farms and pleasant houses.[35]

From 1830, however, people began to worry about soil exhaustion and overcrowding. In the fall of 1837, after several successive bad crops, the first wave of emigration towards the Saguenay was organized by the Sociéte des Vingt-et-un. Neither of the two original seigneurs could have foretold that one day their vast estates would be short of good clearable land. The descendants, who had inherited the responsibility of seeing that the land developed in tune with the rate of population growth, recognized how enormous a task had been accomplished by their pioneer ancestors. And now all the young people of the County of Northumberland were full of praise for the noble cause of colonization.[†]

22 *Mal Bay or Murray Bay* This detail from the topographical map of the province of Lower Canada, drawn by the Surveyor-General Joseph Bouchette in 1815, shows the progress of development of the two seigneuries. Also to be seen is the church of La Malbaie, built in 1805 on land donated by Seigneur John Nairne; it was destroyed by fire in 1949.

AN ATTRACTION FOR SPORTSMEN

From the day of their arrival, the British military were curious about the New World, especially this colony called The Canadas. Several officers garrisoned in Québec or Montréal left valuable sketches made during their stay.

The first view of La Malbaie, dated 1784, was sketched at a distance of three leagues by James William Peachey. Hung in the office of the surveyor-general, Samuel Holland, it is a somewhat technical treatment of the panorama. Some twelve years later, George Heriot, who had learned to be a water-colour artist at the School of Artillery in Woolwich, England, began painting landscapes in a livelier style. During his first tour he traveled in search of the picturesque, moving along the north shore of the St Lawrence from Tadoussac to Québec. He found La Malbaie so charming that he abandoned a somewhat documentary style in favour of an idealistic rendering of the scene. Appointed assistant postmaster at Québec, a post

†The County of Northumberland came into being under the Act of 1791. The name was kept until the revision of the electoral map of Lower Canada in 1829. Thenceforth, Northumberland was split into two counties, Montmorency and Saguenay.

A View of Mal Baye, Bearing N.N.W. distance 3 Leagues, taken 17th Nov: 1784.

he was to hold for almost twenty years, Heriot drew his inspiration from the scenery along the postal routes of the countryside. He was interested in the architecture, flora, fauna, usages and customs of Canada — in short, all the distinctive features of the new colony — and in London in 1807 published an account entitled *Travels through the Canadas*. The book recorded his impressions for the benefit of future immigrants and those who enjoyed dreaming of far-off lands. On the subject of La Malbaie he wrote: "Here the land is cultivated and inhabited for an extent of six miles, in a rich and romantic valley, through which a river, abounding in salmon and trout, winds its course into the bay. The soil which consists of a black mould upon sand, is fertile: and the inhabitants, whose communication with other settled parts of the country is not frequent, possess, within their own limits, an abundance of the necessaries of life."[36]

Heriot loved the colony and its people, commenting that "their address to strangers is more polite and unembarrassed than that of any other peasantry in the world. Rusticity, either in manners or in language, is unknown even to those who reside in situations the most remote from the towns."[37]

When Heriot was preparing to leave Québec for England in 1816, Francis Hall, a lieutenant in the Fourteenth Dragoons, was writing up a report during a visit to Canada and the United States. He had this to say about the people of the Laurentians: "Indeed, the most prominent trait in the Character of this people, is an attachment, to whatever is established. Far different in this respect from the American, the Canadian will submit to any privation, rather than quit the spot his forefathers tilled, or remove from the sound of his parish bells."[38]

Hall left Kamouraska, "a village of some resort during summer, for sea-bathing," and went to La Malbaie, which he described as "a small semi-circle of alluvial land lying at the foot of mountains of a bolder and more romantick character than any I had yet seen in Canada."[39] When he landed

23 *"A view of Mal Baye, Bearing NNW distance 3 leagues, taken 17th Nov 1784"* James Peachey, a British army officer employed by the office of the surveyor-general, dealt with landscapes in technical fashion. This view of La Malbaie is a typical example of the topographical sketch produced by the military.

at La Malbaie, the house offering the best hospitality was pointed out to him as that of "Madame Nairne, the lady of the Seignory." He was given a warm welcome and enjoyed making the acquaintance of the household. From there he journeyed to Québec, where, he remarked, the lovely valleys that opened onto the coastline seemed cramped between the river and the mountains.

24 *Colonel Nairne's settlement at Mal Bay* Born in Scotland, George Heriot came to Québec in 1792 in the service of the British government. He profited from his stay by traveling all over the country, and he frequently visited the banks of the St Lawrence for the picturesque views offered by the Laurentians. During his travels he painted many watercolours, some of which were reproduced in his book *Travels through the Canadas*, published in London in 1807.

In 1823, Doctor John J. Bigsby, in the service of the British army, went on an expedition to study the geology of La Malbaie. When he was leaving on his fourth excursion, he was particularly moved by the beauty of the river and its banks during an Indian summer. Arriving at Kamouraska late at night, he got on board a fishing boat to cross to La Malbaie. Early in the morning, dead tired, he found a lodging in a house of one Antoine Brassard. He related with amusement having inadvertently climbed into the grandmother's bed while she was in it. This incident, much to the surprise of the officer, drew loud laughter from the Brassards, who, as though to make up for the slight embarrassment, served him a splendid lunch before he left for the village of La Malbaie. "I found Malbay, or Murray-bay, as the Seignior likes to have it called, a round indenture in the north shore of the St. Lawrence, about two miles in outer diameter, overhung by steep, pine-clad hills, at whose feet (in the bay) are grassy diluvial terraces, on which stand some houses and a neat church," Bigsby wrote.[40] Five days of exploration prompted him to make additional comments — on geology and meteorology, which he enhanced with a series of rough plans and sketches, and on those pleasant people he was getting to know: "I visited a small farmer's establishment, five miles up the valley, relations of my host, and was pleased with its tidiness and family harmony. They had collected from the rocky wilds around immense pans full of bilberries for food. The young people, men and women, showed no shyness, although their threshold cannot be crossed by a stranger once in twenty years; and they entered into conversation with me agreeably and sensibly."[41]

25 *Mal Bay* Dr. John Jerimiah Bigsby came over from England in 1818. In his spare time he was a geologist and an artist. For more than six years he traveled all over the country, pencil in hand, making sketches that would be used to illustrate his memoirs, *The Shoe and Canoe*.

Although Bigsby was primarily searching for scientific data, he could not ignore his picturesque surroundings. Nor could the explorers Baddeley and Andrews, who in their account of the geophysical aspects of the mountainous hinterland did not fail to mention "the known hospitality of Mr. and Mrs. M'Nicol," their hosts at Murray Bay.[42]† It is surprising to learn from Baddeley and Andrews that already in 1830 "the steamship *Waterloo*" had come to La Malbaie "on a pleasure-trip."[43] This pleasant corner, which had not escaped the curious eye of geologists on the lookout for ore, was also attracting travellers for the charm of its scenery, and perhaps even more, for its plentiful fishing.

It was at the end of June 1830 that Doctor Walter Henry, superintendent of the province's military hospitals, left Montréal on a steamship with

---

†Magdalene, the elder daughter of the Nairnes, had married Peter McNicol, whose son John became in 1839 the last seigneur directly descended from John Nairne.

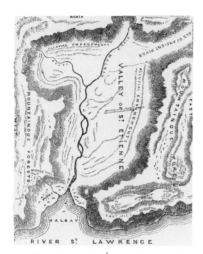

26 *The Valley of St Étienne* During his voyage in 1823 Bigsby, a good geologist, drew this map, which contains some particularly interesting information on the physical surroundings of La Malbaie.

Major Wingfield of the Sixty-sixth Regiment. These two sportsmen were to spend a month at La Malbaie salmon fishing, which was ideal that season. They left for La Malbaie from Québec aboard a schooner. Rough water slowed them down, and it took four interminable days to cover a short distance of ninety miles. Finally they landed at La Malbaie, exhausted, and recouped at an inn run by the Chaperon family. On a Monday morning they went to the falls, six miles in the heart of the St Étienne valley, up the Malbaie River. Henry was familiar with the place, having been there several times before. He had engaged the services of a guide known as Jean Gros and, with his knowledge of French, was able to speak to him. Henry appreciated the locals and the simple if hard lives they led:

> A very quiet and moral population of seven or eight hundred people inhabit this retired valley ... Many of the Malbaie families are very large, and from twelve to twenty children are not uncommon. They marry early, get a stripe of a "concession" from the seigneur, and a house is run up for the young people, more Hibernico, by their relations. They are then cast adrift, but never separate far from their own connexions. There is much social comfort in this custom, but much poverty in its train; for the bit of land is soon exhausted.[44]

This fishing trip allowed them a few free moments; once Henry had filled his creel with a good catch, he relaxed in a shady corner and continued to record his experiences. "We then crossed with old Maitre Jean to the shady side," he wrote, "and reposed ourselves: and having discovered a copious spring bubbling through the gravel, close to the water's edge, we enlarged it into a well, into which we plumped our fish, and a bottle of Hodson's pale ale, covering it with green boughs. We then employed ourselves in collecting strawberries for a dessert to our sandwich, and after lunch enjoyed our cigars and chatted over our morning exploits ... "[45]

But these excursions never went off without a hitch; inevitably the men were attacked by mosquitoes and by "those insidious black wretches the brulôts, who give no warning ... "[46] Then there was the dog who sank his teeth into their horse's nose, the loss of an oar, which resulted in their being carried straight to the rapids, and similar incidents to spice up the trip. But they were happy when they returned to Montréal with two fat barrels of fish to offer their friends. Needless to say, they had not forgotten to thank dear Madame Chaperon—every day she had kindly thought to put roses in the dining-room window of the inn.

If people were beginning to leave for the country, it was because during the dog days the towns became insufferable. Travel, made easier by the new steamboats that cruised the river, was now within people's reach. The towns were also dangerous. Since 1825 the government in London had allowed massive immigration during the warm season without ensuring healthy traveling conditions. In the summer of 1832, because of repeated negligence, a terrible epidemic of Asiatic cholera ravaged the city of Québec, spread to other towns in the St Lawrence valley, and finally reached

Trois-Rivières, Berthier, and Montréal.[†] Those who could afford to immediately left the capital and made for the surrounding countryside. The
epidemic brought considerable change to the social life of Québec, and
curiously enough contributed to the growth of summer resort life near
Sillery and at Ste-Foy and Cap-Rouge.[47] Thus while cities enacted measures
to promote public hygiene, the countryside with its pure air became irresist-
ible, at least for the more fortunate. Now at last, La Malbaie was transformed into a resort area, no longer reserved for friends in the intimate
circle of the seigneurs.

The family of Charlotte Holt Gethings was probably one of the first of
the restricted colony of summer residents to come to La Malbaie for
summer holidays. In her memoirs Charlotte—Madame Macpherson—
recounted the first summer she passed there, around 1840:

> I was still very young when I paid my first visit to Murray Bay on the
> steamboat *Pochahontas*, which belonged to Mons. Price. Although it was by
> no means a boat which would be called first-class today, we were very proud
> to have it, for up till then we had to use schooners to get there. At this period
> Murray Bay was only inhabited—even in summer—by the family of John
> Nairne, the seigneur, his charming wife and their friends, his father-in-law,
> the Hon. Mons. Leslie from Montreal, and his son. There was not even a
> baker or a butcher—we had to eat the black bread of the habitants, which
> was sometimes very sour. Also, we were careful every time to bring not only
> bread and meat, but fruit, and butter, etc. ... One thing we enjoyed at Murray
> Bay was the wild turtle-doves; unfortunately, ignorant people decimated
> them, trying to take them with poison; they are no longer to be seen in
> Canada. Salmon were also found in abundance. Some of the houses were
> occupied by foreigners in the early days. I remember some of the hunters'
> families—the Austins, the VanFelsons, and J. Burroughs and A. Campbell
> (both of whom are now protonotaries in Quebec).[48]

27 *John McNicol Nairne (1808–61)* In
1834 John McNicol, the second son
of Magdalene Nairne, decided to
adopt the family name Nairne, with
royal assent, to preserve the seigneurial lineage. On the death of his
mother in 1839, he became the last
seigneur of Murray Bay. For some
twenty years he carried out improvements to the manor, but showed
little interest in developing his seigneury. The government of Lower
Canada officially abolished the seigneurial system in 1854.

28 *Steamboat wharf, Montréal* This
view of Montréal in 1830 shows the
activities of the port from which so
many sportsmen sailed, lured by the
fish-laden waters of La Malbaie.
James Duncan, who drew this lithograph, came over with the British
army about 1825; he settled in Montréal, where he earned a reputation as
a landscape painter.

†That year cholera claimed more than 3,400 victims in the city of Québec alone (see Pierre-
Georges Roy, "Le choléra asiatique au Québec," *BRH* 12 (1906): 88–92.

The star attraction at La Malbaie was always the fishing. In 1840 another British officer, Henry James Warre, fell in love with it on a trip to Tadoussac. During his trip he did a good number of sketches, and later made twenty or so prints of them, which were published in London in 1848 under the title *Sketches in North America and the Oregon Territory*.

These isolated sportsmen's trips eventually opened the whole area up to travellers. In 1844, thanks to the development of sea and rail transport—New York was now linked to Montréal, and Montréal had long since been linked to Québec—a regular steamboat service took travellers from Québec to La Malbaie for the sum of four dollars. One guidebook described the fruits of such a voyage: "Many families from Quebec visit Malbaie in the summer for the benefit of salt water bathing, the water here being perfectly sea-salt. There is also excellent salmon fishing in the river near the Chute about six miles from its mouth. Sea trout are likewise taken here of a considerable size and several small lakes at a few miles distance afford abundance of trout."[49]

29 *"Mal or Murray Baie"* Henry James Warre, serving in the British army, arrived in Canada in October 1839 and remained until August 1846. During his stay he kept a diary to record his impressions and accompany his sketches. Among these, "Mal or Murray Baie" was used in *Sketches in North America and the Oregon Territory*, published in London in 1848.

30 *Lord and Lady Minto* The seigneury of Murray Bay was honoured by visits from two governors-general of Canada. In 1901 Lord and Lady Minto spent several days at the manor; on their departure, they presented their hosts with this little piece of embroidery as a memento of a pleasant stay. Ten years later, Earl Grey and his family spent several weeks in a house at Pointe-au-Pic.

For steamship cruising, the Saguenay offered some of the most spectacular views a tourist could ever hope to see, according to many of the travel guides of that time: "Few places in Canada can be justly compared with this in beauty of scenery."[50] The long trip by water left Buffalo, explored the Great Lakes, skirted Niagara Falls, and finished up at the mysterious, magnificent Saguenay. Perhaps some knew of La Malbaie through a crazy idea of one William Burr: on a strip of linen, which he claimed was seven miles long, he sketched a panoramic view of all the major North American cities. This "moving picture" was unrolled before an audience at twenty-five sous a head and accompanied by a running commentary and piano music. *Burr's Seven Miles Mirror* allowed the viewer to take a cruise without

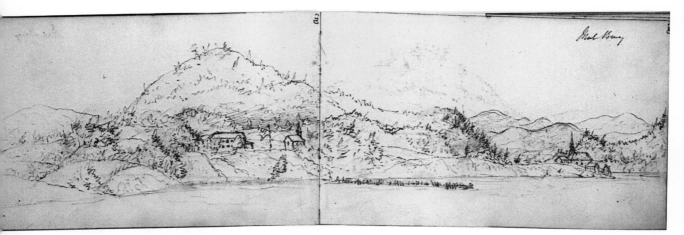

moving an inch and at the same time enticed him into a real trip. Did *Burr's Mirror* mark the beginning of the panoramic cinema? La Malbaie justly won a place in this "pictorial tour," and because of it many people were inspired to take the long voyage.

As for transportation companies, whose main concern was growth, they copublished travel guides giving information about connections, fares, and timetables for railways and steamboats servicing the St Lawrence valley. By 1854, a one-way trip from Québec to La Malbaie cost three dollars, a return trip, five. Prices were becoming competitive.

After that, the hill country was never the same. Commercial activity boomed; new and wealthier visitors arrived with each passing season; everyone was anxious to see the "Big River" and retrace the faint tracks of the people who had settled by its banks. A new era of prosperity had begun. And as though to mark the birth, Parliament chose this moment to name the county after the Jesuit Father François-Xavier de Charlevoix, the first man to show an interest in the history of New France.[51]

31 *The village of La Malbaie, 11–12 July 1840* During his six-year posting in Canada, Captain Henry James Warre traveled frequently in the countryside. He took advantage of several fishing trips to decorate his notebook with sketches that would immortalize the scenery of Charlevoix.

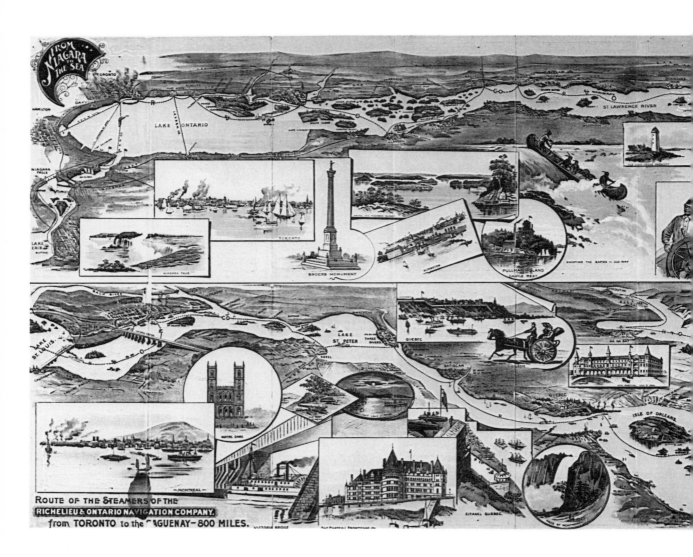

FROM NIAGARA TO THE SEA

ROUTE OF THE STEAMERS OF THE
RICHELIEU & ONTARIO NAVIGATION COMPANY.
from TORONTO to the SAGUENAY—800 MILES.

HOLIDAYS

32 *The Saguenay tour* Map of the 800-mile excursion from Toronto to Saguenay on the inland waterways of Canada.

Destination Murray Bay

THE AMERINDS called the St Lawrence River "the road which moves," and with reason: it is the only waterway in North America to cover so much distance and also reach the heart of the continent. At the start of the nineteenth century, rapid changes were taking place in the two principal cities of the St Lawrence valley, Québec and Montréal. In both, flourishing commercial activity attracted venture capital and a merchant class, an enterprising élite that would encourage technological innovation to further their own interests. These were the merchants who would revolutionize the transport industry and thus improve the economy of Lower Canada. The apppearance of the paddle-boat meant that navigation was no longer subject to the whims of wind and tide. Now more accessible, the inland seaport of Montréal became a serious rival of Québec.

The whole of the St Lawrence valley now made unprecedented economic strides, sustained by demographic growth due as much to a prolific Canadian population as to the ceaseless flow of immigration from Great Britain. Business between Montréal and Québec increased, and there was a constant exchange of businessmen. All this activity was of particular benefit to the shipping companies, who welcomed the opportunity for development. The New York journalist Theodore Dwight, Jr., son of the legal historian of the same name, noted in a travel report that "steamboats are of the utmost importance on this great river, for they contribute extremely to the convenience and expedition of travelling and render most valuable assistance to commerce."[1] Steamboat travel did indeed open up many ports of call and made it possible for visitors as well as businessmen to discover Canada off the beaten track.

PLEASURE TRIPS

The attraction of the St Lawrence is largely attributable to the beauty of its scenery. Past l'île d'Orléans, the river opens out to a width of some ten miles; from Cape Tourmente onward, the Laurentians fall abruptly into what is virtually the open sea. There are islands, too, which stand out from

33 *For Murray Bay and Rivière-du-Loup* Every Tuesday and Saturday in the summer of 1849, the steamer *Rowland Hill* ran a connecting service between Québec, Murray Bay, and Rivière-du-Loup.

the shining waters here and there, adding a touch of the picturesque to the magnificent setting. Many authors have sung the praises of this lovely country, especially around the banks of the St Lawrence; they have an entrancing, dreamy beauty, and in the heat of summer they are an oasis for city dwellers.

Pleasure trips along this stretch of river began about 1830 with the *Waterloo*, which belonged to John Molson's St Lawrence Steamboat Company; a little later, the steamships *Rowland Hill* and *Alliance* were carrying passengers from the cities twice a week. In 1853, construction of a quay on piles at Pointe-au-Pic made it possible to open a regular steamer service between Québec and the Saguenay fjord during the short summer season.

Up till that point, travellers had not stopped often at La Malbaie and then only when the river was calm. None but fearless adventurers and their families came from Québec to spend the summer months there, as W. Norman, proprietor of the Victoria Hotel in Québec, pointed out: "Formerly this voyage was only made by the young and hardy, for no means existed of reaching it except in fishing schooners or open boats. Now, things are entirely changed; steamboats, well fitted for the work, leave Quebec twice a week, and ere this summer's navigation closes probably daily. In many of these the trip may be made in perfect comfort and even luxury."[2]

A tourist itinerary was built up, and soon "Murray Bay, a beautiful grassy valley on the north shore," became a fashionable destination. The river with its boats and schooners, its sailboats and steamboats, attracted Americans first of all—they were already fond of pleasure trips. Merchants and higher officials from Montréal and Québec began traveling for pleasure, as romanticism, with its passionate taste for nature, permeated the arts and

34 *"Loading a Batteau at Low Tide"* To replace stock, the merchants of Charlevoix had to use schooners almost exclusively; for almost a century these remained the ideal type of vessel for transporting goods on inshore waters. About twelve metres in length and propelled by two sails, the schooner was easily beached, since being flat-bottomed it hardly listed at all. Thus at low tide horse-drawn carts could be used for loading and unloading cargo.

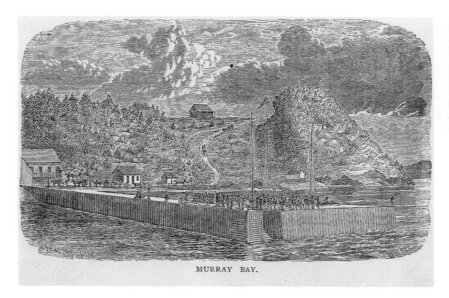

MURRAY BAY.

35 *Murray Bay* "After passing along
Mal Bay, the steamer makes its first
landing at Murray Bay. Here is a long
and substantial wharf, built by the
English government" (Henry M.
Burt, *Burt's Guide through the Connecticut Valley to the White Mountains
and the River Saguenay* [Springfield,
Mass. 1874], 285).

customs of Canada. The trip on the *Saguenay* lasted three days and cost
twelve dollars. The round trip from Québec took two days, the third day
being devoted to a tour of the Saguenay. From 1853 onward, Captain René
Simard made this trip his specialty. The Québec and Three Pistoles Steam
Navigation Company had chartered Captain Simard's boat exclusively for
this excursion.

Let us board the *Saguenay* in the company of an American who described
his trip in *Harper's Magazine* and, guidebook in hand, relive the experience
with him. The vessel leaves Napoleon Quay, in Québec, at nine o'clock
precisely. It promises to be a fine sunny July day.

36/37 *"Excursions to Murray Bay,
River Du Loup, Kakouna, and the
Far-Famed River Saguenay"* From
1853, with maritime transport more
efficiently organized, this type of little
travel guide was used to promote
tourism on the St Lawrence.

> There we met some tourists from New York; several priests in their long
> black cassocks, with pupils of the Quebec Seminary in uniform, just leaving
> to spend their summer vacation at home; three or four nuns going to places
> below; a Protestant clergyman from Ottawa; a gentleman of the bar and his
> family from Montreal; the Seignior of Murray Bay; Sir St. George Gore, the
> notable sportsman lately returned from a three years' hunt in the Rocky
> Mountains, with a part of his attendants; some citizens of Quebec going to
> the summer resorts below, and a few *habitans*.[3]

The ship seems to be floating at the mercy of the placid river; in fact,
Captain Simard is handling her in accordance with an exact timetable,
stopping first at Rivière-Ouelle, then moving to the other bank before
finally reaching La Malbaie to discharge a few passengers and some cargo.
One of our fellow passengers, a gentleman from Philadelphia, writes one
Wednesday morning in July 1855:

> The boat stopped at Murray Bay to land passengers and freight. This place
> seems to be the Cape May of Canada, where the citizens of Quebec and
> Montreal resort in great numbers, for salt-water bathing. The long pier that
> stretches into the river was crowded with ladies expecting friends and relatives

38/39 *On the route to Saguenay* On this three-day round trip, the steamer *Saguenay* tied up for the night along-side the quay at Rivière-du-Loup.

40 *The steamer* MAGNET Starting in 1861, this steamer went up and down the river on the St Lawrence cruise. "By taking this steamer," announced the *Morning Chronicle* for 1 July 1867, "the TOURIST and INVALID will enjoy the refreshing and invigorating breeze, and picturesque scenery of the Lower St. Lawrence ... "

by the boat. During the summer, the ladies of Canada, when at watering places, wear straw hats, with rims of enormous breadth, which afford a marked contrast to the minute fixtures which American ladies affect. The scene was highly picturesque, and called forth much complimentary notice from travelling Americans who were aboard.[4]

We reach Rivière-du-Loup towards seven o'clock in the evening. After a peaceful night a thick fog delays our departure, so we watch Micmacs making wicker baskets until it's time to leave. Naturally, we expect to see something marvellous — after all, that is why we came — but we have never seen anything like this before! Our gentleman traveller is quite dazzled: "I have stood in the presence of Niagara, and there regarded the voice of man as sacrilegious impertinence; but never have I felt the insignificance of human utterance and human effort as when standing still in the presence of those silent preachers of omnipotence, capes Trinity and Eternity, with the broad heavens above filled with the light and the unstable waters below deep and black, where darkness eternally broods. It was a lesson of humility long to be remembered."[5]

During the voyage some locals come on board and we have the pleasure of watching them dance for hours to the lively rhythm of traditional music. Finally, after three days we return contented to Québec. The trip has been outstanding both for the beautiful scenery and for the charm of the inhabitants.

As the years went by La Malbaie acquired more and more of a reputation; in increasing numbers, tourists from Montréal went downstream to Québec aboard the luxury steamships of the Richelieu Company. This shipping outfit did much to establish Charlevoix as a summer resort.

In 1845, Pierre Édouard Leclère had launched the Richelieu Shipping Society with a view to linking Richelieu Valley and Bonsecours Market in Montréal. He hoped to sell agricultural products and thereby stimulate local trade. Leclère expanded his operations quickly, and in 1857 the society

41 *Indians making bark canoe* One of the interesting features of an excursion was to make contact with the Amerinds, who took advantage of the summer months to come to Pointe-au-Pic and sell their handicrafts to tourists.

became the powerful Richelieu Company. When the magnificent *Québec* was built at Sorel in 1865 at a cost of $172,000, Canada's inland water transport did not have to envy American lines any longer. Every day except Sunday this steamer left Montréal at 7:00 P.M., carrying passengers to Québec for a dollar, a dollar and a half first class. At Québec they had to board new ships, such as the *Union*, which from 1867 made the big trip to Saguenay.

The stop at La Malbaie, en route to Saguenay, was not to be missed. James Macpherson Lemoine, an erudite gentleman from Québec who had traveled the lower St. Lawrence on more than one occasion, concluded that "of all the picturesque parishes on the banks of our great river, where our innumerable swarms of tourists swoop down each summer to *take the waters*, none interests the lover of imposing scenery more than La Malbaie. For Nature in the raw, Nature on the grand scale, for broad horizons, one must go to La Malbaie."[6]

The impetuous Arthur Buies expresses this with even more conviction and enthusiasm: "You can't stand it any longer? You're suffocating, you're panting, you're melting? ... The remedy is simple. At seven o'clock in the morning, take one of the St. Lawrence Company boats, and do the Saguenay trip; ... stop off at La Malbaie, the most picturesque and the most poetic of watering-places, Canada's Eden, the poet's dream."[7] In the same account Buies hints at the pleasures of river trips:

> Every morning at seven o'clock a steamer of the St. Lawrence Company leaves the port of Quebec and gets to La Malbaie six hours later, skirting Orleans Island, and then the North Shore – that part of the wild, superb coast where the Laurentides reach their maximum height: where Cape Tourmente, suddenly emerging from the river and rising to a height of two thousand feet, starts a series of mountains which bathe in the St. Lawrence, rising proud and free like giants of stone, casting behind them their dark locks from peak to peak, plateau to plateau, until the eye loses them in a horizon tinged

42 *The Richelieu Company's steamer* QUÉBEC *leaving the wharf at Montréal for Québec* In 1870, the Richelieu Company's *Montréal* and *Québec* linked the metropolis with the city of Québec. The two steamers were filled with travellers who preferred the pleasant trip by water.

43 *Passengers transferring from one steamer to another in Québec* All steamship travellers had to stage at Québec before embarking for La Malbaie.

with all the colours of the clouds ... Tell me, what pick-me-up equals an hour passed with the sun rising over the bridge of the *Union* or the *Saguenay*, while the light of day climbs ever higher up the horizon, bathing all Nature in its light without yet setting it afire: and the air, all full of fragrance, pure and strong, surges through panting throats down into the thirsty lungs! Tell me, what pleasure, what joy can equal this intoxication of the senses, this peaceful, strengthening intoxication which enters the body through every pore, which permeates every fibre, and simultaneously recharges the soul completely? Ah!—from time to time God is truly good to his miserable creatures, and the St. Lawrence Company more than merits every expression of our gratitude![8]

A little further on he adds, "The food on board is remarkably good and varied—besides which things are done with elegance and a sort of prodigality which is, in my opinion, the highest compliment that one could pay the passengers."[9]

The well-known Saguenay tour attracted many outside Canada. By 1877 they were arriving in groups organized by Gustave Leve's Grand American Excursion Party in New York, guided by Leve himself. Meyer Auerbach went with one of these groups in August 1877 and wrote about the benefits youth could derive from travel. Once in Québec, the group embarked early one morning on the *Union*:

> After a good night's rest, we next morning assembled in the parlor, and were then driven down to the pier, where we went aboard the steamer *Union*,

44 *Disembarking at La Malbaie* The steamer *Union* lying alongside the quay at Pointe-au-Pic before her return to Québec.

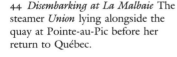

45 *Arrival at La Malbaie from Québec*
The arrival of the cruise-ship was a
social event for visitors and locals
alike.

which was there made fast. Punctually at half past seven they cast the lines
loose that bound the steamer to the dock, and we commenced what turned
out to be one of the most charming water tours, which any of our party had
ever participated in. The steamer was a double-decker, with very large and
roomy saloons and cabins, which were handsomely fitted up. Each cabin had
an upper and a lower berth, which were provided with heavy woolen cover-
lets, which are a necessity in that climate; two cork life preservers were also
prominently hung up in every cabin.

The steamer, as indeed all steamers and ferry boats in Canada, burned
wood and soft coal, and emitted a dense black smoke, which in the night,
looked very pretty, as it was then seen to be interspersed with myriads of
brilliant sparks. By this time we were proceeding swiftly down the St. Lawrence river, which is about one and a half miles wide at Quebec; it soon
widens, however, and the steamer passes the "Isle of Orleans", which is about
twenty miles in length and altogether a very beautiful spot. Arriving at the
eastern end of the island, we found that the St. Lawrence had attained a
width of about six miles; that the mountains, which are very steep and
rugged, came to the very water's edge; and that we were keeping very near
the north shore. After running in this way until noon, the steamer made its
first landing at Murray Bay. This is a very flashionable [*sic*] watering place,
visitors coming here annually in great numbers; during the summer months
several indian tribes make it their headquarters, doing a very brisk trade in
selling indian work and curiosities. Quite a number of passengers here left

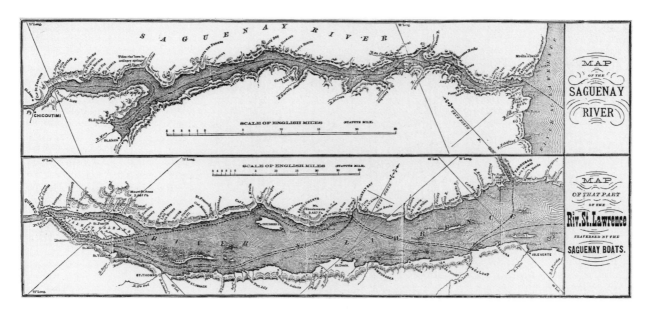

46 *Map of the Saguenay River* From 1872 on, the St Lawrence Steam Navigation Company's steamers *Union* and *Saguenay* made four trips each week from Québec to Chicoutimi, calling at Murray Bay on both outward and return journeys, as indicated on this map.

the vessel, and, after taking on board an immense quantity of wood, the steamer again proceeded on its journey, passing the Pilgrim Islands and reaching Rivière-du-Loup at about four o'clock.[10]

After a trip to the Saguenay, whose beauty awed the Americans, they disembarked for a few hours at Pointe-au-Pic to get a closer look at the Amerinds, whom Meyer had noticed with interest on their first stop: "At ten o'clock that evening we arrived at Murray Bay. The captain, after attending to some necessary duties, accompanied us ashore to the indian settlement; here he unceremoniously entered the first handy hut, aroused the inmates and asked them to show us the goods which they had for

47 *The steamer* SAGUENAY Built in 1853, this steamer was bought by the St Lawrence Steam Navigation Company in 1872. She cruised the St Lawrence between Québec and Saguenay until September 1884, when she was destroyed by a fire off the quay at Pointe-au-Pic.

48 *An Indian village of twenty to thirty hearths, near the quay at Pointe-au-Pic* "One lands at the foot of a menacing promontory, where the waves breaking against its jagged cliff give off a dull, growling echo. Sheltered against the base of this promontory lies an Indian village of twenty to thirty hearths, oddly grouped together; no visitor ever misses paying them a visit, either through curiosity, or because he wants to buy one of the thousand and one little objects the Indians make in willow or ash—baskets, hampers, vases of every description, ear-rings, pendants, etc." (Arthur Buies, *Chroniques canadiennes, humeurs et caprices* [Montréal 1884], 166–7).

sale ... They offered us bead-work, baskets and straw and wooden-hats for ladies' wear; these latter cost only two dollars apiece, and weighed about a pound and a half."[11]

The popularity of the Saguenay grew steadily, and with it, that of stops between Québec and Chicoutimi. Under the presidency of Abraham Joseph of Québec, the St Lawrence Steam Navigation Company replaced the St Lawrence Tug Company and offered first-class service to visitors, who could now travel aboard the *Saguenay*, *St Lawrence*, *Clyde*, or *Union*:

49 *The menu aboard the steamer* SAGUENAY In 1874, many tourist guides acknowledged right away that the *Saguenay* was no cheaper than the St-Louis Hotel in Québec or the St Lawrence Hall in Montréal.

50 *The steamer* ST. LAWRENCE This ship, built in New York in 1852, was 210 feet long, 18 wide, and 19 high. Later bought by the St Lawrence Steam Navigation Company to do the Saguenay tour, she carried out a shuttle service every summer between 20 June and 10 September.

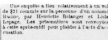

51 *An excursion in 1875* All through the summer season, "the pleasure of a trip on the majestic waters of our river" was regularly advertised.

52 *A first-class cruise ship* The interior of one of the "floating palaces," which offered the most luxurious cruises on the St Lawrence.

"Four times a week in the summer months steamers freighted with holiday-makers and tourists leave Quebec for Tadoussac and Chicoutimi, touching at the various places between these points. To look at the piles of baggage and furniture, the hosts of children and servants, the household goods, the dogs, cats and birds, one might think the Canadians were emigrating *en masse*."[12] The steamers followed a route of endless beauty, which is why the Saguenay trip was so popular. It became known as "the trip *par excellence*," during which casual meetings might lead to a happy ending ...

The American writer William D. Howells soon found material in the region for a novel. Using his travel notes, he published *A Chance Acquaintance* in 1873, later translated by Louis Fréchette as *Une rencontre, roman de deux touristes sur le Saint-Laurent et le Saguenay*. His heroine, Miss Kitty Ellison, was modeled on an eccentric young lady he had met with his wife during their river trip. It is a charming, comic love story about an emancipated, broad-minded girl who encounters her opposite, a "proper

53 *The prestigious décor of the steamer* Richelieu The elegance of the living-room, on the second deck, is self-evident: the refined furniture, the rich mouldings on the ceiling, and, at the far end, the portrait of Cardinal Richelieu.

Bostonian," a faithful upholder of the conventions of his class, on a river voyage. It is against the scenic background of the St Lawrence valley that the differences between the two protagonists are worked out:

> The coast, nowhere precipitous and sheer, looked as though it had been cut by one of those majestic rivers of southern countries, broad and sleepy, reflecting the blue skies above all throughout the day until the setting of the sun. But no palm-tree flaunted its sharp-cut silhouette on these pale-green, regular banks; only the pale birch, slim and delicate, was reflected in these waters, its winter foilage gleaming white.
>
> This was the great desolate river of the terrible country of the North ... [13]

54 *The steamer* MONTRÉAL Built in Toronto in 1903, the *Montréal* was the biggest steamer in Canada in her day; she could accommodate up to 750 passengers. Her career as a cruise ship came to an end when she caught fire in 1926, shortly before she was due to be laid up for the winter near Sorel.

55 *The Richelieu and Ontario Navigation Company* A poster illustrating the tourist attractions to be encountered on an increasingly popular form of travel.

It was not only literature that benefited from these excursions. The whole of the St Lawrence shipping industry was expanding at astonishing speed. From 1875, the acquisition of the Canadian Steam Navigation Company enabled the already powerful Richelieu Company to cover a vast territory, from Toronto to Québec, with a fleet of eighteen steamers flying the flag of the new Richelieu and Ontario Navigation Company. In 1886, this company merged with the Saguenay lines to become absolute masters of the waters from the Great Lakes to the Atlantic. From now on it was

56 *From Niagara to the sea* This illustration by Raoul Barré, father of the Québec cartoon, gives a good idea of what can be expected on a St Lawrence cruise.

57 *The Québec Central Railway* In 1875 tourists could leave from New York or Boston on the White Mountains Line to Richmond Junction in Canada; there they would join the Grand Trunk line, which would take them to Rivière-Ouelle, the embarkation point for Pointe-au-Pic.

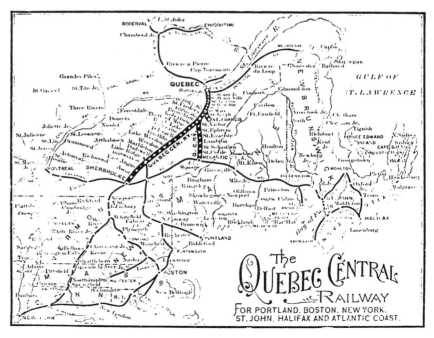

possible to leave Montréal, do the Saguenay tour, and return on the same ship. For these new cruises, almost eight hundred miles from Toronto, the steamers were turned into veritable floating palaces, fast and luxurious.

The ships were decorated in an elegant Victorian style. Wide staircases led down to a vast saloon laid with burgundy-coloured carpet and covered with a richly gilded dome. The *Montréal* had her saloon decorated with bas-reliefs in bronze representing the four seasons. Simplicity, however, was the fashion in cabins, which could accommodate nearly three hundred

passengers. Outside, the vessels were painted white, and the people who lived along the river, who saw them gliding by gracefully like swans in midstream, called them white ships.

The railways also developed. At the start, they were tributaries of the river and depended on its trade. Their task, in effect, was to speed the delivery of goods to major centres. But with the incorporation of the Grand Trunk in 1853 the railways started expanding, and when the government placed the postal service in their hands exclusively, their future was assured.

Starting in autumn 1855, some travellers could go by train from Montréal to Québec by taking a branch line that linked the two cities along the south shore of the St Lawrence and passed through Richmond—the Québec junction with a line that ran from Portland, Maine.

La Malbaie also profited from the railway. By 1875, a network of ferries tied it to the south shore, and Pointe-au-Pic had Pointe-aux-Orignaux as a liaison port at Rivière-Ouelle, "where the *Rival* came in every morning at nine o'clock, and a coach left immediately to carry passengers and baggage to the Grand Trunk station eight miles further on."[14]

61 *Flying the R & O flag* This illustration shows nine of the twenty-five steamers that comprised the fleet of the Richelieu and Ontario Navigation Company at the turn of the century. Their continued desire for expansion led the R & O in 1913 to join the conglomerate that ultimately became the maritime-transport giant known as Canada Steamship Lines.

NINE *of the twenty five* STEAMERS
Comprising the fleet of the R. & O. NAV. CO.

62 *The steamer* CANADA *alongside Cap-à-l'Aigle quay around 1900* Built at Sorel in 1866, the *Canada* ran between the ports of Montréal, Québec, and Saguenay; she was officially put into service in the year of Confederation (whence her name). She was enlarged in 1905 and renamed *St Irénée*. During her last years she was known as the *Cape St Francis*.

63 *Destination Murray Bay* The quay at Pointe-au-Pic was built in 1853; it was enlarged and strengthened a dozen years later to handle cruise ships, which had become veritable floating hotels.

64 *Captain H.W. Gagné (1873–1961)*
The arrival and departure of a cruise
ship drew a crowd onto the quay.
Captain Wilfrid Gagné was proud
to welcome passengers as they
boarded his ship. Among the great
families of Charlevoix navigators, the
Gagnés had been at the helm of
"white ships" for 187 years!

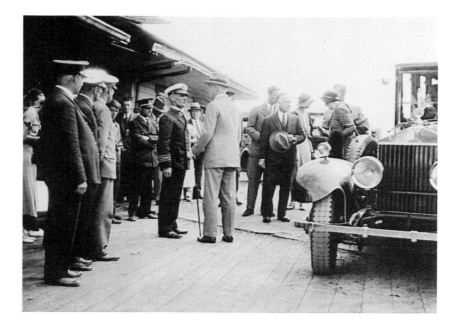

A number of boats served as connections between the *Rival*, on which
Arthur Buies traveled in 1877, and the *Champlain*, which ran a daily service
in 1903 between Pointe-au-Pic and Rivière-Ouelle; the *Admiral*, *Folger*,
Lévis, and *Eureka* were but a few. This line was kept going until 1919, when
the deputy for Charlevoix, Rodolphe Forget, obtained a railway for La
Malbaie, finally linking it with Québec. However, the speed of rail service
did not outdo the charms of steamers, and boat transport reigned supreme.

65 *The steamer* RICHELIEU In 1927, a
fleet specially constructed and
equipped for cruises on the St Lawrence and the Saguenay flew the
new black-and-red flag of Canada
Steamship Lines. The most prestigious of the four ships, the *Richelieu*,
was almost invariably chartered for the
week-long cruises that left Victoria
Quay in Montréal every Monday
with more than two hundred passengers aboard. For their comfort, a
series of alcoves had been built on the
second and third decks, which
replaced private balconies and the
usual promenade around the decks.

In 1894, control of the Richelieu and Ontario Navigation Company passed into the hands of a financial group headed by Louis J. Forget. Under his leadership the company strove to modernize itself; great strides were made, owing largely to a commercial strategy which consisted of maximizing services to the semi-captive clientele aboard steamers. Hotels were acquired, first at Tadoussac and then at Pointe-au-Pic, for which the white ships provided guests. In the end, every part of a cruise, on land or water, was run by the company.

66 *For a real holiday, take a cruise!* When the *Québec* was destroyed by fire at Tadoussac in August 1950 the three other "little ships" of Canada Steamship Lines, the *Tadoussac, St Lawrence*, and *Richelieu*, kept the hundred-year-old tradition of cruising going until 1965.

LIFE IN THE HOTELS

Charlevoix's career as a tourist attraction started modestly. At first there were hardly any visitors except those who came to see the Nairne and Fraser families. Then came a few explorers and adventurers, soon followed

67 *Central House* "The centre of all
the action was without question
Duberger's. There was a ballroom
there, a billiard-room, a bar, a skit-
tle alley, and a telegraph office. The
long façade of the main building
had two porches, one above the other,
where the summer residents would
often sit and watch the eternal and
ever-changing spectacle of the sea.
To the right of the central door stood
a hundred-foot-high maypole flying various flags, which moved lazily
in the summer breeze. Jets of water
played in two huge green tanks,
where there were sometimes fish
swimming, and during the calm,
quiet summer nights one could hear
the flowing water singing quietly to
itself in the fountains" (Alfred De
Celles, "Villégiature d'autrefois et
d'aujourd hui," *La Revue moderne*
[September 1923]: 20).

68 *The hotelier Georges Duberger
standing between his parents* "M.
Duberger is the most welcoming of
hotel-owners, and the prices in his
establishment are so moderate that
when all's said and done, one finds
that one hasn't spent more than one
would at home" (Anonymous,
« L'hôtel Duberger, à La Malbaie »
L'Opinion publique [25 August 1881]:
397).

by sportsmen attracted to the lakes and rivers. In the beginning only
schooners came to Charlevoix; the first steamers did not appear until about
1830. And it was not until 1853 — when the dock at Pointe-au-Pic was
standing firmly on piles — that ships of heavy tonnage started bringing in
tourists. This was the birth of a famous tourist centre in eastern Canada.

During the early years, some of the locals began opening their houses
to visitors. The Chaperons' inn built up a good reputation in varied circles.
But such accommodation could not satisfy the needs of the growing crowds
arriving day after day. The first establishment dedicated exclusively to the
reception of visitors was built and established at Pointe-au-Pic in 1860, by
Georges Duberger. His hotel, very simply furnished, could accommodate
a hundred people comfortably, and it had a concert hall to seat three
hundred. It was the biggest and the best situated in the village, which won
it the name Central House.

According to Laurent-Olivier David, co-founder and editor of the illustrated weekly *L'Opinion publique*, summer resort living had already taken
various forms by 1870: "The strangers adopt several different life-styles.

Some of them shut themselves up in hotels; others rent houses and do
their own cooking; a good many of them board with local smallholders.
Staying at a hotel costs a *piastre* a day; boarding with smallholders varies
from two to four *chelins*."[15] A year later David was back again, in July; this
time he gave some details about the hotel he was staying in:

> I will merely add today that La Malbaie has several good hotels, and that
> Duberger's in particular offers its visitors a charming place, where they will
> find a good table and good rooms, billiards, bowls, bagatelle, music, and
> dancing for those who want it. It is impossible to describe the trouble they

†The *chelin*, the French version of the English *shilling*, was worth twenty-five cents. There
were four *chelin* to the *piastre*, which was equivalent to the dollar.

go to to satisfy everybody, and the prices are very reasonable; but many tourists simply do not understand how difficult it is to run such an establishment for just two months in the year, in the country. And those who complain most are those who pay least.[16]

A year later, Arthur Buies wrote about this little summer resort hotel, making special reference to the kindness of the proprietor's mother, who went to all sorts of lengths for the clientele:

> At Duberger's Hotel, there are skittles, and billiards, and high spirits, and free-&-easiness; and above all there is Madame Duberger Senior, a heroic woman of seventy, who is a real prodigy of prodigies. Always on her feet, alert and lively, she never gives herself a moment's rest. Her guests are her children. You should see her at table, calling to her serving-girls on all sides, controlling them, spurring them on, stamping her own indefatigable activity onto them. Her voice dominates all other voices, and it is a truly pleasurable sight to see this incomparable matron darting now right, now left, foreseeing every wish, dividing every appetite. Last week, she dropped dead from fatigue; we thought she was gone, she received the last sacraments—and two days later her voice was resounding once again amongst the tables filled with astounded and delighted guests.[17]

Throughout these years the summer residents flowed in; the calm, the simplicity, and the freshness of the climate made La Malbaie an ideal place for rest. Life was accommodating—so much so that in an article for the *Canadian Illustrated News* in 1871 a traveller could not conceal his astonish-

69 *Arthur Buies, a regular resident at The Hotel Duberger* The journalist, columnist, and pamphleteer Arthur Buies was known as an ardent "back-to-earth" supporter. He was also an eccentric, with bushy moustache and piercing eyes, one of "the most reckless of our heroes of the written word." He got himself into hot water with his pen at La Malbaie, and as a consequence fell victim to one of his contemporaries. Here is the reporter reported on: "Town dress and town style are well known: but they look like simple easy morning undress against the array of finery that greets the rustic sun in resorts that are in the least fashionable. Cap-à-l'Aigle changes its clothes three times a day, at the very least; Pointe-au-Pic, four times; Buies is the only person I have seen sloppily dressed ..." (Napoléon Legendre, *Echos de Québec*, vol. 2, Québec [1877]: 66).

70 *"Pier at Murray Bay, St Lawrence River"* Dozens of dog-carts, traps, and calashes patiently await the army of tourists who would shortly be disembarking at the Pointe-au-Pic quay.

71 *The Canadian calash* "Carriage! Carriage! Carriage! sings out a chorus of voices and, presto! the long lines of carriages are seen winding up the roads" (Irene Todd, "The Newport of Canada: Murray Bay," *The Canadian Magazine* [June 1923]: 145).

72 *Xavier Warren's house about 1890* This Pointe-au-Pic house, with a wing added, offered — in the words of the visitors who followed one another there — "the best rooms and the fullest meals."

ment at the buggies dashing around: "After a rush up and a rush downhill, and a rush along a level road for about a quarter of a mile, I was landed safely at a hotel kept by one Xavier Warren ... The meals and accommodation at the hotels are everything that can be desired, and from personal experience I would recommend mine host Warren, as one who is ever indefatigable in his efforts to make his guests feel comfortable."[18]

The columnist Arthur Buies, who kept coming back to this "unique watering-place" year after year, had equal praise for it: "Now comes the Warren Hotel, split into two houses, one beside the other, and both the youngest in the place; they have the best rooms, and serve the best meals. The owner bears a Scottish name, but that does not stop him also being as good a Canadian as the purest Jean-Baptiste."[19] Indeed, the Scots name of the proprietor was a bit deceiving; there was a touch of humour in one visitor's voice as he discussed it with Alfred D. Decelles, the renowned librarian of the Canadian Parliament: "Since I don't know a word of

73 *Riverside House, Murray Bay* The name of this country hotel is shyly displayed on the second floor, above the entrance. It was said at the hotel that Abraham Lincoln's widow came there for a rest in 1873.

French (he said to me), I didn't want to stay with some Frenchman called Duberger; but it turns out this Warren's a Canadian like yourself! What sort of a fraud is this?"[20]

If there is any one man who left his mark permanently on Murray Bay, it is without doubt Monsieur Chamard, who may be said to have been the Pointe-au-Pic hotelier *par excellence*. Jean Olivier Chamard was a Montréal grain merchant of delicate health; in 1868 he decided to rent the Riverside House from Georges Warren and make it his new business, far from the bustling city. In 1872, the place was renamed Chamard's Lorne House, in honour of the Marquess of Lorne, who later became the forty-second governor-general of Canada. That summer, the establishment welcomed more than 250 guests; the following year, 370; and in 1874, a total of 577. The registers of those days were like social notes where the Dows and Caverhills rubbed shoulders with the Drummonds and Molsons from Montréal, the Sewells, Prices, Garneaus, and Lemesuriers from Québec, and of course the Blakes from Toronto. Nothing succeeds like success; and for the 1878 season Monsieur Chamard had a new hotel built on top of the cliff, much bigger than the first, with a clear view over the river.

> It was in the wooded part of the cliff, immediately overlooking the river; the eye took in a limitless panorama, full of variety, apparently stretching to infinity, and protected by its very position against any inconvenient buildings nearby. Here Monsieur Chamard, the welll-known proprietor of *Lorne House*, wished to build a large hotel with a capital of fifty thousand dollars, divided into 2,000 shares at twenty-five dollars each; and in the immediate neighbour-hood a certain number of isolated cottages, all dependent on the hotel, which would accommodate families who wanted to live separately ... Monsieur

74 *Jessie and William Chamard around 1880* Jessie and William were happy to work in the family business, assisting their widowed mother; they helped the hotel prosper, and its reputation spread way beyond the Canadian border.

75 *Chamard's Lorne House (1878–98)* Though it wasn't smart looking, this hotel was the busiest one in Murray Bay. With a touch of humour, it was said the partitions between the rooms were so thin one could hear one's neighbours changing their minds! But William Chamard's legendary good nature made guests forget such shortcomings. Seen here posing proudly in the doorway is the corpulent proprietor, whom guests liked to address as Uncle Bill.

Chamard proposed to build his hotel in such a way that it could be successively enlarged as the need arose. The hotel would start off ... 120 ft. long by 40 ft. wide, and would consist of three stories, the second above the first, and the third above the second, in the normal fashion. It would be sited in the midst of the pine woods and through every door and window would come that delicious bitter-sweet smell composed of the mingled odours of the sea and the woods.[21]

After Chamard's accidental death, his widow and two children, Jessie and William, took over and further improved the hotel. By careful administration, they managed to keep prices low—seven dollars a week for a full pension. That price included a room, a wooden tub for washing, a jug of cold water, and another of hot. In the dining-room trout was plentifully served, and partridge in season; tea was available from three o'clock in the afternoon and also in the evening. A horse ride cost twenty-five cents, and to hire a buggy for the whole day cost a dollar and a half. The golden age

76 *The new Chamard's* Built at the beginning of this century, the Chamard family's second hotel overlooked the Murray Bay golf-course. A story is told of an American tourist who failed to find a room at Manoir Richelieu and was forced to look elsewhere. Arriving at Chamard's, he said to Uncle Bill in a haughty tone, "Monsieur, your hotel looks exactly like a stable!" To which Uncle Bill replied with a sly smile, "Perhaps so, Monsieur, but there's nothing but thoroughbreds inside!"

CHAMARD'S LORNE HOUSE, Murray Bay, P. Q., Canada.

of Chamard's Lorne House lasted until 1898. Then the Richelieu and Ontario Navigation Company acquired the land on which the hotel stood, and the Chamards had to rent it back from them. The new owners decided to build the first Manoir Richelieu there; and so in 1901 Jessie and William Chamard started constructing another building on a promontory not far from the boundary of La Malbaie, with a fine view over the golf-course.

Despite the increasing availability of hotel accommodation, many tourists preferred to board with a local family, which was cheaper. Cap-à-l'Aigle was a popular place for this: "crowds of tourists go each summer, ... renting the farmers' houses for a couple of months."[22] As an industry, agriculture had peaked; thus an influx of visitors from outside ensured a sizeable extra income. Hiring a summer cottage or farmhouse became so popular that Cyrius C. Duberger, a surveyor and civil engineer, published the *Murray Bay Atlas* in 1895, containing twelve maps of La Malbaie and its surroundings, divided into twelve sections showing every property together with the name of its owner. The atlas suggested walks to take, listing points of interest along the way, including lakes, rivers, waterfalls, and the paths that led to them.

> Many families have their own pretty country-houses, but a favourite plan is to take a *habitant*'s cottage just as it stands, and to play at "roughing it" with all the luxuries you care to add to the rag-matted floors and primitive furniture. Those who want more excitement find it at the hotels, where in the evening, there is always a dance, a concert, or private theatricals, to wind up a day spent in bathing, picnicing, boating, driving, trout-fishing, tennis, bowls, billiards, and a dozen other amusements. It is a merry life and a healthy one; you can live as you please, and do as you please, and nobody says you nay.[23]

77 *To let at Cap-à-l'Aigle!* Letting the house to tourists during summer months brought considerable addition to a farmer's income.

78 *Thomas Bhérer's farm at Cap-à-l'Aigle, 1896* Mr and Mrs William Kerry and their children, Esther and Arthur, accompanied by their little friend Keith Notman, all lodged with the farmer.

79 *The Bhérer barn, Cap-à-l'Aigle* The Notman children and Kerry children enjoyed playing around the barn-cum-stable during their holidays at the farm. The Bhérer barn, a typical Charlevoix building, had a thatched roof; the overhanging upper storey was a sort of penthouse.

THE CONVALESCENT HOME, MURRAY BAY.
From a sketch.

80 *The convalescent home, Murray Bay*
For almost a century, from 1874 to
1964, this nursing home allowed the
underprivileged from the Montréal
region to enjoy a summer holiday in
La Malbaie.

81 *At the village of Pointe-au-Pic* Here
and there, boarding houses offered
accommodation to those in search of
peace and quiet.

82 *Between fresh water and the sea* At
Pointe-au-Pic, the banks of the river
attracted several tourists who had
come seeking the bracing blend of
sea air and refreshing mountain
breeze.

While some preferred the hotels with their endless activities, others
sought peace and quiet. For those who lacked financial resources, Miss
Hervey and her friends launched with donations from welfare societies the
Convalescent Home in 1874. This rest-house was reserved exclusively for
about a hundred invalids and sick patients sent by charitable organizations
in Montréal. Its administration was carried out by members of the summer
colony, who felt it an honour to take up the responsibility.

As mentioned, the transport companies did not remain unaffected by
the general affluence. They took the opportunity to widen their range of
services, opening hotels where their boats put in, at Tadoussac and La
Malbaie. To do this, the Richelieu and Ontario Navigation Company
bought all the land that overlooked the dock at Pointe-au-Pic, on top of
the cliff where Chamard's Lorne House stood. In 1899 the new owners had
a hotel built, to the plans of Maxwell and Shattuck of Montréal; it was

three storeys high, built entirely of wood, and completely covered in cedar shingles. With pomp and ceremony, it was given the name Manoir Richelieu. The season ran from 15 June to 15 September. Two hundred and fifty rooms could accommodate nearly four hundred guests; the rooms were luxurious, covered in the best Brussels carpet, and had adjoining bathrooms supplied with both salt and fresh water. This was a far cry from rustic establishments like Duberger's Hotel, which had vanished in a fire that destroyed the centre of the village of Pointe-au-Pic. The ambiance of the *manoir* was sumptuous, and the services offered to its smart and distinguished clientele became more and more sophisticated. Guests could now bathe in a salt-water pool behind the hotel, or play tennis on well-kept courts; a billiard room and a bowling-alley relieved the boredom of those who did not enjoy rainy days; the big lounges on the ground floor were comfortable, and the dining-room had a magnificent view over the river. The food could please the most discriminating palate. Each day tables were laden with vegetables from a magnificent kitchen garden; there were fresh fruits, too, and flowers to brighten up the dining-room. On spacious verandas guests could sit and watch the steamboats gliding smoothly down the mighty river. The *manoir* orchestra played every afternoon for the guests and also gave four concerts a week. Nearly every conceivable service was available: a barber's shop, a ladies' hairdresser, a manicurist. There was even a resident doctor.

83 *Hotel at Murray Bay* This first-class hotel was the work of the Montréal architects Maxwell and Shattuck. Constructed in 1899, it had 250 handsomely furnished rooms and could accommodate four hundred guests.

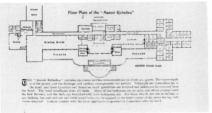

84/85 *A daring construction* The construction of this monumental type of architecture was an event in 1899. It required the importation of semi-skilled labour to assist the local work force.

The hotel was a vast pavilion in a fragrant balsam forest on the brow of a cliff. People there might well have imagined themselves guests of some remote seigneur, lost in wonderland. The climate, into the bargain, was a perfect mixture of dry mountain air and the salty sea breeze from the river. Not far away lay a charming little village with a certain flavour of Normandy and bonny old Scotland; it satisfied the visitor's taste for the picturesque. This combination of modern hotel and traditional hamlet made Manoir Richelieu the perfect summer resort place.

Before long the *manoir* was joined by the Château Murray, on which work had started in 1903 for John Warren. The architect was his son J.-Charles. This new building filled the gap left by the destruction of Hotel Duberger. If the atmosphere at the manor was fashionable, at the Château it was cosy. Indeed, the intimate, Franco-Scottish hospitality of the Warrens won them a faithful clientele, composed mainly of French-speaking lawyers' families from Montréal and Québec. Most of the guests were wives with their children, joined by their husbands on the weekends. There were few organized activities at the Château; the reputation of the little hotel rested mainly on the peace and quiet it offered townsfolk. The day might consist of meals eaten in the dining-room and a stroll down the main street in the evening. There were, however, endless card games to liven things up, especially when the players, as they often did, took things too seriously. Three generations of Warrens held the reins at the Château; then the day came, in 1978, when the all-wood structure had to be demolished for reasons of safety.

86 *Manoir Richelieu* This hotel complex, which offered a full range of modern services, earned a reputation as a veritable palace of luxury.

The first Manoir Richelieu had a much shorter life span: at the end of the 1928 season, after thirty years of operation, this monument was completely destroyed by fire. On the following day, T.R. Enderby, director-general of Canada Steamship Lines, informed a reporter for the Montréal *Gazette* that work would start immediately on the building of a new *manoir* even

87 *A salt-water pool* The swimming-pool attracted not only swimmers but also those who came to "rubber-neck."

88 *Quite a sight!* Passengers on "floating palaces" always found Manoir Richelieu a spectacular stop.

bigger than the first. The architect John S. Archibald submitted a design that the company accepted immediately; the lines of a Norman château, with turrets and pointed gables, would make the new *manoir* a symbol of the French heritage of Charlevoix and underline the historic character of La Malbaie. It is of interest to note that at that time the château style was very much the fashion for big hotels; the same firm designed Château Laurier in Ottawa.

At the insistence of the engineer William H. Coverdale, president of Canada Steamship Lines, a concrete structure was chosen; this had the advantage of being fire-proof. Another novel idea, carrying out the construction underneath an immense wooden hood that could be heated, made it possible to pour concrete all through the winter season. Operating with two teams of five hundred workers each under the direction of Davie Shipbuilding of Lauzon, the contractors Wilde and Brydon kept the work going day and night throughout the eight months of winter. This feat accomplished, the new Manoir Richelieu was able to open its doors on the usual date, 15 June 1929, without missing a season.

Besides being fire-proof and earthquake-resistant, the building was to remain open in winter. During the first two seasons, the new hotel drew quite a crowd, who spent the Christmas holidays skating, skiing, and tobogganing. Unfortunately, the experiment was doomed to failure, partly because of the distances guests had to travel to reach it, but mainly because of the troubles flaring up in the cities.

For reasons of economy and safety, Archibald had put a raw-concrete finish on the interior, leaving it to the painters, through a skilful choice of light colours, to beautify it. The rest was a matter of decoration, which was placed in the hands of one Coverdale, who worked with the Arden Studios of New York. Furniture, carpets, chandeliers, and *objets d'art* were imported from France, and some examples of Canadiana were added — maps, prints, and paintings illustrating the history of the country. The

89 *Château Murray (1904–78)* This American-inspired hotel was built by J.-Charles Warren; the architectural style was typical of the Atlantic coast. Situated in the centre of Pointe-au-Pic and facing the river, it had a special appeal for French-Canadian visitors.

90 *The new Manoir Richelieu* The second *manoir*, built entirely in concrete, was an admirable reproduction of a château with its Norman turrets and pointed cornices piercing the copper roof in perfect harmony. Its 350 rooms accommodated up to 600 guests, making it the most spacious summer hotel in America.

91 *A peaceful interior* The simplicity of the décor, enhanced by historical paintings by Jefferys, set the guest's mind to dreaming.

92 *Triumphant ostentation* An impressive staircase led to the upper lobby with its princely foyers and its valuable collection of *objets d'art*.

"Coverdale Collection" rose from fifteen hundred items when the *manoir* first opened to three thousand; among the most beautiful works that accumulated over the years were those of Short, Smyth, Peachy, Cockburn, Bartlett, and Jefferys.[†] In the Pink Lounge and the dining-room hung the most popular works, among them 220 ornithological plates from the Audubon collection. In such elegant surroundings, protocol was strict. Men had to wear jacket and tie in the dining-room and ladies were required to dress formally, even at breakfast.

93 *Elegance is all* To give the *manoir* a sumptuous look, a large part of the furniture was imported from France, but the paintings specialized in Canadian subjects.

[†]Except for five paintings still hanging on the walls of Manoir Richelieu, this collection is now held in the National Archives of Canada, in Ottawa.

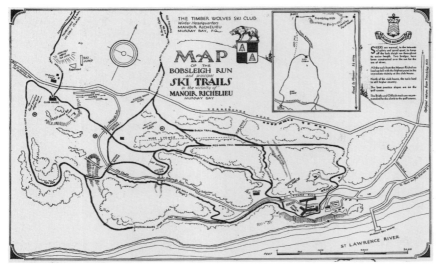

94 *Winter sports* Early in the 1930s the *manoir* took guests in the winter. One could indulge one's taste for tobogganing, skiing, or skating, or even go for a sleigh ride, muffled in warm layers.

The summer visitor had an almost embarrassing choice of activities. There was an eighteen-hole golf-course about a thousand feet up the mountain, with magnificent views. There were pleasant trail rides for amateur equestrians, archery, lawn bowls, and croquet for the more sedentary. For the competitive, there was always tennis; a serious tournament was organized every season. A few steps from the *manoir* lay the Casino, where in a large salt-water pool people could swim to the murmuring sound of a breeze in the cedars or the lull of an orchestra. There were dances too, every Thursday and Saturday evening, featuring the Romanelli Orchestra. They played for more than twenty years.

95 *Music!* Since 1938, the name Romanelli has been intimately associated with the musical life of Murray Bay. On the dais, first Luigi, and later his brother Leo, entertained summer guests for more than twenty seasons. Eddie Alexander, Frank Shurben, Bobby Gimby, Roy Roberts, and Peter Duchin were members of the Romanelli Orchestra. They kept the Manoir Richelieu tradition going, which meant entertaining bathers at the pool every afternoon.

Manoir Richelieu hummed with activity from morning to evening, and the colony of summer residents that occupied fine villas on Boulevard des Falaises were glad to join in. Many of them held their own big receptions at the *manoir*; many were guests at cocktail parties given for prestigious visitors. The Duke of Kent, Charlie Chaplin, the Tiffany family, Brenda Diana Duff Frazier, the American president Theodore Roosevelt's Uncle John, the King of Siam, Mary Pickford, or Mrs Alfred Gynne Vanderbilt — such were the people who gathered at Pointe-au-Pic, especially during the Second World War when, for obvious reasons, transatlantic voyages were restricted.

This remarkable group included the chairman of the board of the Bank of Montréal, Sir Frederick Williams-Taylor, and his gracious wife Lady Jane. Having lived a long time in England, they enjoyed spending their holidays in a place that reminded them, in many respects, of old Europe. Invariably one of the best tables was reserved for them in the dining-room; and all the guests secretly hoped for the honour of being seated close by. Sir Frederick's arrival in the hotel bar was an event in the evenings. On one of these theatrical occasions, he let his cape slide from his shoulders to the floor and asked the waiter in a penetrating voice, "Anyone remarkable or distinguished here this evening?" And the barman replied imperturbably, "Well, *you're* here, sir!" That was the sort of spirit that made life at the *manoir* seem like life in a castle.

96 *The magic of the setting* "But how gripping, too, is the view that we have from the Terrace at the Manoir, facing the vast River, the waves of which beat at the foot of the cliff. Harmonies between the wind of the waves, aromatic perfumes from the forest so close at hand, mingled with the sea-breeze and the healthy smell of seaweed, walks along lonely paths — all these are part of the Manoir's charm" (Camille Pacreau, *Un voyage au Saguenay* [Montmagny 1944], 44).

Summer Resort Life:
A New Art of Living

IN THE NINETEENTH CENTURY, if people still believed that an idle mind in an idle body was the devil's workshop, they were also beginning to realize the virtues of a good long rest. It was essential that the new city dwellers break their humdrum routine and get away from their surroundings — which meant moving from town to country. The migration of city dwellers to regions far from the madding crowds gave birth to summer resort life.

This new art of living made those who enjoyed it feel, for some time at least, like aristocrats. The summer vacationer might set himself up in a villa as if it were a château, surround himself with servants, and do as he pleased. I must repeat that the story of Charlevoix is not only the story of a region, it is also the story of a life-style unique in America.

97 *A life-style unique in America* The holidays are split between fishing and golf, swimming and playing croquet; between the picnic and teatime come photography and water-colours.

> We have seen what happens to Pointe-au-Pic at the end of July every year. It is the favourite retreat of all the city-dwellers who are fleeing from the heat and dust of the cities. It is the rendezvous for those who want to freshen up and revive their weary bodies in the ice-cold waters of the bay, to breathe in the odour of seaweed and the salty tang of the sea and the balmy breezes from the resinous woods that crown the mountains.
>
> In a word, it is the Tréport† of Canada, and there are to be found all the lucky people from Toronto, Ottawa, Montreal, and Quebec, who can afford a few weeks of summer holiday.[24]

Or, to quote the twenty-seventh president of the United States, William Howard Taft, who for nearly forty years spent his summers in Charlevoix, "The invigorating air of Murray Bay exhilarates like champagne without the effects of the morning after." The fresh air was much valued by the vacationer, as were the fishing, golf, bathing, picnics, photography, and water-colour painting with which he parceled out his days.[25]

---

†A seaside resort on the English Channel, near Dieppe, France.

98 *Pointe-au-Pic, La Malbaie, St Irénée* "It's a splendid summer resort we'd gladly call the Trouville of Canada—if one could hunt bear and caribou at Trouville, and if almost virgin forests swept down to the beach in Normandy. There's also bathing in the sea, quite unimproved—that refers to the salt, of course—for it's as cold as it can be" (Th. Bentzon, "Saint-Laurent et Saguenay," *Revue des deux mondes* [1898]: 523).

SPORTS AND PLEASURES

Charlevoix fast became a fashionable destination because of its virginal character and innumerable resources. Fishing fills the first volumes of the history of La Malbaie. Seigneur de Comporté tried to commercialize beluga fishing, but the cost of transport swallowed up his profits. Then in the days of the Scottish seigneurs, salmon fishing drew a good number of officers from the garrisons at Québec and Montréal. Friends of Nairne and Fraser even crossed the Atlantic to fish in the river that watered the valley between their two estates. Fishing was so plentiful that the seigneurs had to regulate it almost immediately. Many fished with the aid of torches from the banks of the river, an Amerindian method that left the salmon no chance of escaping. This method, practised without restriction, could alone account

99 *Fishing by torchlight* With his spear in his hand, the Amerindian fisherman used to stand up in the bow of his boat so that he could spy his prey without being noticed.

for three or four hundred catches every tide, and threatened to exhaust the valuable resource that had originally helped make La Malbaie's reputation.

Fishing in the freshwater lakes upstream of the Malbaie River also brought in sportsmen, men attracted by big stretches of water in untouched country, teeming with trout. The British military soon popularized this once select sport and turned La Malbaie into a celebrated fishing spot. During the months of June, July, and August, the favourite lakes were Comporté, Morin, Gravelle and Jacob, Grand Lac, and Petit Lac. Small, generally rudimentary buildings sheltered fishermen and hunters around the shores of isolated lakes in the mountainous regions of the hinterland.

100 *Prohibition against fishing by torchlight, 27 April 1793* Although the seigneur had the right to every eleventh fish caught in his rivers and streams, John Nairne and Malcolm Fraser were bitterly opposed to the full-scale fishing of salmon, which could be done by torchlight.

101 *A typically Canadian scene* The English officers on garrison duty in Canada collected hunting and fishing trophies and displayed them in romantic style.

The first summer residents were crazy about fishing; the men would install their families in cottages, which enabled them to take longer and more frequent fishing trips. These devotees were particularly prevalent among the magistracy, who formed the core of the colony of summer residents. In 1879 at Murray Bay, Archibald McLean began organizing expeditions along the north shore in the *Galiote*; men were taken to rivers were the salmon were plentiful—the Godbout, Ste-Marguerite, Moisie, La Romaine, and Mingan.

102/103 *The benefits of rustic life* On the high plateaus, in the heart of the forests of the hinterland, a simple log cabin built beside a lake full of fish was enough to satisfy any experienced sportsman.

104/105 *Lawyers on holiday* Magistrates saw the annual closure of the law courts as an opportunity to go on a fishing trip.

106/107 *Local guides* Thomas Fortin of St-Urbain, together with his son Thomas-Louis, knew where to go for the best catch. The half-breed Nicholas Aubin won the admiration of his clients for his mastery of Amerindian techniques of hunting and fishing.

Excursions into the hinterland led to the progressive discovery of what would become Laurentides Park and its principal lakes: Petit Lac Malbaie, Emmuraillé, La Galette, and La Roche. William Hume Blake was the most passionate and faithful friend of Charlevoix, forever praising the unsuspected resources of its woods. For nearly forty years, accompanied by local guides, he roamed over the vast mountainous land. Years of exploration and reconnaissance made him an expert on the Laurentian environment and an ardent defender of a project to make Park Laurentides into a game and fish reserve.[†] More than a thousand lakes water the high mountain plateaus and turn autumn into an unforgettable spectacle of iridescent colours.

108 *To sportsmen, fishermen, and tourists* Many schooners like *La Galiote* turned out to be ideal for fishing expeditions on the north shore.

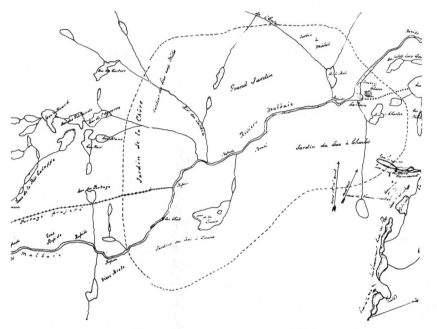

109 *Les Grands Jardins, in the heart of Laurentides Park* "According to Thomas Fortin, it was no exaggeration to say there were at least 10,000 caribou inside the Park, particularly in what was called the Grands Jardins, which stretched for about a hundred miles. This was truly Caribou Kingdom" (Damase Potvin, *Les Oubliés* [Québec 1940], 123).

Inspired by his experiences as a dedicated sportsman, William Blake wrote about local men who followed old traditions and lived in harmony with nature. Their prototype, who inhabited the wild and mountainous hinterland of Charlevoix, was Thomas Fortin. Fortin accompanied Blake on his expeditions and was also friend and guide to hunting and fishing enthusiasts such as Lord Grey, governor-general of Canada, and the Honourable Sir Lomer Gouin and Louis-Alexandre Taschereau, who were premiers of Québec between 1905 and 1936. Among this distinguished group, Fortin was respected for his knowledge of the forest. For more than seventy-five years he made a passionate study of the vast open book of

---

†This was the first park in the province of Québec, established by a provincial government law in 1894. Within its boundaries there were many private hunting and fishing clubs; among the best known were La Petite-Malbaie, La Roche, La Chaudière, Prémisse, Bonne-Veine, Tourelli, Triton, and St-Vincent.

110 *The camp of Club La Roche* A hundred and fifty miles up the Malbaie River, the Club La Roche — so called because of a huge rock sticking out of the water just in front of the camp — was founded on 10 September 1880. This building, which housed three generations of Blakes and Fortins, was unfortunately destroyed when the area was forested.

111 *Thomas Fortin (1858–1941)* This woodsman took deep satisfaction in watching his clients "struggling with a big trout."

nature. To everyone, people of Charlevoix and outsiders, rich or poor, Thomas was the hunter, the fisherman, the man of the woods *par excellence*. He knew the country inside out, people said. Head keeper of Laurentides Park, supreme authority second only to God, he looked after the protection and integrity of this reserve, larger than the state of Rhode Island and sheltering one of the richest faunas in the world.

Golf, which is said without prejudice to have originated in Holland, was first popularized in Scotland in the sixteenth century, then exported by the Scots. It took some three hundred years before the first golf-club in North America was founded, in Montréal in 1873. The craze grew, and the game became a full-fledged sport; 1876 saw the formation of the fourth association of North American golfers, the Murray Bay Golf Club at La Malbaie.

Unfortunately, there are no records of the club's activities during its first few years. At the start the game was informal, played within the bounds of Pointe-au-Pic and La Malbaie, in the fields of Madame Hubert Warren and of the notary Charles Angers. There being no spot in the whole of Canada better suited for use as a golf-course than the nearby grazing grounds of the seigneury of Murray Bay, with its conical hillocks, a group of thirty-five golfers decided on 24 July 1894 to erect permanent facilities there. In 1895, the club rented the grounds from Monsieur E.J. Duggan and arranged the hours of play so that cows and sheep could graze undisturbed, thus keeping the fairways nicely cropped.† The rules were adjusted to suit the circumstances: if a ball should hit an animal, the shot could be replayed without penalty. Sunday was ruled a day of rest, as much for the golfers as for the course they had thronged all week. Those who complained drew a standard answer from the local priest: "Even if you don't need a day of rest each week, the worms do!"

---

†In 1925, the Murray Bay Golf Club bought the meadows lying west of the seigneury, then belonging to Archibald Gray.

In 1897 inter-club competitions were organized, and the Murray Bay Golf Club swept the field on many occasions. On 26 August 1901, the *Québec Daily Telegraph* reported a victory for La Malbaie: "The Murray Bay Golf Club administered rather a severe defeat to the Quebec Club on the latter's links on Saturday, the game being played under a pouring rain." In 1905, when the club's membership numbered seventy-five and a season ticket for the whole family cost ten dollars, the new club house was inaugurated. It soon became an important centre of social activity. Each tournament was an excuse for receptions and dances, organized by the women. Two tennis courts were built next to the clubhouse during the twenties, by which time the Murray Bay Golf Club membership had reached 110. In 1925 the course was officially recognized by the Royal Canadian Golf Association, and international matches were held there. Its prestige was due partly to its exclusive membership, partly to those who handled its affairs. Among the best-known members was former president William Howard Taft, who ran the club from 1914 to 1921. His children were said to have admired him more in this capacity than as president of the United States—though they felt his term of four years had been too short.

112 *Camp Ronevsorg on Lake Chaudière, St-Placide* This block of five little rudimentary huts contained, *left to right*, a dormitory for six, a dining-room, a kitchen, an ice-house, and the "usual offices."

113 *The game of golf* Since the previous century the royal and ancient game, as it was called, had gained adherents of every sort.

114 *Murray Bay Golf Club around 1900* Founded after the Montréal, Toronto, and Québec clubs, the Murray Bay Golf Club was the fourth association of golfers to come into being in Canada. More than a simple sport, golf was the heart of a lively social scene.

With the numbers of tourists increasing every year — most of them drawn to Manoir Richelieu — the Murray Bay Golf Club felt it was being invaded and deprived of its intimate atmosphere. The management of the *manoir*, for their part, liked to keep clientele closer to home, and commissioned the architect Herbert Strong to build a modern golf-course. In 1925, to the delight of golf enthusiasts, an eighteen-hole course of competition class was opened. Strong, the genius who had created The Engineers and Inwood on Long Island and Lakeview in Toronto, had literally sculpted his course out of the wooded highlands of the Laurentians. For the panorama from each of its tees, for the variety of the course as a whole, and for the excellence

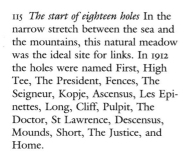

115 *The start of eighteen holes* In the narrow stretch between the sea and the mountains, this natural meadow was the ideal site for links. In 1912 the holes were named First, High Tee, The President, Fences, The Seigneur, Kopje, Ascensus, Les Epinettes, Long, Cliff, Pulpit, The Doctor, St Lawrence, Descensus, Mounds, Short, The Justice, and Home.

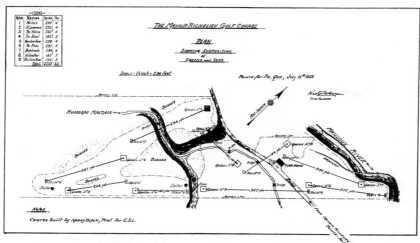

116 *The Manoir Richelieu golf-course* Around 1907, the golf professional Harry Black suggested a nine-hole course to Canada Steamship Lines clientèle.

of its greens, the Manoir Richelieu course is a living tribute to Herbert Strong. The course also owes something to Hector Warren, the *manoir*'s first director of golf; with his training as an engineer, he insisted from the first on the highest standards for landscaping.

Several international tournaments established the reputation of the *manoir*'s course and attracted many well-known players eager to carry off the Manoir Richelieu Golf Club shield. In 1951 the highly select Cardinal Club was established, a society of 114 gentlemen golfers, each of whom had to defend his entitlement annually to remain a member.

117 *A lady golfer around 1930* The panoramic view from the Manoir Richelieu golf-course, in an exceptional mountain setting, drew the following from Herbert Strong, the architect who created it: "The scenery surrounding the Manoir Richelieu Golf Course at Murray Bay is the most impressive setting for a links of which I have knowledge."

118 *The inauguration of golf at Manoir Richelieu* Among those present at the opening ceremony on 18 July 1925 were (*left to right*) Messrs William Coverdale, William Howard Taft, Hector Warren, and Herbert Strong.

Fishing and golf were not the only summer recreations. Lawn tennis, which had first been played in England in the middle of the nineteenth century as a sort of open-air adaptation of the game of "real tennis", was introduced to Canada after rules and regulations had been set, in 1877, at the first championship in Wimbledon. The first Canadian club was formed in Toronto, where tournaments were organized starting in 1880. In less than twenty years tennis developed from a mere social pastime into an exacting sport. And those who considered it too exhausting for the heat of summer threw themselves into it wholeheartedly on the courts of Manoir Richelieu, where a constant breeze kept the air fresh and cool.

119 *Pocket money for the kids* Who from Pointe-au-Pic or La Malbaie cannot remember having acted as an unofficial caddy, even if only for one season? One thing is certain, the experience will never be forgotten by those who for hours on end braved the links at Nordet, Terrebonne, Cap Noir, Trait Carré, Cap-à-l'Aigle, Chamard, Les Éboulements, Le Maire, Trou des Fées, Étang, Chapelle, La Baleine, Savard, Cartier, Kamouraska, Nairne, Grande Anse, and Malbaie.

120 *A semi-aerial sport* "Nature herself created this perfect spot ... There is the widest, loftiest sky in the world overhead (even America has that), the whole effect is aerial — you feel as if you were asked to drive a ball from cloud to cloud" (H.N. Wethered and T. Simpson, *The Architectural Side of Golf* [London 1929], 105).

La Malbaie was quickly numbered among the most fashionable wateringplaces on the St Lawrence. Napoléon Legendre probably listed all the reasons for this in his *Échos de Québec*, published in 1877:

> Now we have reached the time when everyone leaves for the watering-places, either from habit or under doctor's orders.
>
> It is a fact that seabathing and sea air are a universal panacea. They are used for slimming, or for gaining weight, depending on the need of the moment; they cure colds and rheumatism, high-blood pressure and anaemia. Many patients have even found them an excellent remedy for baldness.
>
> But I believe that basically what people are looking for most of all in these salt-water holidays is diversion and amusement. In any case, that is what they usually find while looking for everything else — and I bet there are no complaints about it.[26]

121 *Lawn tennis at Manoir Richelieu in 1902* "The crude beginnings of tennis go back to the eighties. It gave excuse for an occasional afternoon gathering" (William Hume Blake, *In a Fishing Country* [Toronto 1922], 55).

122 *Tennis on clay courts* From the simple pleasure that it was originally, this racket sport has moved quickly to ever more complex techniques, and is governed by a rigid code of rules.

123 *The Beach at Murray Bay* "This water is salubrious and hygienic; hundreds of persons cured every year from rheumatisms and kindred affections, bear testimony to the efficacy of the sea baths of Murray Bay" (J.C. Langelier, *The Quebec and Lower St. Lawrence Tourist's Guide* [Quebec 1875], 134).

124 *Bathing, a public event* At Atkinson Rock, Pointe-au-Pic, bathing costumes added a cheerful note to the social scene.

125 *A quick dip in the sea* Children sometimes lacked the courage to duck in the icy waters of the river, but they were quite happy to warm themselves in the sun and pose for the photographer.

It must be admitted that the river's allure has not been the same at all times. Should this be attributed to the hardiness of an earlier generation more resistant to cold, or merely to the possibility that in former days the waters of the St Lawrence were warmer? The answer is not clear. However, it seems probable that at the turn of the century technological progress would have permitted salt water to be drawn from the river and heated for the Manoir Richelieu swimming-pool. This practice has been maintained almost without interruption up to the present. On the other hand, there have always been those who prefer the sand and icy tides; as soon as access is made available by car they will be able to go to the beach at St-Irénée, as Rodolphe Forget forecast at the turn of the century.

Often a whole family would take a trip into the surrounding countryside for a picnic. The long summer days lent themselves to excursions through the woods, which left people dog-tired but proud for having made the effort. In his memoirs, *God Packed My Picnic Basket*, about the exploits of a group of young upper-crust New Yorkers in Charlevoix, Reginald T. Townsend recalls a visit to a place called the "Trou," when they gorged themselves on splendid country bread covered with wild strawberry jam. Come nightfall, they sat around the camp-fire singing Canadian folk-songs. The British historian Bradley, who visited the area at the turn of the century, described with a touch of nostalgia how happily the lovely summer evenings slipped by for those who knew how to enjoy them:

> Many picnics were held on the St. Lawrence in the evenings, from which one came home by moonlight. On those occasions, big bonfires were laid, made of driftwood washed up by the river; and when they were set afire, and the flames flickered over the surface of the water, and on the woods, and the canoes tied up in a bunch at the river's edge, there were always people with a whole repertoire of French-Canadian songs to sing. Then it was back to the oars or the paddles, under the stars, in the shadow of the overhanging cliff. That was the sort of life one led, with many other diversions and amusements too, on the banks of the St. Lawrence at holiday-time.[27]

126 *The "Trou"* "I shan't mention this strange, unique spot known as the "Trou"—a deep pool formed by a fold in the mountains, sprung from the very bowels of the rocks; the locals, who always find the right word—coarse though it often is—have given it this name, which fits it perfectly" (Arthur Buies, *Chroniques, humeurs et caprices* [Québec 1873], 172).

Elsewhere, children went on cart rides, planting themselves comfortably on a thick bed of straw. The parents, of course, preferred the calash. Others took trips in sailboats, which gave them a taste of what a real voyage of exploration was like. A spell aboard a St Lawrence river skiff was less fun; it could quickly end up at the nearest dock, victim of the river's ugly currents.

127 *Lunch "al fresco"* A picnic at the Cabots in Cap-à-l'Aigle about 1930.

128 *Giddyup!* A carriage ride to Lake Nairne could be as long as twenty miles.

129 *A ride in the cart.* Fun for all the family in the cart!

130 *A habitant's house around 1890* Those who wandered deep into the countryside might come across some interesting old places.

This variety of activities was what brought the same families back to La Malbaie year after year; they found it the perfect place to suit the tastes of every age. As one promotional brochure, boldly trying to outdo the others in the eloquence of its message, proclaimed: "Murray Bay is a stronghold of good society and fashion, both Canadian and American, and growing more and more so every year. It has already all the equipment, the elegant social life, the amenities, the amusements and conveniences of a high-class modern summer resort, while its facilities for healthful exercise and sport in the shape of walking and driving, bathing, picnicing, fishing, golf, tennis and other diversions are innumerable."28

Oh, the pleasures of summer! The innumerable wonders of Charlevoix!

131 *Through the meadows* Parasols in
hand, summer residents enjoyed
strolling freely through the meadows.

132 *Afloat and ashore at Murray Bay*

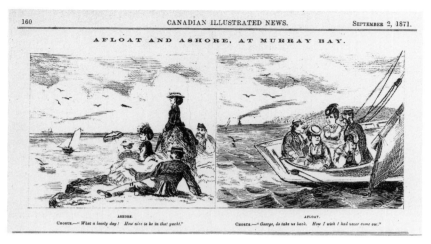

133 *Enjoying the river* From the top of Cap Blanc, one could watch sailboats moving in the wind off Pointe-au-Pic.

134 *Makeshift marina* One of the traditions at Charlevoix was sailing, much in favour with sportsmen who frequented the waters this far up the St Lawrence.

SUMMER RESIDENTS

As the ideal spot for summer holidays, Murray Bay was first discovered by Seigneur Nairne's guests. The first Americans who visited the place had not chosen to come there; they were rebels imprisoned on the property of the seigneur, who was loyal to the British crown. After them, a few adventurers and explorers risked some exploratory trips, sometimes briefly writing up their observations. Later, sportsmen identified the rich resources of the Malbaie River and its surrounding lakes in the hinterland. But the nineteenth century was half over before the citizens of Québec in their turn discovered this al fresco paradise, as the Victorian idiom would have it. It was aboard the *Waterloo*, and then the *Alliance* and the *Pocahontas*, that they came to Pointe-au-Pic. These families were not put off by uncertain facilities; they came, and the following year came back again.

A little colony of Montréal and Québec lawyers and merchants had taken root at La Malbaie ... ; the first cottage west of the quay belonged to Mr.

W.H. Kerr. Messrs Lamb, Gibb, Henshaw, McLimont, D.C. Thomson, and Madame Vannovous and many others, built themselves charming summer residences in that area. Mr. Thomson owned a whole village of attractive little cottages, occupied by The Honourable Alex. Morris of Ottawa, by Mr. Champion, Dr. Sewell, Mr. Bonner of New York, and others like them.[30]

These summer residents, as James Macpherson Lemoine stressed in 1872, were lawyers and businessmen who came in search of the peace and quiet offered by the bay. One of them, the Montréal lawyer William Busby Lambe, was kept busy by the company he had founded in 1867; with Jean Olivier Chamard among his associates, he developed Pointe-au-Pic as a resort. Trade also had to be organized, because families were ordering their food from town each week, not wanting to depend on the hotels.

During these early years, Pointe-au-Pic became the Eden of the St Lawrence for those in search of beauty and tranquility: "So strongly is the spirit of conservatism intrenched here that the same families come year after year from Quebec, Montreal, and even Toronto, to occupy the same room or cottages."[31] Among the families Annie Howells Fréchette mentions in her article of 1884 were the Blakes, well-known Toronto lawyers and politicians. The first to come was William H. Blake, solicitor-general of Upper Canada in the Baldwin-Lafontaine administration. As a deputy, he was called to attend the pre-Confederation parliament, which sat periodically in Québec. From there he, and his wife and children, Edward, Samuel, Anne, and Sophia, discovered Charlevoix. After that, the Blake family never missed a single season, though they already owned a second house on the outskirts of Toronto. For them, nothing could take the place of those weeks at La Malbaie. When Edward, the eldest, grew up, he built himself a villa called the Maison Rouge — inspired, it seems, by his political convictions, for he was known as an ardent defender of rights and liberties under the banner of Canada's Liberal Party. This reformist led federal

135 The first Protestant church at Pointe-au-Pic This is the original building, constructed entirely in wood in 1867, to the design of the architect Scott; it was named Union Church. Here, the ecumenical spirit reigned from the start; as soon as the church was established, it held both Presbyterian and Anglican services.

136 The Murray Bay Protestant Church From 1860 onwards, Protestant vacationers met regularly for Sunday services. Father Narcisse Doucet, the clergyman at Murray Bay, was somewhat displeased when John Warren first leased a small house to the "outsiders" as a chapel. Doucet's intolerance did not stop these faithful from building their own church in 1867; construction was completed in August of that year. In 1909, the trustees decided to add a stone face to the building, leaving the interior unchanged.

137 *On the steps of Maison Rouge in 1892* For the Blakes, holidays were splendid family gatherings.

138 *In front of Mille Roches* It was mainly because of the children that the Blakes chose long holidays at Pointe-au-Pic. Here, nearly all of them can be seen wearing long striped socks, known as Murray Bay socks, which are still the fashion with visitors today.

139 *George MacKinnon Wrong (1860–1948)* This intellectual was a pioneer in the field of Canadian history. Here seen proudly sporting his jacket of country cloth, Wrong used La Malbaie for several years as his chosen place for "rest and recreation."

forces until he handed the reins over to Wilfrid Laurier, the deputy from Arthabaska, in 1887. His frail health kept him close to his family, who spent more and more of their time at La Malbaie. As for Sophia, she married George M. Wrong, a young history professor at the University of Toronto who had spent several holidays at La Malbaie. The university profited from these long stays—during them he prepared *A Canadian Manor and Its Seigneurs*; this was first published in 1908 and is today recognized as a classic of Canadian history. The work bears eloquent witness to the author's love for Charlevoix. He spent several summers carrying out research in the outbuildings of the Nairne's manor.

The Blake's house was always full of friends and guests, who came for a day, a week, or a month. Maison Rouge had four double bedrooms, nine single rooms, and three camp beds. The love of big gatherings was shared by Samuel, Edward's younger brother, who was also a lawyer. In 1873 he bought a plot of land from William B. Lambe, not far from the future Chamard Lorne's House, and there built a spacious summer residence called Mille Roches. He had three children, Mabel, William Hume, and Katherine. His only son showed a talent for law and letters and a deep interest in nature. However, the law courts held little attraction for William Hume Blake, and he gave himself up to literature. The author of *Brown Waters, In a Fishing Country*, and *A Fisherman's Creed* was so attached to and knowledgeable about Charlevoix that he was the obvious choice to translate Louis Hémon's great novel, *Maria Chapdelaine*, and later Adjutor Rivard's *Chez Nous*. Through his literary work, Blake would immortalize the rich beauty of this fishing country.

The Ontario Irishman loved the people who lived in the deep forests of Charlevoix and the *coureurs de bois* who served as guides on his many expeditions in Laurentides Park. He married Jeanie Law of Montréal in the Protestant chapel at Murray Bay, a peaceful spot where he later chose to be buried. His epitaph was a paraphrase of Napoleon's: "I wish my ashes to rest on the banks of the river amidst these people I have loved so much."

Blake's descendants have kept up the custom of vacationing at Murray Bay. Among the best known was Hume Blake, a Canadian diplomat living at Pink Cottage while waiting for Round Court to be built on the cliff-top. Others, such as Edward Francis Blake and those of his line, the Wrights and the Verschoyles, preferred Cap-à-l'Aigle.

140 *William Hume Blake (1861–1924)* One of French Canada's truest friends, this man of letters — transformed, as often as not, into a man of the woods — wrote a series of novels extolling the mysterious beauty of nature.

141 *On the terrace of Le Caprice* Mr and Mrs Edward Blake were admired for their air of distinction. In 1898 they had an imposing house built for them; each of the three floors had a broad balcony, and there was a terrace at roof level overlooking the vast countryside. As though to excuse their fancy, they called it Le Caprice.

Another Canadian family, the Buchanans, distinguished as much for their skill in law as for their innate business sense, came direct from Montréal. In 1881 they bought land on the hillsides of the bay, fragrant with conifers. Alexander Brock Buchanan was the first to buy, in 1886; he built New Bold Cottage at Pointe-au-Pic, later known as White Cottage. His family grew larger, and in 1893 Buchanan built Blairvocky, a villa with six bedrooms plus two for the staff. In 1894, Clareinch was added, and later Cedar Cottage, Huis Ten Busch, Boulevard Cottage, and Stoneycroft. For nearly a century, the Buchanans kept their rendezvous at Pointe-au-Pic in the family.

James Macpherson Lemoine notes in his article of 1872 (see note 30) that a man named Bonner was part of the growing colony of summer residents. Even if he was considered a New Yorker, George T. Bonner was Canadian by birth, and came from an English family. The Bonners had immigrated to Canada in 1820 and settled in Québec; almost immediately they made money in the timber business. As a child, George stayed several times at Cap-à-l'Aigle, on the farm at Fraser Manor. At the age of sixteen, after completing his studies at Queen's College in Kingston, he went to New

142 *St Anne-in-the-Field, Pointe-au-Pic* This second Protestant church was built by Samuel Blake in 1899; the Episcopal service was celebrated here. The church stood at the corner of today's Boulevard des Falaises and Côte Bellevue. It was better known to the local population as the "mitaine", a corruption of meeting-house.

143 *Alexander Brock Buchanan (1832–1917)* Originally from Montréal, this well-known financier used to boast about having himself discovered far-off Pointe-au-Pic for his vacations.

York to join his elder brother John, who was already well established. There he found a job with a firm of agents whose business was mainly with France.

His knowledge of French soon won him an important position within the firm, which he left when he reached his majority to launch his own. Enormously successful, he moved into a house on Staten Island called Stadaconé, after his birthplace. In 1869, at the age of thirty-two, he married Isabel Sewell of Québec, with whom he spent all his holidays at Murray Bay. They loved this place more than any in the world, and except for a

144/145 *Then and now* Proud of his Scotch heritage, Erskine B. Buchanan, a familiar figure to locals, wore his clan's tartan for the long walks he loved so much.

few trips to Europe spent every summer there with their three daughters, Maud, Mabel, and Isabel. In 1898 they built a villa near the riverbank at Pointe-au-Pic, following the example of Susanna Shaw Minturn, who was already installed in her big house close to the Protestant church. Three years later a friend of the Bonners, Alfred C. Chapin, mayor of Brooklyn, bought a huge estate on the rest of the point.

The eldest of the Bonner girls, Maud, married Francis Higginson Cabot. In 1902, her father purchased the seigneury of Mount Murray for fifty thousand dollars and gave it to her. She thus became seigneur of Cap-à-l'Aigle—a role she played with the enthusiasm that came naturally to her. For more than fifty years Maud Cabot, known to her intimates as Mootzie, was the driving spirit of the place. The Cabot family maintains to this day the tradition of holidays at Charlevoix. Lac à Gravelle lies within the seigneury, which formerly comprised an immense territory of ninety square miles; the best trout are still caught here, in a mountain setting. The seigneury of Mount Murray has managed to preserve its prime function as a farm that works in harmony with the ecology of the rural neighbourhood; the family's holidays are working holidays devoted to the upkeep of the farm. The Cabots' respect for nature in all its forms is doubtless the reason they come back every summer to Les Quatre Vents, Chouette, and Cache-Cache.

The atmosphere that had hitherto characterized Murray Bay was in the process of changing. The coming of the Americans upset established habits and ways of thought: "But with the coming of the Americans, everything gradually changed; Americans built new, better and bigger houses, they

146 *George Thomas Bonner (1837–1924)* Because of a cholera epidemic that hit Québec in 1842, George was packed off to Cap-à-l'Aigle when he was barely five. From then on he spent every summer of his childhood at Beach Farm Cottage with the Frasers, the seigneurs of Mount Murray.

147 *The Cabot family going to church* Maud Bonner Cabot and her children, Higginson and George, pause for the photographer on their way to church.

148 *Maud B. Cabot* Here is "Mootzie" in 1952, as she could often be seen in the gardens of the seigneury of Mount Murray at Cap-à-l'Aigle.

149/150 An invitation to Mount Murray Manor The manor needed major repairs after the damage caused by an earthquake in 1925. In the seigneury, the Cabot tea parties were among the most sought-after events.

151 The Morgans In 1931 two American painters, Maud Cabot and her husband, Patrick Morgan, combined their talents and their dynamism to create a friendly haven for creative art at La Malbaie.

152 The grandmother at the centre of everything The Minturns had been coming to Murray Bay since 1887, with Madame Susanna Shaw Minturn reigning affectionately over all. Their aristocratic style left its mark on summer life in the area.

furnished them more luxuriously, they brought ways that they had been used to at home, if not really urban and sophisticated, yet more so than those of the Canadian pioneers."[32] The American writer Sedgwick considered that the new summer residents brought with them a more modern outlook. Susanna Shaw Minturn, the first American woman to build a villa on the riverbank, in 1895, was inspired by summer residences along the coasts of New England. Up till then, the Minturns had rented cottages overlooking the bay; now they chose a location giving directly onto the river. Her summer residence encouraged the establishment of a small all-American colony that included the Stokes, the Sedgwicks, the Bowditches, the Harlans, and the Olivers; together, they seemed to constitute a sort of clan, bound together by a common passion for this area. However, they were not the only Americans; the Taft family from Cincinnati had already started coming to Pointe-au-Pic.

It was love at first sight when William Howard Taft and his wife Helen first called at Murray Bay. They chose Pointe-au-Pic as the site for their summer residence and returned there faithfully for more than forty years. Although they found the Chamards' hotel charming, they chose for several reasons to rent a cottage next to it before finally settling in at Fassifern Cottage. The way its renovation proceeded showed what sort of people the Tafts were. As a start, they rebuilt the cottage in a style resembling that of the traditional Québec house. Then over the years, as more children and grandchildren came along, they added a room, a wing, and an annex, until finally they had twenty bedrooms and a dozen bathrooms. The Tafts were a real tribe with their thirteen grandchildren and their close friends — the Semples, the Extons, the Ingalls, and the Noels. Their villa was lavishly decorated with things from the Philippines, where William Howard Taft had been governor from 1901 to 1904. Each summer brought them back to Pointe-au-Pic, except during Taft's term as president (1909–14).

153 *The young Taft family around 1895* To this Cincinnati family, whose friendliness was legendary, a vacation was not a vacation unless the house was full of family and friends.

154 *Summer 1924* The twenty-seventh president of the United States, surrounded by his family.

155 *The president and his descendants* Like their grandfather, the Taft grandchildren had a long-standing affection for Charlevoix.

The villa was perched on Cap Blanc, the peak of an enormous rock. At the foot of the slope lived Nicholas Aubin, a metis, or half-breed, from Tadoussac who came every summer to rent out boats and canoes to the residents. A fine summer afternoon was just the right time to go for a row on the river. Rowers could go as far as the beach of Grand Ruisseau and farther when the tide permitted. But the high moments were picnics. Several times a year, everyone would go in calashes to Cap-à-l'Aigle or Fraser Falls and have a banquet in the open air. On those occasions Mr. Taft—who disliked picnics because of his corpulence—would go off by himself and watch the dancing colours of the river and enjoy the sea air.

Among the local villagers this former president, who later became chief justice of the Supreme Court of the United States, was known facetiously as the Little Judge on account of his remarkable waist measurement. In those days, it was the custom for summer residents to order a suit in locally made cloth. Mr. Taft, complying with it, went to visit Madame Bouliane at Pointe-au-Pic. As this seamstress, no stringbean herself, diligently took his measurements, every one of them made her cry out in amazement. Some years later, when the Little Judge's suit was handed down to his chauffeur, there was enough material in it to clothe six of the man's sons. Or so the story goes ...

156   The Taft family song

TAFT FAMILY SONG

I

Once there was a President whose name was William Taft
He came to La Malbaie on a great big river raft
And when he saw the Pointe au Pic
He said, "That's one for me,
I'll go ashore and build a house and raise a family."

Chorus

Fat Tafts, thin Tafts, any Tafts at all
Come to the Manning house and have yourself a ball.
Be sure to park your rods and your golf clubs at the door
and you'll hear such caterwauling as you never heard before.

II

Bot, he was a senator and Charley, quite a boy
Helen was the only girl, her Papa's Pride and Joy;
And these had thirteen children who have mostly made their mark
They are as diversified as animals in the Ark.

Chorus

Fat Tafts, thin Tafts, any Tafts at all
Come to the Manning house and have yourself a ball,
Be sure you park your rods and your golf clubs at the door
And you'll hear such caterwauling as you never heard before.

The last event of the Tafts' summer season was William Howard's birthday party; this was held outside, rather like a village fête. Helen Taft served up to thirty lobsters, four turkeys, and a dozen chickens to eighty guests, seated at little round tables arranged informally. Among the best-known Canadians invariably invited were the former chief justice of the Supreme Court of Canada, Sir Charles Fitzpatrick, who later became the twelfth lieutenant-governor of the province of Québec; Sir Lomer Gouin, premier of the province from 1905 to 1920; Albert Sévigny, chief justice of the Supreme Court of Québec; and Montréal businessmen Gordon MacDougall, George Caverhill, and Tancrède Bienvenu. As for the Americans, one was sure to see Mabel T. Boardman, the "queen mother" of the American Red Cross for more than thirty years; Elisabeth H.S.T. Binsse, woman of

Ex-President Taft. Pointe a Pic. P. Q. Mfg. by European Post Card Co.

157 *Ex-President Taft at Pointe-au-Pic* At the end of the season, William Howard Taft's birthday, on 15 September, was a good reason for a party.

the world and great benefactress, who split her time between New York, Boston, Washington, and Pointe-au-Pic; Francis Sydney Bancroft, a New York banker and a Canadian by birth; and most certainly Charles J. Livingood, who had built a new town called Mariemont on the outskirts of Cincinnati. These people, though sometimes of divergent opinions, basked in the atmosphere of cordiality that William Howard Taft created.

158 *At the Monument des Braves, Cap-à-l'Aigle* A monument was dedicated in August 1919 to the memory of those from Cap-à-l'Aigle who had fallen in the First World War. Shown here (*left to right*) are David McGoun, the Honourable Rodolphe Lemieux, Sir Charles Fitzpatrick, former president William Howard Taft, Sir Arthur Barrett, A.H. Campbell, and Sir Lomer Gouin — all faithful summer residents of Murray Bay.

At the turn of the century, the presence of another family began making a deep mark on the Charlevoix scene. This was the family of Rodolphe Forget, a Montréal financier whose named figured on almost every important board of directors of the day. Starting in 1901, the Forgets spent their holidays at Gil'Mont, on a vast estate that spread over the St-Irénée tableland between La Malbaie and Les Éboulements. By the sheer size of

159 *Sir Charles Fitzpatrick (1853–1942)* This daring sportsman and water lover was as happy swimming long distances as he was paddling his canoe on Lake Nairne.

160 *Mabel Thorp Boardman (1861–1946)* This great Victorian lady, who devoted the whole of her active life to the Red Cross, had the happy knack of turning a big dinner with fifty guests into a simple meal enjoyed by all.

his fortune, Rodolphe Forget was one of the first to give the lie to the dictum, The English for finance, the French for eloquence. Politics appealed to this accomplished millionaire; as the Conservative Party candidate in the district of Charlevoix, he was elected in 1904, 1908, and 1911. His major accomplishment as a deputy was undoubtedly the construction of the railway linking La Malbaie to Québec, but he was also anxious to diversify the regional economy.

161 *Elizabeth Hewlett Scudder Thébaud Binsse (1869–1957)* Mme Binsse loved gardening in the peace and quiet of La Malbaie.

162 *Harry Lorin Binsse de St-Victor (1905–71)* Journalist, historian, translator — Harry Binsse enlivened the cultural life of La Malbaie. He also ran the restaurant Sur La Côte, where, in addition to an excellent table, the host offered food for the spirit.

To this end, he developed an infrastructure for the growing tourist industry by constructing two big hotels, one at Tadoussac, the other at Pointe-au-Pic, both owned by the Richelieu and Ontario Navigation Company. Rodolphe Forget was known to all his electors; he enjoyed visiting his constituency in his red convertible (though the Conservative Party's colour had been blue from time immemorial). However, his noisy engine was more than once soundly cursed by vacationers who had come from the city's hubbub in search of peace and quiet.

163 *At Pointe-au-Pic, an ideal spot* According to some of the metropolitan press, Pointe-au-Pic was famed as much for the quality of life as for the society people who stayed there.

164 *Sir Rodolphe Forget (1861–1919)* This Napoleon of the Montréal Stock Exchange came regularly to St-Irénée-les-Bains in search of rest, accompanied by his close friends Adolphe B. Routhier, Joseph Lavergne, and Louis Fréchette.

165 *Gil'Mont, sonnet to Mme Rodolphe Forget* This unpublished piece by Fréchette can be found in the visitors' book at Gil'Mont.

166/167 *Gil'Mont, St-Irénée-les-Bains, 1906* So called in honour of the eldest in the family, Gil'Mont welcomed three generations of Forgets. The main house, known by the villagers as the Château, included sixteen bedrooms and a dining-room that could seat twenty-four in comfort.

168/169 *Gil'Mont, St-Irénée-les-Bains, 1906* In earlier days, the Forget estate comprised about a dozen buildings. In 1901, it was the only house in St-Irénée that had electricity.

Gil'mont

Sonnet — à Mme Rodolphe Forget

*Cette villa qui brille au soleil, et dessine
Sur le fond vert des bois ses paradis rêvés,
Cette villa qui tient les regards captivés
Vous fait bien des jaloux, ma charmante cousine.*

*On dit qu'un jour, au fond de la forêt voisine,
Pour oncer ce palais féerique, vous avez,
Précieux talismans par vos soins retrouvés,
Acheté les secrets de quelque Mélusine.*

*On prétend, à l'appui, qu'autour du gai manoir,
Une baguette en main, sitôt que vient le soir,
Une femme apparaît de longs voiles coiffée.*

*Mais, moi qui vous connais, je sais, même de loin
Que pour charmer ainsi vous n'avez eu besoin
Du secours de personne, et que c'est vous, la fée!*

Louis Fréchette

1er juin 1902

Gil'Mont, St Irénée les Bains

Le "Living-Room".

L'escalier des parterres.

La serre.

It was a different story with the McCagg family. Ezra B. McCagg, originally from Hudson, had studied law in New York before going into practice in Chicago, where he settled permanently. He became interested in works of art and rare books. He loved the countryside, as did his wife, who appreciated flowers, shrubs, and landscaped gardens. They bought a small estate at Pointe-au-Pic, which they called The Spinney. In 1899, for the final design of the garden, they engaged the firm of Frederick Law Olmsted, the landscape gardeners of New York's Central Park. The McCaggs, like so many Americans, were shocked by the loss of green space in urban centres and hoped to preserve Charlevoix's virgin beauty.

The Presbyterian pastor Alexander B. Mackay and his young family arrived in Montréal on 4 May 1879 from Great Britain on an Atlantic ship of the Allen line. The following year his daughter Katharine, an asthma sufferer, fell gravely ill, and the doctors advised him to spend the summer away from the city. So the Mackay family went to Murray Bay, renowned for its healthy climate. Every summer after that the pastor left his Crescent Street parish in Montréal and spent his holidays in Charlevoix with his wife and their four children. One day, when the family was riding in Gonzague Tremblay's cart—he was trying to let his house at the end of the

170/171 *The Spinney, Pointe-au-Pic, 1906* Built at the edge of a small wood, The Spinney offered a new way of communing with nature, through both its architectural style and its location.

172/173 *The Spinney, Pointe-au-Pic, 1906* The inside of the house was furnished as simply as possible, and the gardens were laid out so that they blended with open green spaces and wooded patches; the place seemed to follow an entirely new concept of what life at a summer resort should be.

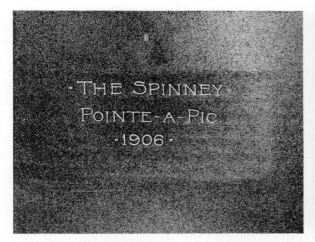

THE SPINNEY
POINTE-A-PIC
·1906·

They say, what they say, let them say,
With thee conversing I forget all time.

Drawing room.

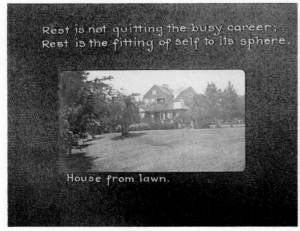

Rest is not quitting the busy career;
Rest is the fitting of self to its sphere.

House from lawn.

In Belmont is a lady richly left,
And she is fair and fairer than that word.

Miss Neff and foxgloves.

road to Cap-à-l'Aigle, at a place called Mont-Murray—Madame Mackay was so taken with the view of the river that she decided then and there that the house would suit them perfectly.

The Mackays took the place at once, and the Tremblay family moved into the kitchen for the summer.[†] Reverend Mackay's children occupied the loft, where the bedrooms were separated by simple pine planks. When the Mackays came back to the Tremblays' house next summer, they were surprised to find that the partitions had disappeared—they had been used to heat the place during the hard winter. The Mackays bought the farmhouse in 1891 and named it Auld House.

174 The Reverend Alexander B. Mackay (1842–1901) "Rev. Dr. Alexander B. Mackay for nearly twenty-five years conducted most of the Presbyterian services and is still kindly remembered by many of us. Vigorous in person, unmistakably Scotch in speech and showing his warm, Christian convictions in all his words and ways, his was a strong and winning personality" (Sarah B. Tibbits, *The Murray Bay Protestant Church for Fifty Years, 1867–1917* [1917], 14).

175 The Cap-à-l'Aigle church (1889–1962) This little chapel, which could accommodate about a hundred worshipers, was built of grey clapboard and crowned with a roof of shingles painted red. It was built in 1889 at a cost of $488.92, with Gonzague Tremblay in charge of construction. Intended as a centre for Christians of all denominations, it was situated at the heart of the Cap-à-l'Aigle summer colony. The chapel was owned by the Mackay family until 1962, when it was removed to make way for a new road.

A.B. Mackay died in an accident during a fishing trip to Sept-Îles in 1901, but before then he had installed an observation gallery on the upper floor of Auld House that gave a clear view of Pointe-au-Pic and its bustling quay. Although the place was without running water, electricity, or any other comforts of the city, five generations of Mackays came back in succession, fascinated by the river and the unforgettable spectacle of white ships passing up and down it.

Among the oldest families to take their holidays in Charlevoix were the Burroughs and the Pelletiers. The first was John Burroughs, the protonotary of Québec; he made his first visit around 1840. Later, his daughter Alice introduced her husband to the area; he was Elzéar Pelletier, a doctor practising in Montréal. These two enthusiasts started a lasting family tradition. In 1899, the Pelletiers built Mont Plaisant, a little cottage in the heart of Cap-à-l'Aigle; then in 1901 they bought some land from Adhémard Lapointe, bordering on the river, where they built Le Sorbier and then Le Gîte. Their son, Burroughs Pelletier, lived in Le Gîte with his young family and spent his holidays exploring the area as an amateur historian.

Like all the summer residents, the Pelletiers enjoyed the splendid annual fête organized by Alfred E. Francis on his big property Twin Poplars, which he had bought from Georges Savard in 1922. Held for the benefit of the Red Cross, the whole of Cap-à-l'Aigle turned out for the occasion—

[†]At that time, it was quite common for habitants to let their house for the summer months and move into the summer kitchen.

the Hydes, the Kyles and the Adairs (who were related), the Cundills, Kerrys, Wrights, Greenshields, and D'Arcys, the Urquharts from Montréal, and last but not least, the Robbs, Bancrofts, and Popes.

Valuing the rural life as they did, residents usually built their villas in the least productive corner of a farm, where they could enjoy the animals and the gardens and the meadows with their wild fruits. Being near the farm gave them close daily contact with people of the soil, and close friendships formed in the diverse community. The families of Honoré Bhérer, Ferdinand Guay, Henri Tremblay, and more recently those of Paul Desmeules and David Lapointe, responded to the influx of summer residents by turning their homes into guest-houses. When the visitors returned faithfully year after year, it was just like family reunions.

Around 1860, the Reverend Fothergill of St Peter's Church in Québec decided to spend his holidays at Cap-à-l'Aigle and rented a cottage from Joseph Collard. When he arrived, he was disturbed to discover there was no place to celebrate mass. He solved the problem by inviting summer residents to his cottage for Sunday services. As the years went by, the number of celebrants grew and he had to find a bigger home. On a slightly raised site in the village stood an abandoned barn. The owner, Madame Vannovis of Québec, agreed to let this building be transformed into a chapel in the summer of 1872. In due course Reverend Allnatt succeeded the original incumbent and for the next thirty-three years ministered faithfully to St-Peter-on-the-Rock. In 1907 the church was consecrated by the Anglican bishop of the diocese of greater Québec, but it retained its

176 *Malbaie, 1885* One of the oldest families in the summer colony was the Burroughs-Pelletiers, who first started coming to Charlevoix for summer vacations in the early 1840s.

177 *The young grow up* ... For six generations of Hydes, as for Kyles and Adairs, the uplands of Mount Murray brought back unforgettable memories of happy childhood days.

Angie Burroughs Maman   Elziar Pelletier Papa   John Burroughs

malbaie 1885

178 *St. Peter-on-the-Rock, Cap-à-l'Aigle* This Anglican building was constructed in 1922 by Charles Warren; in all respects it was an architectural copy of the original building.

179 *I dreamed I went to Murray Bay ...* "Murray Bay for years has been considered the 'Newport of the North' but there has always been this great difference. Those who summered at Newport came to splash their wealth in a heady round of elaborate earth-shaking frivolity and lavish hurdy-gurdy — always contingent in the process of 'social arriving'; while their more select counterparts at Murray Bay came to commune with nature and to rusticate away from the social tumult for the pleasures of the more simple life which seems to appeal to those who know they already have arrived" (Gustavus Arnold, "The Manoir Richelieu," *Michigan Society of Architects Monthly Bulletin* [April 1961]: 29).

autonomous status, remaining in the hands of the congregation. In 1922, the parishioners decided to reconstruct the little church along the lines of the original plan. Maud Cabot, owner of the seigneury at Cap-à-l'Aigle, took pains to see that the presbytery was comfortable. Among other men and women who made this chapel a living centre of worship, mention must be made of Mary Gill, who left many paintings and water-colours extolling the beauties of the countryside, and Beatrice Pope and Esther Kerry, each of whom wrote with great affection a short history of the community.

Among the families who have left their mark on this history are the Kennedys. Their presence dates back to the start of this century, when Harold Kennedy, a native of Liverpool, England, arrived in Québec to keep a closer eye on his shipping and lumber businesses. From their very first years in Canada, and despite the fact that they visited London regularly, the Kennedys spent each summer at La Malbaie in a house called La Surprise, built in 1903. The following year, Harold's brother Murray built a somewhat more modest villa, which he called Ça Nous Va. In the years to follow, their descendants would gather around them — the Mackenzies, Wanklyns, Coves, Porteouses, and Patersons.

Other families, other faces have flocked to Charlevoix in the summer: on the American side, Admiral Thébaud and his wife, the Fortune Peter Ryans, Mrs Henderson Robb from New York, the Honourable Hamilton Fish from Washington, as well as the McGraths and the Sloanes from Virginia; and on the Canadian side, the Timminses, Daweses, Commons, Gillespies, Gravels, and Choquettes from Montréal, and the Kernans, Sévignys, and Amyots from Québec. And of course there were the Donohues — George, Mark, and Charles — the family of industrialists who decided to link their destiny to that of the region.

So there we have it, the élite who through successive generations have brought a new style of life to the countryside of Charlevoix. Whether their ancestors arrived for the first time aboard ship, whether they stayed in a luxury hotel or a comfortable family pension, all of them were captivated by the intimate relationship between nature and the local inhabitants. Since then, their descendants — drawn from the worlds of the bench, finance, and politics — have met in the summer and together participated in the full range of outdoor activities. And they have raised monuments to summer resort life, the new art of living; their splendid villas invest Pointe-au-Pic and Cap-à-l'Aigle with an air of magic that crowns the bay with glory.

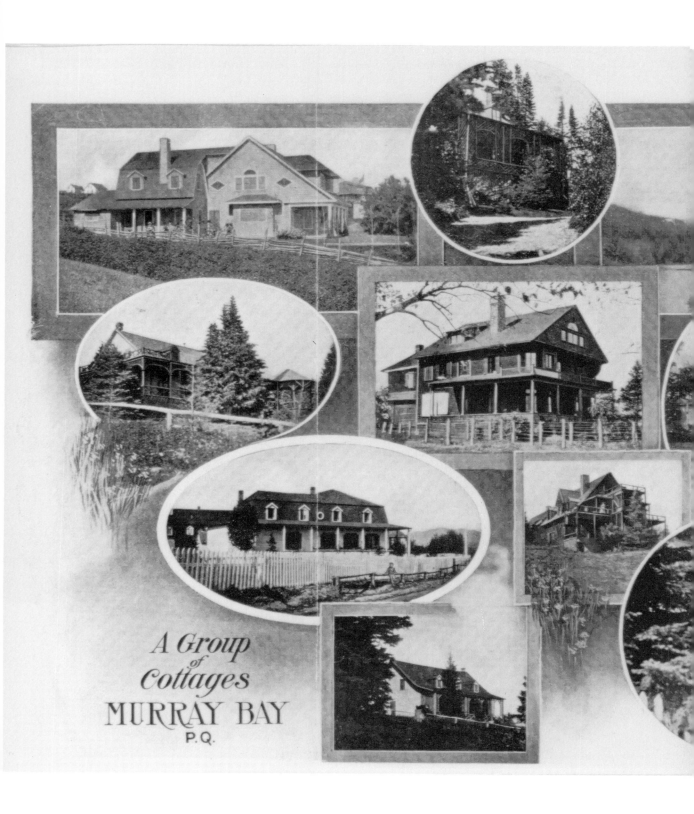

A Group
of
Cottages
MURRAY BAY
P.Q.

VILLAS ON THE CLIFF

180 *Unity amid diversity* This selection shows the variety of architectural styles seen at the end of the century, a period characterized by its eclectic taste. Resolutely inventive, the "seasonal" architect was unique in his search for originality.

IN NINETEENTH-CENTURY NORTH AMERICA, as industry took root in a world that up till then had been essentially agricultural and mercantile, population and resources began to concentrate in cities. Taking advantage of circumstances, an élite with great business acumen carved an enviable place for itself. In Québec and Montréal, the new bourgeoisie managed to graft itself onto the ruling class of British military and civilian administrators that formed the colonial government. A few reached the highest ranks of the social hierarchy. This class at once adopted a new way of life that expressed the change of circumstances. Masters of their own time, they were able to escape the discomforts of the city in summer and take long spells in the countryside, where they built elegant and spacious villas, comfortably fitted out. The trend fostered a new style of building in Québec that came to be known as "free architecture"; it was inspired primarily by the country houses of England with their studied purity of line, in turn influenced by the tradition of Italian villas of the sixteenth century.[1]

The new way of life was defined by the romantic concept of a return to nature, distancing oneself from the hubbub of the city. It had started when, as improvements in transportation made traveling easier, the search for peace and quiet drove devotees beyond the suburbs of the city into regions farther afield. By about 1830, many had already discovered places like Kamouraska, Cacouna, and La Malbaie. These summer vacationers, who first came predominantly from Québec, were following the lead of those who peopled the hillsides of Sillery, Ste-Foy, and Cap-Rouge in summer.

The flocks that disembarked on the coasts included families who had acquired a taste for lengthy holidays in Charlevoix. Now hotels could not adequately meet their needs, for many wanted to come and stay for an entire season. Gradually they built summer homes and formed a colony of summer residents concentrated at Pointe-au-Pic, some distance from the hotels and the dock. In the countryside of Charlevoix a new architecture developed that contrasted with traditional housing styles.

A man called Bentzon, who was on board the *Saguenay* in the spring of 1897, noticed "the pretty villas" as he came into the bay; they were ranged in tiers along the cliffs, a natural amphitheatre:

> The boat stops at Pointe-au-Pic, one of the two points of the bay—the other being Cap-à-l'Aigle; on these two promontories, at some distance from the town, are built the hotels and the pretty American villas, made of wood, in a smart ultramodern style totally different from the solid old Canadian homes with no aesthetic pretension.[2]

Mr. Bentzon might have noted the variety of styles: Norman, English or the "shingle style" so typical of New England.[3] On the other hand, he could never have suspected the contribution to this style made by such well-known architects as Staveley of Québec or the firm of McKim, Mead and White of New York; still less could he have imagined that a local master builder, Jean-Charles Warren, would leave his mark on a good number of villas built on the cliff overlooking the river.

Jean-Charles Warren, Master Builder[4]

IN CHARLEVOIX, the name of Warren is directly linked to a sort of local dynasty that has lived in Pointe-au-Pic for many generations and whose reputation is closely associated with summer residents. Their Scottish ancestor, John, was a good friend of John Nairne. After settling down and marrying in Baie-St-Paul, where he was a shoemaker by trade, he took a concession at Pointe-au-Pic in 1819. This man, known for being "gentle, kind, blythe, frank and free," was Jean-Charles Warren's great-grandfather.[5]

Jean-Charles, baptized in the church at La Malbaie on 26 October 1868, was the fourth child of his father Jean's first wife, Délima Girard. He lost his mother at an early age and boarded with the Sisters of Charity at Youville Convent in Québec, together with his sister Lydia and brothers Edward and James, until his father's remarriage in November 1875 to Elizabeth Duchesne. At that time, Jean Warren owned the general store at Pointe-au-Pic, which his second wife ran with care; he kept his end up building schooners and, later, summer houses. As his affairs prospered, the contractor entered the village school at the age of forty and learned to read, write, and handle figures.

During the summer, Charles was ship's boy in his father's crew, Jean occasionally serving as captain of his fishing boats; Charles also helped build schooners and the little fishing boats called *pines*. At the Pointe-au-Pic school, the young man showed great aptitude. It was probably during these years at primary school that he decided to become an architect, having inherited a practical ability for building and a strong taste for design.

181 *Young Charles and his brother Edouard* Standing beside his elder brother, Charles is wearing a bonnet recalling his Scotch origins. Both boys are wearing Murray Bay socks, a typical item of "folklore" clothing favoured by summer residents.

HIS APPRENTICESHIP

His mind made up, Charles Warren left the village where he had lived all his twenty years and took a job as a designer in a project-study office in Cleveland, Ohio. In his spare time, he studied fine arts and learned more and more about architecture; in due course, he was put in charge of the architectural department of the Cleveland Engineering Company, with the chance gradually to put his name to personal projects. In August 1893, he wrote to his brother, James, in somewhat fractured French, to tell him of his future plans:

> I've done a splendid set of plans for a hotel at La Malbaie, which I'll have built when I have the money; it can be built very cheaply, and will bring a good return. I hope you'll come in with me financially; it's based on American plans. [†6]

Now confident and sure of his ability, Charles returned to Pointe-au-Pic in 1894 to lend a hand to his father, who could hardly cope with the needs of a growing number of summer residents. Among them was Susanna Shaw Minturn, who had been coming to Murray Bay since 1887. She decided to build a villa on the river's edge, west of the Protestant church at Pointe-au-Pic. Making use of a new concept perfected by the American architect Charles F. McKim, Warren designed and built her villa in pure shingle style. This first project gave him a solid grounding in modern planning and construction, from which he went on to a productive career whose span — 1895 to 1925 — marks the golden age of summer residence in Charlevoix. During those thirty years, Warren designed some sixty villas and many public buildings. Following in his father's footsteps, he was recognized as the most skilled constructor in the region.

HIS WORK

In his dogged search for a new kind of building, Charles Warren made every effort to use local materials, even though the American influence was

182 *Jean-Charles Warren (1868–1929)*
In 1900, Charles Warren married Cécile Lajoie of Cap-à-l'Aigle, who worked for several years in the general store of the man who was to become her father-in-law. Six children were born of this union, four of whom left descendants in Canada and the United States.

183 *Château Murray, Pointe-au-Pic*
This hotel is the first known project of Charles Warren; it was made possible by financial assistance from his father. In private correspondence the young architect mentioned the American origins of his design, the inspiration for which was perhaps drawn from the pattern books of the day. Built in 1904, the hotel was named Château Murray to honour the birth of Charles Warren's fourth child.

CHATEAU MURRAY. POINTE AU PIC P.Q.

†J'ai fait un joli plan pour une Hotel à la Malbaie que je ferai batir quand j'aurai de l'argent elle peut être batit très bon marché et rendre une bonne interet. J'espère que tu investra avec moi elle est fait sur les plans Americain.

recognizable in the forms his buildings took. His lack of theoretical train-ing, and above all his professional status as a builder, probably explain Warren's drifts into so-called carpenter's architecture; everything he pro-duced reflected the work of his men, whose skilful solutions to problems were a feature of all his buildings.

Working with their architect-builder, his clients would decide the loca-tion of their summer house based on the view they wanted. On a makeshift step-ladder, future owners could see what sort of view they would get from various parts of their house. The structure would be set in wooded surroundings, in a carefully cleared area, its foundation generally on piles set at the desired level on sloping ground; on this would be raised a vertical open-work skeleton,[7] floor by floor.

Charles Warren would propose a house that was designed to meet the client's needs and yet harmonized with the site he wanted to develop. After often protracted discussions, he would make a proposal that satisfied the owners' tastes as well as his creativity. In this simple and direct way, the architect of Pointe-au-Pic built up a numerous and faithful clientele. It is easy, however, to imagine — Warren being the area's sole contractor — the difficulties he had in proposing original styles of architecture in a district scarcely ten kilometres long, where all the owners met each other regularly.

184/185 *Plans of the Minturn house* In partnership with his father, Charles Warren soon completed his appren-ticeship in domestic architecture with waterside villas. On his first proj-ects, he profited from the technical and architectural knowledge he had acquired in the United States.

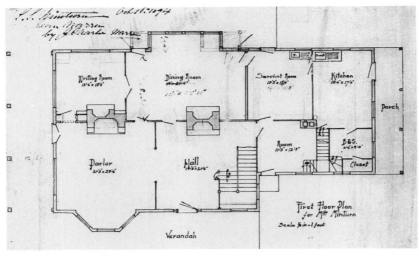

186 *Susanna Shaw Minturn's house* This house was a perfect example of the colonial revival style in vogue in the United States at the turn of the century. Having been strongly influenced by British picturesque, American architects resumed earlier practices in the conversion of colo-nial houses into summer residences.

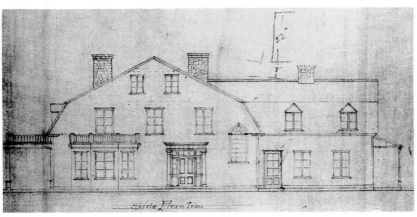

He took the challenge up, exercising freedom in his choice of forms. When the Aymar family of New York ordered a house from him in 1898, Warren made no bones about borrowing features from rural architecture and using the long ground plan characteristic of farm buildings. He added an eccentric feature at the entrance—a tower that could be taken for a grain silo. Furthermore, his dormer windows were upturning circumflex accents, running through the walls in the ogival shape found in certain Gothic Protestant churches. This free-and-easy building, called Yellow Cottage, was a perfect example of the work of a man not yet entirely skilled at playing with shapes and volumes, voids and asymmetrical outgrowths—but who early exhibited a sense of proportion and an almost theatrical talent in the treatment of the outside of buildings. On the other hand, his bold approach did not prevent him from following the prevailing style when dealing with more conventionally minded clients. Having been initiated into fine arts and architecture in America, the master builder of Pointe-au-Pic surprised many by borrowing a style as common as colonial revival.

With his facility for assimilation, it was not long before his work showed a slant toward the traditional Québécois models that many summer residents chose in their desire to integrate with the surrounding countryside. An example is Miss Ethel Louisa Maclean's residence. In 1914, this Montréal lady, fond of the cottages of Charlevoix, commissioned him to build a typically rural house adapted to the requirements of a summer residence. Despite its rustic appearance, the villa was modern in its framework of light materials and in the organization of its interior space. In any case, the experienced eye could quickly detect anachronisms, as Jean M. Donald affirmed in memoirs published in 1940: "Among others, we saw a rose-and-nigger-brown mansion looking much too sophisticated, and a very

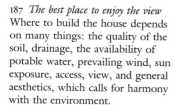

187 *The best place to enjoy the view*
Where to build the house depends on many things: the quality of the soil, drainage, the availability of potable water, prevailing wind, sun exposure, access, view, and general aesthetics, which calls for harmony with the environment.

pseudo-cottage with about ten bathrooms, judging by the ventilation pipes, producing an air of self-conscious rurality very trying to behold."[8] Donald, a connoisseur of old houses, was not easily taken by imitations, but he did not do justice to what was a praiseworthy attempt at a modern interpretation of traditional housing. In Miss Maclean's villa, a clear line was drawn between the zone reserved for domestic chores and the area provided for the rest and recreation of the occupants. Warren also saw to the interior decoration, sparing no detail. This way of designing a house—not merely

188/189 *Building a villa* The position of the two workmen, one in front of the rounded section of the foundation, the other at ground-floor level, gives us some idea of the size of the building. Built on a half-timbered framework, this villa exemplifies a standard system of construction in wood, very modern for the times.

the outer shell and the inner space, but also the furnishings and decor—was thoroughly modern.

At this time, there were said to be two industries in Pointe-au-Pic: Manoir Richelieu, owned by Canada Steamship Lines, and Charles Warren's construction company. Warren had thirty or so workers, including those in his furniture workshop, where the best carpenters were employed all year round. With a disciplined, competent staff, the builder could carry out the whole of a project himself, without having to go through an intermediary. The work

190/191 *Building a villa* The ground plan is almost rectangular, with a porch running halfway around it; in the centre of one side it swells out to include a turret. The house is completely covered in cedar shingles. It was built for Tancrède Bienvenu, a Montréal businessman.

192 *"Summer Residence, for a Sea-Shore-Place"* The lines of this sketch show the influence of the Queen Anne style, which makes skilful use of volumes. It became popular in the United States in the 1880s, when it was used by fashionable architects like Richardson, Emerson, and Stevens, all natives of New England.

Summer Residence.
for a Sea Shore-place,
Jean C. Warren Architect.

193 *The Donohue house* This façade, a collection of disparate architectural elements, is pulled together by the uniform texture of the cedar shingles. The arrangement of the siding gives a certain horizontality to the building and thus better balance to the whole.

was completely his; from the first sketch to the final polish on the furniture, his handiwork was everywhere in evidence — and this despite the fact that he had lost his right hand in a planing machine in his cabinet shop. So great was demand that Warren never stopped working; the construction market opened up for him in an unexpected fashion, even though the economy slowed down during the First World War.

Warren wanted to make Murray Bay a little paradise for tourists, where careful planning would preserve the area in its natural state, and where his

194 *Rayon d'Or* First called Yellow Cottage, and forming a trio with Pink Cottage and Blue Cottage, all belonging to the same owner, this summer residence is now called Rayon d'Or; it has retained its original colour of wheaten yellow.

buildings enhanced its natural beauties. This did not necessarily call for enormous financial resources, but the idea itself was essential. Maja Chatka (in Polish, My Little Hut), constructed for a nurse from Montréal in 1917, brought the following comment in the May 1928 issue of *Canadian Homes and Gardens*: "This pretty summer place at Murray Bay, Que., is set among

195 *A simple and spontaneous construction* Built by Charles Warren in 1898, this house is set on a natural promontory; it takes the form of a half-moon, as though it were ready to swallow the neighbourhood in one fell swoop.

silver Birches and facing a delightful, rambling garden. The house is painted oyster white with windows and doors in marine blue. The interior is trimed [*sic*] in unfinished Pine, characteristic of the district, and in the living room the habitant chairs and table, gay chintz and stone fireplace are inviting."[9] The interior of the house attracted the attention of the writer as much as its exterior, whose observation about the interior pine trim being character- istic of the region is notable. "In the Manner of a Normandy Farmhouse," in the same magazine, described another of Warren's buildings as unique among the Murray Bay villas, though its interior arrangement was much the same as anyone else's.[10]

196/197 *Le Barachois* Warren's virtu- osity included the colonial Ameri- can style, which was coming back into fashion. A ground plan with two axes crossing each other gave an attractive view of the river from three sides of the house. It was a com- pact, rather tall house, which looked as though it wanted to capture the immensity of the countryside and the light that flooded it. The word *barachois* is French Canadian for little harbour or place of refuge.

198 *Interpretation of the traditional style* Although the dimensions of this cottage are bigger than those of a traditional house, it is clearly rustic. The arrangement of the interior, where each piece of furniture has its own function, reflects an essentially modern, urban way of life. Around 1925, the New York banker Francis Sydney Bancroft, Canadian by birth, moved into Mon Rocher with his wife Beatrice F. Jordan and their three children; they changed the name of the house to Darly Fields, after an ancestral village in the north of England.

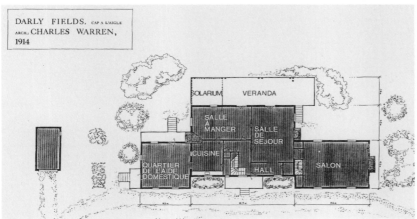

DARLY FIELDS, CAP A L'AIGLE
ARCH.: CHARLES WARREN, 1914

SOLARIUM VERANDA
SALLE A MANGER SALLE DE SEJOUR
CUISINE
QUARTIER DE L'AIDE DOMESTIQUE HALL SALON

199 *Darly Fields* This ground plan, with its three large rooms for living and entertaining, shows how summer residence calls for a particular architectural arrangement.

200 *One of Charles Warren's characteristic interiors* The rustic look of his interior is directly connected with the lines of the outer shell of the house. The simplicity with which all the internal space is furnished expresses a return to nature. The arrangement of the furniture is just as important as its style or material.

201 *Comfort with a country accent* Technical progress is skilfully blended into the villa's rustic features. Why should one be deprived of modern comfort?

202 *True to life* The strongly regional character of such an interior derives from the furniture and fabric, which all come from Charlevoix. No authentically rural house has a purer look to it.

203/204 *Bel Adon* Formerly known as Maja Chatka, Bel Adon was for more than fifty years the property of Miss Esther W. Kerry of Montréal. Its name came from a local expression used in William H. Blake's *In a Fishing Country*. Sailing one day off Charlevoix, the author had been becalmed on the river; a wind from the north-east saved him. The captain of the boat described this breath from heaven as *un bel adon*, a happy coincidence (William H. Blake, *In a Fishing Country* [Toronto 1922], 45).

205 *Penteaves, with its Norman charm* The set-back conical tower stresses the French character of this seigneurial farmhouse. But one must not be deceived by its old-fashioned appearance; built in 1923, it had underground electricity and a central-heating system that was very advanced for those days. The owner, active in the real-estate business, was familiar with technological advances in building.

206 *Penteaves* The plan divides the interior space into two distinct parts: one for the owner, the other for domestic servants. This simple and functional plan, in the shape of an H, made the living-room the central element of the building. Both the internal and external planning of Penteaves stress the intimate aspects of summer residence. The garden was designed by Isabella Pendleton, a friend of the Livingood family.

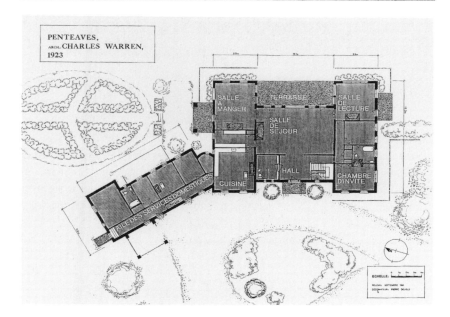

PENTEAVES, ARCH. CHARLES WARREN, 1923

Charles Livingood of Cincinnati was not indifferent to the idea of a global approach to architecture.[11] His residence, Penteaves, in the Norman style, fit in perfectly with the site on which it stood. This building demonstrated Warren's mastery of his trade; he used brick for the outside, leaving the upper parts of the vertical framework exposed, and for the roof he made skilled use of rounded cedar shingles, which gave something of the effect of thatch. He was also a master of the use of space. Upon entering the front door the first thing one saw was an enormous, breathtaking bay window in the living-room. Also, the arrangement of the furniture and the symmetry of its dimensions showed how deeply skilled the fifty-year-old architect had become in the use of every device that architecture could bring to the creation of a functional habitat.

207 *Skilled techniques* This house is built of stone and whitewashed brick, with half-timber showing. Its thick roofing of rounded cedar shingles recalls the Norman-style thatched roof.

208 *Les Hirondelles* Charles Warren, in association with the architect Pierre C. Amos, made good use of his talent to create this house with its sweeping roof. In a spare style, corresponding to the clean lines of the traditional house, the architect took pains to impart a picturesque look to a modern building. The facing of whitewashed stucco and the blue shutters were concessions to bring the building into harmony with its environment.

At the summit of Warren's career, new commissions kept coming in. His last summer house, Les Hirondelles, was built in 1925 for Mr. and Mrs. Sidney Dawes of Montréal; this project was evidence of full maturity, especially in the play between depth and protuberance and in the sweep of the long eaves-troughs, which harmonized with the curved dormer windows. After thirty years of practice, the inventive builder had gone far beyond his original dream of helping develop his native village tastefully.

Smitten with arteriosclerosis, which caused him grave loss of memory, Charles Warren slowly drew nearer to nature for consolation. His youngest son Robert managed somehow or other to carry on his business for a few years; but the Great Depression slowed down the development of Charlevoix. On 4 June 1929, at the age of sixty-one, Charles Warren died, carrying with him the secret of his architectural dreams. There is no written record of his professional ideas after his youthful years in Cleveland, though he did tell his daughter Charlotte on several occasions that all along he had been striving to create a distinct Laurentian architecture.

209 *The nobility of simplicity* Interiors of natural pine are a mark of the style appropriate to summer homes in Murray Bay. This dining-room has an elegance rarely found in a simple summer house. The furniture and the big hooked rug display local craftsmanship.

CREATING A LAURENTIAN ARCHITECTURE

Self-taught, Charles Warren managed by sheer determination to broaden his outlook, first by leaving his birthplace to apprentice as a designer in America, then by traveling.[12] About the latter, unfortunately, very little is known. In 1910 he set up a furniture factory in Montréal with his brothers James and Edouard. But after a year he came back to Charlevoix, convinced that city life was not for him. A dozen years later he went on a business trip to Rio de Janeiro, where a group of architects asked him to join them — probably because of his influential contacts with Charlevoix's summer residents, whose names figured in the international "blue books." A few years later this same group invited him to Vancouver, where he took part in several large-scale projects. However, his love for Laurentides Park brought him back to the banks of the St Lawrence every autumn, when he went hunting with his friend William Hume Blake. Both were strong supporters of the idea of turning the vast wilderness into a natural park. Such experiences and contacts doubtless helped mould the unique architect that was Charles Warren.

Because he had mastered English in his youth and, as a consequence, was familiar with the English milieu, Warren understood the needs of his clientele. Though he lacked a formal degree, he was a true architect insofar as he propounded an architectural programme adapted to the environment of his market. He was above all a builder of houses, master of the most recent technological advances, who made a point of incorporating practical and comfortable space into every one of his creations. Even the former Provincial Bank at La Malbaie and the clubhouse at the Murray Bay Golf Club resemble family houses, both in dimensions and general appearance. Each fit in with its site wonderfully well, and its shape and materials seemed to blend naturally with the mood of the locale. With his knowledge of physical and human environments, Warren was predisposed to landscape

210 *One form of development* This map, drawn by Charles Warren in 1924, shows part of the Murray Bay region. The list of properties gives a good idea of the number of summer residences. About sixty of them were built by Warren alone.

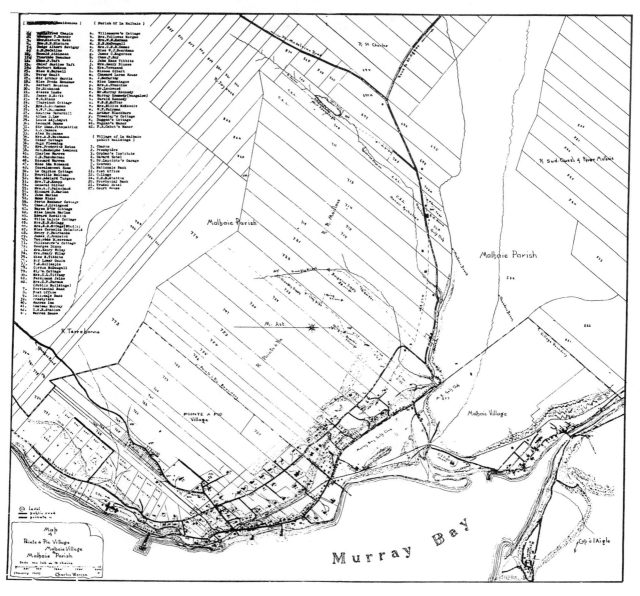

his work; the opening of the Boulevard des Falaises at the beginning of the century bore witness to his intentions along these lines.

To Warren, the view from a villa was of fundamental importance in its planning. The actual location was dictated by the view, as was the shape of the house. The building itself, as we have seen, developed in accordance with the fashions of the day. However, one trademark was to be seen in all of the architect's creations: his use of interior space, which in some way or another idealized the rustic aspects of Charlevoix. Warren always remained true to that, for he wanted the occupants as if by osmosis to melt into the surrounding countryside. Probably through intuition, but also from his personal experience with northern houses, the architect used his interiors to express something entirely his own. Combining the various styles he had worked with in boat building, in the American firm, and in his adaptations of traditional houses, he arrived at some original ideas that amounted to a new style of life for his clients.

In building summer mansions that reflected the spirit of Charlevoix, Warren was probably not far from his idea of a Laurentian style of architecture. The building must in effect grow out of the ground like a plant at the beginning of summer. According to him, his best work from the point of view of style was Pins Rouges, built in 1920. His concepts of scale and height, of balance and the use of open spaces, were combined in the most ingenious manner, intuitive rather than theoretical.

The overall picture of his work reveals an independent personality. The practical training during his formative years led to a facile and free-flowing creativity and helped him develop a level of skill sufficient to overcome the many material difficulties he encountered in carrying out his plans. He had no mentor that we know of, except perhaps his father, from whom he learned to make the best use of his workman's ingenuity. He would cer-

211 *Les Pins Rouges* This seventeen-room house was built in 1920 for Henry Parker Fairbanks; it was designed by Charles Warren, who melded several different styles into a charming and logical whole. The gambrel, sloped roofing over the terrace, the shutters with their shapely tops, and the embrasured gallery—all harmonize perfectly in this cruciform design, which sets a judicious limit to proportions that would otherwise look gigantic.

8893 MURRAY BAY FROM THE HILLSIDE   NOTMAN MONTREAL

tainly have wished to see the architecture of summer homes taught the way he himself practised it — that is, as a method rather than a style. With his villas, Charles Warren created an environment that harmonized with the sea and mountains. He set his works here and there on the tiers of a natural half-moon amphitheatre, as if putting the finishing touches to a spectacle of rare beauty.

212 *A choice location* The large house on the right, photographed by William Notman of Montréal, was called Blue Cottage; it formed part of a celebrated trio, the Yellow, Pink, and Blue Cottages. From the plateau on which it stands, this monumental house, today called Porte-Bonheur, commands an unspoiled view of the bay.

The Architects

THE ARCHITECTURAL LANDSCAPE of La Malbaie has for more than a century prompted all sorts of comment, from the unbridled swoonings of extrovert enthusiasts to the more restrained ecstasies of the gentry. All are unanimous in their praise, as the French are in speaking of their châteaux on the Loire or the English their country houses. The villas in Charlevoix are monuments evoking the elegance of a golden age. Several of them, perched on the cliff, were designed and constructed by Charles Warren, whose style is to a large extent responsible for Murray Bay's reputation as the Newport of Canada.[13] But other architects have played their part, enriching and diversifying the region with their master-pieces — some of which, unfortunately, no longer exist. In all, some fifteen professional architects have exercised their talents at Pointe-au-Pic and Cap-à-l'Aigle between 1874 and the present. La Malbaie and its environs are thus a crossroads of architectural styles, all of which, ultimately, serve a common purpose: to house summer residents.

Villa architecture in Charlevoix has only two origins, two sources of inspiration: one American, the other Canadian. Our cousins to the south, especially in their earliest creations, were preoccupied with the idea of creating a distinctly American architecture. Their homes soon showed the influence of the Beaux Arts; it was through these homes that the French influence came to the banks of the St. Lawrence. For the Canadians, this interest in an indigenous style was less evident;[14] it was not until the later constructions of the twentieth century that it made itself felt. By and large, however, one fact remains: the conception of a residence specifically for summer occupation allowed the architect to go beyond the bounds of the strictly theoretical and venture into the realms of the new, where he could express himself with greater freedom and spontaneity.

THE PIONEERS

Of all the buildings in Charlevoix attributable to a professional architect, Maison Rouge is probably the earliest. In 1874, Edward Blake decided to

213 *Harry Staveley (1848–1925)* Staveley was a founder of the Association of Architects of the province of Québec, incorporated in Québec on 30 December 1890. He was the second vice-president in 1892–93.
214 *Maison Rouge* Built in 1874 to the

settle down at Pointe-au-Pic; he called on the services of Harry Staveley, a young architect of twenty-six who had already worked four years for his father. The Québec firm of Staveley and Son had considerable experience in villa architecture, having already built Mount Pleasant, Holland House, and Cataraqui, all in the neighbourhood. Harry had already drawn the plans for Bijou, on the Ste-Foy road, with complete self-assurance;[15] now he did the same for Maison Rouge in Charlevoix.

214 *Maison Rouge* Built in 1874 to the plans of Harry Staveley, this house was named not for its bright red roof but rather for the colour of the Liberal party, to which its owner, Edward Blake, belonged. The house "high above the St. Lawrence with its sweep of pine and water" was destroyed by fire in 1917 (Joseph Schull, *Edward Blake: Leader and Exile, 1881–1912* [Toronto 1976], 196).

There was no similarity between these two homes, in either style or size. Bijou had "all the characteristics of the Second Empire architectural style,"[16] while Maison Rouge, with its facing of planks laid horizontally, the sober ornamentation of the framework of its balconies, and the asymmetry of its solid and hollow parts, introduced a new type of construction in Charlevoix, the ornate cottage. It was characterized by numerous openings that gave access to the vast countryside and by verandas stacked one above the other, which offered a variety of views. Harry Staveley had certainly been won over by the charms of the area, for it was reported in the summer periodical *Le Touriste* that he had moved into a cottage at Cap-à-l'Aigle with his family to spend the summer holidays of 1885.[17]

Some ten years later, Susanna Shaw Minturn turned to Charles F. McKim, of McKim, Mead and White of New York, the most fashionable firm of the day, for the design of one of her houses at Murray Bay. In 1894 he designed a building for her that combined order and simplicity.

After a period at the École des Beaux Arts in Paris — he was in Daumet's studio in the early 1870s — McKim was employed as an architectural draughtsman for two years with Henry Hobson Richardson, creator and unchallenged master of the shingle style. Under his influence, McKim made free use of cedar shingles for outer facing. In 1877, with his future partners Mead and White, McKim covered New England in search of eighteenth-century architecture, hoping in colonial architecture to rediscover the sources of an authentic American style. His frequent stays in Newport probably gave him a taste for the neo-colonial style, which he

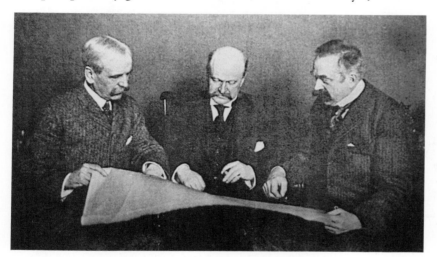

215 *The firm of McKim, Mead and White in 1906* (*Left to right*): William Rutherford Mead (1846–1928), Charles Follen McKim (1847–1909), and Stanford White (1853–1906). These architects established their firm in autumn 1879, when McKim was thirty-two, Mead thirty-three, and White twenty-six years of age. They adopted the motto *Vogue la galère* ("Let the worst happen"), as though to show their confidence of success. In thirty years of practice, they put their name to 785 projects in North America, half of which were public buildings. The dynamism of this group was largely responsible for the rebirth of American architecture.

216 *A building designed by Charles F. McKim* Sober lines and numerous references to the past make the Minturn house (see figs. 184, 185 and 186) a classic New England–style summer cottage.

217 *Georges Janin (1853–1917)* Born in Poitiers, France, this civil engineer, a former member of Paris's Department of Bridges and Highways, was one of the most active members of the French colony in Montréal. His works in that city's water-purification system were a great tribute to his professional talents and business acumen.

used to good effect in his many summer residences, blending cedar shingle and natural stone. His training as a mining engineer, which he received at Harvard before becoming interested in architecture, also stood him in good stead, for he showed great mastery of space. When he turned to colonial architecture for a formal touch, it was to give new direction to interior arrangement rather than to copy former styles.

This "engineering" approach was also noticeable in the work of Georges Janin. A civil engineer, Canadian by choice, Janin arrived from France in 1892. Later, he specialized in the water-purification system of Montréal, where he met Doctor Elzéar Pelletier, at that time in charge of the city's Bureau of Hygiene. Through his wife, Alice Burroughs, Pelletier was connected with one of the first families to take up summer residence in Charlevoix; he adopted Cap-à-l'Aigle for life, as though to contradict the old saw, Marry a husband, marry his country. The house Janin built for him at Cap-à-l'Aigle in 1899 was quite modest, yet it lacked nothing of the spirit of a summer residence.

Alfred C. Chapin, the former mayor of Brooklyn who was now a senator, had higher ambitions for his "country house," as he called it when he commissioned Stanford White to do the plans in 1901. White, the son of an art critic, had started at the age of nineteen as an architectural draughtsman in Richardson's office. His artistic sense soon gave him an insight into the creative possibilities of architecture. He absorbed every nuance, every

218/219 *Mont Plaisant* The square plan of this house, with its kitchen jutting out at the rear, is a good example of the ambiguity existing between the professions of engineer and architect. Despite a somewhat naive treatment of perspective, the proportions of this building give an impression of strength and harmony.

subtlety in the work of the prolific Richardson, and after six years of apprenticeship went on a tour of Europe. A year later, he joined the already-established partnership of Charles F. McKim and William P. Mead.

Passionately fond of beauty, White visited Europe nearly every year to buy brocades and paintings and old pieces of marble for his clients, even sections of walls or paneled ceilings. His untiring correspondence with his client Chapin discusses their mutual interests—for instance, in a mantelpiece they finally decided to have reproduced in New York.[18] The care for detail in internal fittings contributed to the reputation of White, who

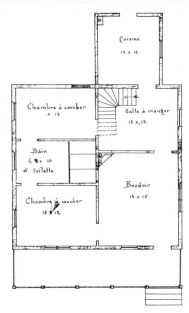

brought to the firm his feel for small-scale work and decoration. White was a devotee of salmon fishing, which drew him regularly to the Restigouche Salmon Club in the valley of the Matapédia; during these intermittent flights from reality he could forget the busy office and ponder his work in peace and quiet.

In 1906, America was shocked by Stanford White's assassination, which made the headlines in every newspaper. That same year, Susanna Minturn was planning a second cottage at Murray Bay with her son-in-law Isaac Newton Phelps Stokes. Stokes had been trained in business administration at Harvard, and his first start had been in banking; but in 1893 he studied architecture at Columbia University in New York. He completed his education with three years at the École des Beaux-Arts in Paris, then went into partnership with John Mead Howells in 1897. In his younger years he had met Elizabeth Minturn, whom he married on 21 August 1895 at Pointe-au-Pic. Stokes had vivid memories of his first contact with Charlevoix: "I was fascinated by the simple life — different from anything I had seen before in America — and especially by the beautiful views over the river, and the wonderful sunset effects. The Minturns knew most of the summer residents, many of them Canadians, and we went on numerous picnics and informal evening parties, where the habitants sang their native songs and danced their simple, rather awkward, dances."[19]

This was how Stokes, some ten years later, came to be drawing the plans for the second Minturn house. Inspired by the lines of the first one, designed by McKim, he positioned the service wing leading away from the main body of the house and reduced its volume, thus forming an eminently practical surface plan. One of this architect's trademarks was the natural effect; the Protestant church at Pointe-au-Pic, the rebuilding of which was carried out under his direction, was entirely covered in ashlar to preserve the natural wood interior.

220 *Ground plan of Mont Plaisant* The arrangement of cubes betrays the geometric stiffness brought to the practice of architecture by an engineer.

221 *Beau Jardin* This little villa retains all the distinction of the original; it even extends the romanticism of Mont Plaisant to the garden.

222 *Stanford White (1853–1906)* He was a big tall man with a face enlivened by a tuft of red hair sticking up from his skull. He was known as vigorous, quick to act, and sure of himself; he always knew what was good and what was bad — his taste was infallible. At the age of fifty-three he was the victim of a crime of passion, which put an end to the days of "the captain of the ship of Beaux-Arts in America."

223 *Bord de l'Eau* Ornamentation was an integral part of this villa. The composition of the front face was classic, with a picturesque touch cleverly incorporated in the rich texture. With his rectangular surface symmetrically divided and balanced, White demonstrated his talent as a decorator.

224 *View over the river* This house on the St Lawrence is an eloquent testimony to the architecture of the pioneers, which was to give more direct access to the river. American architects were the first bold enough to set their houses at the water's edge.

225 *A refreshing interior* The central chimney acts as a pivot around which the interior arrangement opens quite freely. The bay windows draw the eye outside, toward the widest possible panorama. The living-room/hall, with the hearth and the staircase off to the left, carries Stanford White's unmistakable signature.

226 *Mr and Mrs I.N. Phelps Stokes, 1897* This portrait of Stokes with his young wife Edith Minturn was done by the great American painter John Singer Sargent the year Stokes went into partnership with Howells. Stokes and his wife were married in the Protestant church at Pointe-au-Pic in August 1895.

227 *Isaac Newton Phelps Stokes (1867–1944)* This architect by training became known for the publication of his six-volume *Iconography of Manhattan Island*. He was a member of the firm Howells and Stokes from 1897 to 1917 and designed several buildings on the campuses of Yale, Columbia, and Harvard.

228/229 *The second Minturn house* The location of this house, east of the Protestant church at Pointe-au-Pic, called for an elongated plan that would allow full enjoyment of the wide horizon surrounding it.

230 *Ground plan of the Minturn house* This L-shaped plan has the advantage of separating the service wing from the main body of the house, thus making best use of the horizontal site.

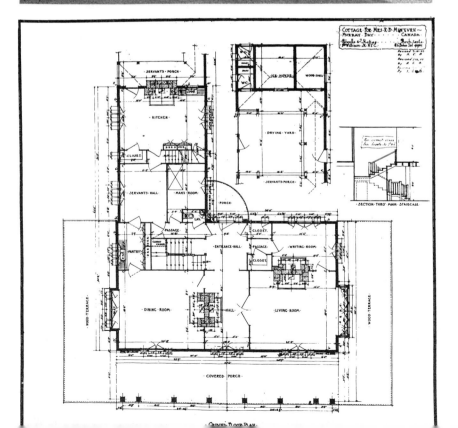

231 *Elevation of the Minturn house* Numerous openings in the walls flood this house with light. The colonial style gives the back-to-nature effect so sought after by summer residents.

232/233/234 *The Murray Bay Protestant Church* "The Church edifice had become very shabby and dilapidated on the exterior and, at the Annual meeting of 1909, under the leading of the trustees, plans were formulated and steps taken to make the building at once durable and beautiful, by encasing it in the stone of the country, while preserving unchanged the interior which is endeared to so many of us by long and hallowed associations. The estimated cost of this work was $6,000 ... I.N. Phelps Stokes, Esq., added greatly to the impetus thus given by his kind contribution of the architectural drawing made by his firm, Messrs. Howells & Stokes of New York" (Sarah B. Tibbits, *The Murray Bay Protestant Church for Fifty Years, 1867–1917* [1917], 9–10).

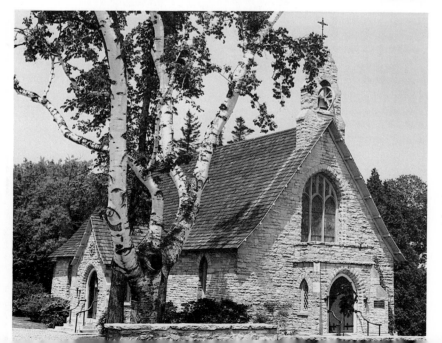

Like the Americans of Pointe-au-Pic, some Canadians at Cap-à-l'Aigle wanted to be near the banks of the St Lawrence, though the cliff kept them at a certain altitude. The second cottage of Doctor Pelletier, built in 1908 and called Le Sorbier, sat on a promontory at the extreme southern end of the farmer Adhémard Lapointe's land. The site dictated the layout of the cottage; the living-rooms, extended by a veranda rounded off at its

235 *Plan of Doctor Elzéar Pelletier's property* This parcel abutting Farmer Lapointe's land had little value for agricultural use, especially since access to the beach was reserved for the Mount Murray seigneury, except under payment.

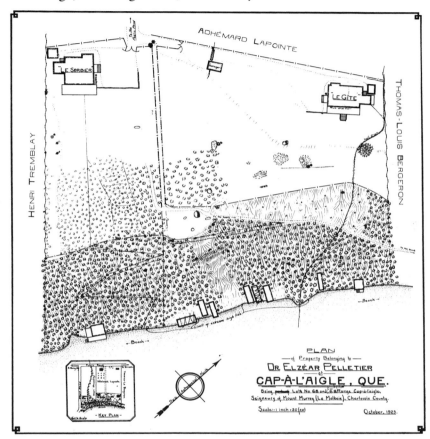

236 *Le Sorbier* The steep roof, pierced by a central chimney and dormer windows of varying shapes, covered a modest house of rectangular plan. The bold feature was the promontory it sat on, which dominated the river.

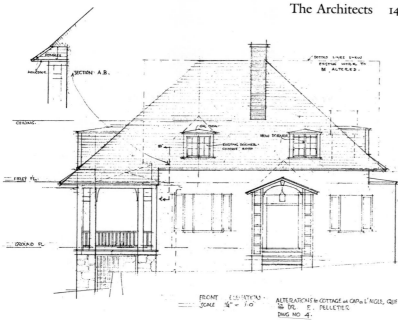

237 *Front elevation* Modifications to the original plan made this a less angular structure; the new and more enveloping shape was better suited to the requirements of summer residence.

ends, faced the river. Incidentally, his use of the slope of the ground to accentuate the way the house projected into the landscape was a good example of the way architects tried to meet the demands of owners.

In the same spirit, the Pelletier family asked the Montréal architect David Shennan to modify the roofing of Le Sorbier so that the house and veranda would be under the same roof.[†] This alteration made the building look more compact and whole and sheltered it from aggressive north-east winds. In 1913, the same owners asked Shennan to draw up plans for a cottage a few hundred metres from the first one. Le Gîte was noticeable for the quiet simplicity of its lines, the curve of its roof, and the delicacy of the vertical framework supporting its flared eaves.

[†]This architect, born in Scotland in 1880, trained at Castle Douglas; he arrived in Canada in 1906 and joined the firm of John S. Archibald. Among other large-scale projects, the firm drew up the plans for the second Manoir Richelieu.

238 *Le Sorbier after renovation* Conversion of the roof into a four-sided pavilion lowered the house by several metres, so that it looks as if it is clinging to the ground.

239 *Le Gîte* Set lengthwise and facing the river, this house on pillars opens to a broad panorama.

Pre-Construction Sketch, by David Shennon, Architect, 1913.

The Cottage, when built, 1914.

Le Gîte, Cap-à-l'aigle.

240 *Panorama over the St Lawrence* The banks of the majestic river alter with every change of the tide and the sky.

THE INFLUENCE OF THE ÉCOLE DES BEAUX-ARTS IN PARIS

The years of plenty and prosperity at the end of the nineteenth century had fostered the search for comfort and beauty. At the same time, art was showing a reaction against the austerity of earlier years, and architecture became smitten with elegance and refinement. The tone was set by Paris, which explains why so many architecture students attended the École des Beaux-Arts, or a school in London or New York that pursued the Parisian ideal of beauty. The practice of architecture consists of the capacity to blend aesthetic ideals and the more practical demands of construction. The teaching at the École des Beaux-Arts, which encouraged the borrowing of historic styles, improved the general quality of North American architecture and exercised a visible influence on a generation of American architects.[20]

241 *William Adams Delano (1874–1960)* The quintessential young American architect of his day, Delano profited greatly from his years in Paris, enriching his vocabulary with the noble architecture of France.

242 *Mur Blanc* Built in 1907 by Charles Warren from a sketch by William Delano, this villa harmonized perfectly with the surrounding landscape. People in the area said that Mur Blanc ought to be called Mur Bin Net ("very clean"). One of the favourite guests of Madame Rowley, its owner since 1928, was the Right Honourable R.B. Bennett, prime minister of Canada from 1930 to 1935.

William Adams Delano received the education typical of his times. The eldest of a well-to-do New York family, he took an arts degree at Yale in 1895, then enrolled for two years in the Columbia School of Architecture. Full of enthusiasm for his subject, he spent a year as a designer in the office of Carrère and Hastings in New York. Next he set out for Paris and entered the École des Beaux-Arts, where he received his diploma five years later. During this apprenticeship he met his future partner Chester Holmes Aldrich, with whom he founded the firm of Delano and Aldrich in New York in 1903.

While studying in Paris, young Delano courted the beautiful Lois Swan, who spent summers with her family at Murray Bay. He accepted an invitation to visit the Swans in Canada and after his stay, in the usual bread-

243 *Designed for the site* The materials, together with the fine lines and high, narrow doors and windows, are distinctive marks of French architecture of the eighteenth century. The central staircase gives balance and emphasizes the well-placed volumes, while the lines subtly prolong the promontory on which the villa is built.

and-butter letter to his hostess, enclosed a sketch for a summer residence; later, Emma Swan had it built by Charles Warren and called it Mur Blanc. The New York architect's style showed the influence of old French farmhouses. Throughout their careers, Delano and Aldrich remained true to their alma mater and spread architectural principles based on harmony with the environment. Like one of their summer mansions in Newport, Mur Blanc gave an impression of serene uniformity. Its elegant lines softened the severity of near-naked white walls. Delano—who died at the age of eighty-four—was fortunate to have practised in the early years of this century; he was quite conservative, and fought the idea of the extensive use of glass in modern architecture.

244 *Summer mansion on Ocean Drive, Newport, Rhode Island* It is tempting to compare two villas by the same architect, built some fifteen years apart. Mur Blanc, a work of Delano's youth, has a typically French character, while the summer mansion at Newport is an American adaptation of the original model.

245/246 *Projecting dormer windows*
The rich texture of the cedar-shingle roof foretells interiors in natural wood.

Louis-Auguste Amos, a Montréal architect, shared Delano's aesthetic ideals. In 1890, after completing an engineering degree at the Royal Military College in Kingston, he turned to architecture at McGill University. There he studied under the well-known professor Arthur Cox, whose partner he became for the next twenty years or so. In 1911 his sister Alice married the premier of Québec, Sir Lomer Gouin, who had been a widower for seven years. When Gouin decided to build a villa on the cliff at Pointe-au-Pic, naturally he called upon his brother-in-law. The result, inspired by Norman architecture, looked like a fortress; clinging to the side of the mountain, it seemed ready to protect itself against seige.

Similarly, James Hampden Robb, a Boston architect, took a personal approach when his mother, Beatrix Henderson Robb — Mrs Swan's sister — asked him to plan a summer residence in 1932. Mrs Robb, who had long had a taste for French antiques — her good friend William Coverdale, president of Canada Steamship Lines, collected them for the new Manoir Richelieu — adopted the style of a Norman country house. Les Falaises was a small-scale replica of a Renaissance château. The historical style was dictated by the choice of furniture, which had been made prior to construction, and also by the pre-eminently French heritage of Charlevoix, which appealed so strongly to the imagination of American residents. As Les Falaises indicates, the influence of the École des Beaux-Arts was beginning to exert itself: it seemed natural to an architect trained exclusively at the Columbia School of Architecture to make use of French models.

It was the same story with Frederic Rhinelander King, who tackled the problem of designing a residence in French provincial style on foundations that had survived a fire in 1956. King spent his childhood in Newport

247 *Louis-Auguste Amos (1869–1948)*
In 1925, a few years after the death of Arthur Cox, Amos went into partnership with his son Pierre-Charles, who had just completed his studies at the School of Architecture at McGill University. The firm of Amos and Amos existed in Montréal until 1976.

before attending Harvard, from which he received his diploma in 1908. Dissatisfied with his brief training, he left for Paris, the international rendezvous of the cultural élite. Enriched by his studies at the Beaux-Arts, he returned to America and joined the firm of McKim, Mead and White in New York. During the First World War he returned to France with the American army. When it was over, he founded his own firm in New York with Marion Wyeth. Though not an acknowledged specialist, he built many residences as well as some churches and public buildings. His classical training showed in all his work, which maintained the formalist tradition, and probably made it hard for him to turn to what he considered inferior modern and commercial architecture. On the other hand, he excelled in

248 *Verte Feuille*
It's sometimes gay at La Malbaie,
And Pointe-au-Pic, they say, is chic,
But for a really striking sight,
Verte Feuille wins without a fight!
(a poem by Arthur Amos, taken from the Verte Feuille guestbook, 21 August 1921, collection Mme Thérèse Gouin-Décarie).

Built in 1918 to the plans of Louis-Auguste Amos, this villa bears the name of a farm in Normandy which, as reported in *Le Figaro*, 8 June 1918, heroically resisted occupation by the Germans.

249 *James Hampden Robb (1898–1988)*
The young Robb received his diploma from Harvard in 1921—the year of his marriage to Ruth Winsor Minturn—and then proceeded with three years of study at the Columbia School of Architecture; most of his professors there had been trained at the École des Beaux-Arts in Paris.

250/251 *Les Falaises* Built in 1933, this villa resembles a small Norman château. The French elegance of its lines gives it a unique gracefulness that tones down the symmetry of its proportions. The inner courtyard houses the main entrance, where a turret accommodates an elegant wrought-iron staircase.

the use of the sober lines of French Renaissance architecture, and had the taste to eschew rich interior decoration. King belonged to an age when only architectural grandeur could satisfy the wealthy's desire for elegance.

The Renaissance châteaux of the Loire were imitated to express patrician values, not for historical exactitude or modern comfort. The architects of the Beaux-Arts tradition perpetuated the style of sumptuous French mansions with their sharp, pointed towers. The chateau style also sought to glorify the French manor farm, which had defined the cultural heritage of French-Canadians.

252 *Les Quatre Vents* This is a successful adaptation of the judicious French use of brick and stone together. With its many aristocratic touches and its tower and gables, this villa is inspired by the châteaux of the Loire; in Canada, these have been imitated most frequently in public buildings and the prestigious hotels of railway companies.

253 *Elevation of Les Quatre Vents* The perfect proportions of the main body of this little château with its outstretched wings give it an undeniable charm.

SOUTH ELEVATION

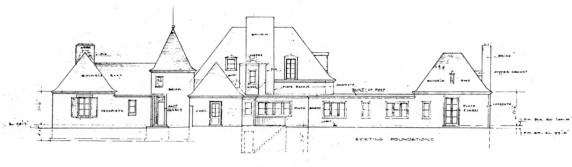

NORTH ELEVATION
SCALE ⅛ = 1'0"

254 *Noblesse oblige* Perched on a plateau, this villa is exposed to the sweep of the winds. Its French features are in the best of taste. The villa is flanked by well-proportioned wings; the rooms are flooded with light and give direct access to the gardens. The precise lines show clearly Frederic R. King's preoccupation with aesthetic rationalism. The construction of Les Quatre Vents in 1957 was supervised by Charles Warren's godson, the Montréal architect Walter Warren. Since the foundation of the Association of Architects of the Province of Québec in 1890, it has been customary, in the construction of a building designed by a foreign architect, to engage the services of one of its members to oversee the work.

257 (caption opposite)

In Canada, such multiple historic references were first successfully tested by the American architect Bruce Price, who planned the Château Frontenac in 1892–3.[21] This hotel in Québec City was the first of a series of French-inspired buildings associated with patrician luxury. It was followed by Montréal architect John Smith Archibald's second Manoir Richelieu.

Despite the dictates of aesthetics, the prevailing consideration in the château style was to derive the maximum picturesque effect from a site. A building that rose naturally from the ground and offered the best possible view — that was the dual aim of architects who opted for this style, and it resulted in houses, from Mur Blanc to Quatre Vents, that cannot be confined to a single category. In addition to their style, they had — like the other villas in Charlevoix — features appropriate to the architecture of summer residence.

255 *A project by Edward J. Mathews (1903–80)* Trained at the Yale Architectural School and the École des Beaux-Arts in Paris, this architect collaborated in many prestigious projects in the city of New York. His avant-garde style made him one of the first American practitioners of the international style. In the layout of this little farm at Cap-à-l'Aigle the architect expressed his daring.

256 *A small model farm at the entrance to Les Quatre Vents* Mathews's interpretation of traditional farm buildings is more of a modernist abstraction. Here, stylistic dichotomy has worked well for the architect, who has chosen a closed-in arrangement to give a wind-break effect.

257 *A certain vision of space* Les Quatre Vents has an exceptional, wide-angle view over the river. The landscaping was the work of Currie M. Cabot's brother, Edward J. Mathews. As early as 1936 this architect superimposed a four-sided pyramid on a cube — though post-modernist architects arrogantly claim this innovation as their own.

258 *The new Manoir Richelieu* John S. Archibald of the firm Archibald and Schofield adopted the château style, which is most often associated in Canada with hotel architecture. The sloping roofs pierced with narrow dormer windows and the tower set in the front façade call to mind Gothic characteristics of the Norman mansion. It is easy to imagine what an influence this sort of building has on the architectural taste of summer residents.

259 *Donald Mackenzie Waters (1894–1968)* A fervent propagandist for Canadian architecture, Waters, centre, was one of the members of the Diet Kitchen Group, which shared with the Group of Seven the desire to ameliorate the situation of the Canadian arts by encouraging the choice of an authentically national content.

CONTEMPORARY ARCHITECTS

In Canadian architecture, the modern movement began at the end of the 1920s, when in Europe use of historic styles, seen as a backward, was already out of date. A new attitude came into being as soon as formal borrowing was discarded. A generation of young architects, rebelling against docile reference to the past, began the search for a genuinely Canadian form of expression. Without claiming to create a style, they tried to devise a form of architecture capable of meeting the demands of the twentieth century. Acceptance of new forms first came with recognition of the intrinsic value of materials and structures, intensified by a sudden national awareness; since architecture was a part of Canadian life, it must henceforth incorporate Canadian characteristics.

It was during this time of change that seven architects and artists, who regularly dined together in The Diet Kitchen, a restaurant on Bloor Street in Toronto, decided in 1927 to form a group devoted to the spread of Canadian architecture and arts. They planned exhibitions and conferences to encourage the development of a distinct Canadian style. Mackenzie Waters was one of the seven. In his buildings he tried to combine modernism and nationalism, drawing inspiration from Canadian sources. Born at Belleville in Ontario on 1 October 1894, he took his degree in applied sciences at the University of Toronto in 1920. His career was interrupted by both world wars, in which he served as a senior non-commissioned officer in the Canadian artillery. He retired from his profession as architect in 1960.

In the summer of 1932 Hume Blake, the owner of Pink Cottage, which had just been destroyed by fire, decided to choose a new site; he found a suitable one on the other side of the Boulevard des Falaises, a high plateau with an exceptionally fine view of the river. Looking for a Canadian architect who could design a villa to satisfy his tastes, the distinguished Torontonian engaged Mackenzie Waters in 1935. Waters's design turned out to be a masterpiece that plunged into the heart of the twentieth century while maintaining respect for the attainments of the past.

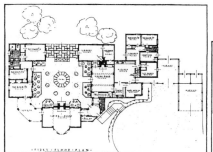

260 *High Acres* This building by Mackenzie Waters is a good example of architecture that unites two schools of thought, one modern, the other traditional. Restrained in aspect, the house is flooded with light; its lines are drawn by logic on shapes imposed by tradition.

261 *A unique plan for a summer residence* This groundplan by Mackenzie Waters was inspired by Mediterranean villas where an inner courtyard ensures the maximum amount of sunshine. The architectural elements, framed in wood for emphasis, add a modern look to the traditional character of the building.

262 *An interior courtyard* The court-yard at High Acres is not only a distinctive, stylish touch; it also solves the problem of natural lighting. The result is a pleasant, open-air place in which to relax.

In 1940, the neophyte Robert W. Humphrey took on a sizeable challenge; his father, a New York financier, commissioned the plans of Sunnybrae Farm from him. That same year, the young architect began studying for his master's at Princeton University; two years later he received the degree after designing an art gallery for Lord Rothermere. Meanwhile, he gave his best effort to building the grand mansion for his family. He

263 *An interior kept deliberately sparse* The furniture was designed by the architect himself to preserve the integral character of the house. Mackenzie Waters uses materials that recall tradition to marry the rationalism of his day and the richness of the past.

blended several characteristics of Canadian architecture more or less happily, but his knowledge of traditional architecture was poor and his borrowings of style, made without an assimilation of the spirit of past achievements, were prompted mainly by his imagination. Nevertheless, his work helped initiate him in country-style architecture and perhaps gave him a taste for Canada, for he moved to Montréal in 1946 and joined the firm of Fetherstonhaugh, Dunford, Bolton and Chadwick. His enhanced knowledge of regional architecture stood him in good stead when he undertook his first professional contract at La Malbaie, a commission from Mr and Mrs F.P. Ryan of New York.

The sources of his model were immediately apparent in what had been *le rang du Nordet* (Northeast Row) at La Malbaie. Humphrey was wise to base his plans on existing homes. Perhaps to express the nobility of Québec mansions, he made reference to the mansion of Alfred Bouliane; a photograph of the place had appeared in Pierre-Georges Roy's *Vieux manoirs, vieilles maisons*,[22] but the architect might have made a personal study of the mansion's four-sided mansard roofs. In any case, he succeeded in giving historic reality to his building through the manipulation of dimension and proportion.

Such faithfulness to the past did not mean Humphrey was averse to modern ideas. The Bourne's house, standing next to the Ryan's (Défense de Passer), was proof of that. Built in 1950 to plans drawn by Humphrey, the residence was balanced and restrained, recalling the elegance of former days without denying the new aesthetics. This became his trademark, and it was what he was relying on when he quit the firm in 1951 to work independently. Until his death in 1972, Humphrey came back to Pointe-au-Pic every summer, as though he were happy to be discharging a debt of gratitude to Charlevoix.

At the end of the summer of 1950, Sir Charles Fitzpatrick's granddaughter, Madame Pierre Sévigny, née Corinne Kernan, and her husband commissioned a young Montréal architect named Guy St-Aubin Mongenais to draw up plans for a new house to be built on family land. Mongenais had been trained at Montréal's École des Beaux-Arts and was sensitive to the charms of Québec mansions, which had been extolled in the classic *Old Architecture of Quebec*;[23] he recovered materials from a hundred-year-old house that had to be destroyed because its framework was decaying. The new house included a ground floor that could be lived in all year round. When the house was in use, the temperature could be kept at a comfortable minimum; and the hall, kitchen, master bedroom, and big living-room could be quickly warmed up, thanks to the fireplaces fitted with central-heating ventilators.

The exterior interpreted the lines of Québec architecture freely. A vertical elevation gave it the look of a suburban building, while the interior layout gave it the freedom of movement appropriate to a summer residence. The living-room took up more than half the floor space of the house because

264 *Robert Walker Humphrey (1916–72)* After obtaining his diploma at Princeton in 1942, Humphrey made his debut with Fetherstonhaugh, Dunford, Bolton and Chadwick of Montréal. After 1951 he had his own firm. Later he went into partnership with Patrick Séguin, an architect originally from Rigaud.

265 *Sunnybrae Farm* Built in the summer of 1940, this villa shows little orthodoxy in its eclectic borrowing of features from traditional architecture. Humphrey scorned the old rules of proportion but gave his building a spaciousness of volume that radiated freedom. The name of the house was later changed to Ciel sur Mer, which suits it perfectly.

266 *Ciel sur Mer* The architect used up a good part of the villa's extraordinary site by building a terrace that dominates the river at ground-floor level.

267 *An exotic interior* In keeping with
the taste of the day, Humphrey
designed the dining-room Chippen-
dale furniture and added touches
inspired by the Orient.

268 *A fine example of traditional architecture* The Habitation Alfred Bouliane had a mansard roof, its four sides prolonged by short, curved gutter overhangs. Although French in origin, this type of well-proportioned roofing, in fashion during the second half of the nineteenth century, seems to have been popular in the United States before being adopted by the Canadians.

269 *Elevation of Défense de Passer* In the four-sided mansard roof of the Ryans' house, the architect added symmetry that was lacking in the Boulianes'. The regular spacing of the dormer windows on the upper floor fitted in well with the French windows on the ground floor.

270 *Défense de Passer* This house, built in 1947, shows Humphrey's easy mastery of the mansard style. The roof, delicately pierced by gabled dormer windows, sits on the house like a hat.

there was no wall between it and the dining-room. It was thirty-five feet by fifteen, and had wide windows that opened onto the gardens and distant river. With this marriage of essentially traditional exterior and modern interior, Mongenais showed flexibility and adaptability; he integrated his form into the surrounding landscape and succeeded at the same time in fulfilling the requirements of a summer residence that could also be used throughout the year. Mongenais, seen by his contemporaries as a master of his art, was at one time professor of architecture at the University of Montréal; today he works with the O'Keefe and Associates Society of Architects.

271 *The nicely curved profile of the Fraser Manor* This house, so full of history, must surely exert an influence on those within. The mansard roof replaced the early roof in the 1900s. It is an elegant and practical way of converting an attic into liveable space and gives a reassuring feeling of protection to the inhabitants.

272 *The predominant roof* Built on a rectangular plan, the Bournes' house has a mansard roof, which permits better use to be made of the upper floor. Dormer windows give enough light to make it comfortable.

As for the younger generation of architects, there is often a tendency to minimize the influence traditional architecture has had on their formal vocabulary. Philip Mackenzie, however, openly acknowledges that the barns of Charlevoix, with their purity of line expressing necessity so directly, have left their mark on him. The young Mackenzie, grandson of William Hume Blake, used to spend his vacations roaming the woods of the huge Laurentides Park with the Fortins of St-Urbain. The young man has never forgotten the countryside; in 1960, when his aunt by marriage, the artist Sybil Kennedy, asked him to design a studio with an interplay of space and light, and this within a strictly limited budget, he drew on his memory to find the precepts of the "architecture of necessity."

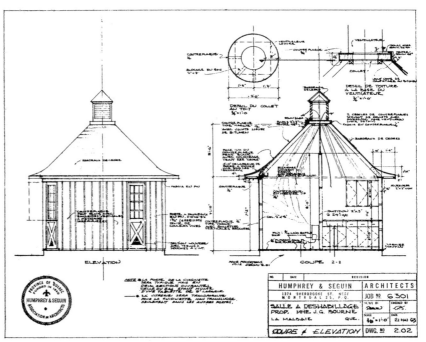

273/274 *Rotunda designed by Humphrey and Séguin* This firm, located on Sherbrooke Street in Montréal, knew the ups and downs of the architectural profession. It made a point of handling every aspect of design with complete virtuosity.

Having first attended Montréal's École des Beaux-Arts, where he was the only anglophone, he went to the University of Michigan in 1952 to complete his training. On his return, he practised in Montréal for some fifteen years before retiring from a profession he no longer found satisfying.

At one point, Mackenzie designed some prefabricated houses originally intended for the Tower Company of Montréal; in 1960, he got hold of material for one of the houses and had it shipped in trucks to Sybil Kennedy's property in Murray Bay. There, plywood panels were unloaded—for the walls, roofing, and floor—together with joists, doors, and windows. The infrastructure had already been completed; foundations had been laid down and the plumbing installed. Ten days later, the artist moved into her studio; the décor was neutral, so no particular style was forced on her. Nearly twenty-five years later, nothing has been changed

275 *Recycled materials* All the doors and windows, which originally belonged to a house more than a hundred years old, were skilfully salvaged by the architect. By including them, Guy Mongenais produced his own version of the traditional house.

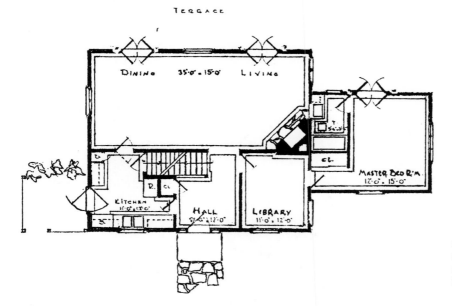

276 *A plan by Guy Mongenais* The combination dining-room/living-room was the centre of this household's activity.

except for a coat of paint to brighten the exterior. Still in perfect condition, Kennedy's house has been a complete success, much better built than a traditional home and at a cost nearly thirty per cent less.

It was built with plywood panels of standardized dimensions, eight feet by four. The ground plan is forty-eight feet by twenty-four, giving a balanced rectangle twelve panels long by six panels wide. To provide light

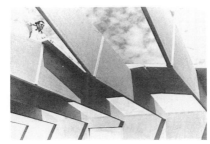

277/278/279 *An industrial building*
This prefabricated construction has
its origin in the functionalist concept
of "machines to live in," which
dates back to the 1930s. The absence
of ornamentation allows the recov-
ery of utilitarian shapes.

280 *Architect's sketch* The plan of the
interior is reduced to its simplest
functional form. The organization of
space indicates that the architect has
made maximum use of the area at his
disposal.

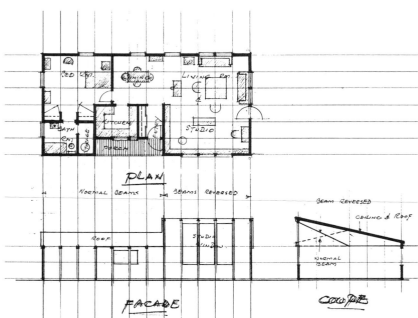

281 *A bungalow on the cliff* This little
bungalow, made in sections and
semi-portable, offers a flexibility
much sought after these days, the
direct result of industry's making
strictly functional use of materials
and refusing to treat them as conven-
tional symbols.

in the artist's studio, roof trusses are reversed, making the front wall higher. The framework of the ceiling is visible, and the lack of partitions in the studio proper gives the impression of a big open space. As for decoration, the departure from traditional romanticism is a good argument for leaving everything bare here. The colouring is muted, a light grey, and the door and window frames are painted pale yellow; this is balanced by the somewhat severe tone of the furniture and its careful positioning. In the middle of it all is a Franklin stove, the only source of heat apart from the glass panels of the front wall, which let in the sun's warm rays. What style can this be called? As the architect himself puts it in a letter, "Architects like to label buildings with a style ... [P]ure construction like this omits conscious style. Would they ... call it 'Non-Architecture'? Whatever the answer it seems likely that structures built from necessity only cannot go out of fashion. Is it claiming too much to associate the spirit of this prospect with that of the old barns of Charlevoix?"[24]

That should convince sceptics about the authenticity of the approach professional architects take today. Contemporary architecture, which technological discoveries rendered partly possible, claimed its own forms only after the exhaustion of historical imitations. The product of science and industry, it obeys the logic of the present-day spirit, which recoils from

282 *A constant search for the essential* New materials call for strictly geometrical treatment. The tendency is toward purity of line and simplicity.

déjà vu. Contemporary architects have laboriously blazed the trail for those who seek to forget styles and stick to the essentials, for those who hope to respond in the best way to the demands of our time.

All the architects who have worked in Charlevoix, from the very first to those of today, have tried to forge a new way of life through their creations. Because of the seasonal character of the region, they have often had to experiment with adaptable structures, which above all express a close relationship with nature's ever-present panorama. Each in their fashion, the architects that have worked in Charlevoix have followed the spirit of the landscape painters of the nineteenth century, who overcome with the beauty of the country sought feverishly to express the emotions, the admiration, and perhaps the meditative state that it inspired.

Summer Resort Architecture²⁵

RESISTANCE TO THE URBAN LANDSCAPE inspired the romantic movement and its stress on the countryside; and the first architectural forms to come out of it were mainly rustic. At the start of the nineteenth century, people went to Charlevoix principally to hunt and fish. Accommodation reflected the countryside itself; it was natural, unfettered by historic precedent, and above all bore the mark of local character. Local housing—as painted by Cornelius Kreighoff or idealized by Philippe Aubert de Gaspé—appeared more pure to sportsmen because it had not been sullied by technology. The idea of summer residence became associated with the typical Québec house, an austere cottage with a steeply sloping roof prolonged by projecting eaves and pierced by symmetrically placed dormer windows. The sportsmen's wooden dwellings, whose humble simplicity was their sole attraction, were the first manifestations of the growing taste for the picturesque.

MODEST BEGINNINGS

The first summer homes, like the traditional homes of the habitants, were built of timber—tree-trunks squared off by the axe and placed in layers. The building, capped with a two-sided roof covered with cedar shingles, was constructed exclusively of local materials. The house was usually built to a rectangular plan with gables at either end. Construction methods were traditional, passed down from family to family since the early days of New France. It was essentially indigenous architecture, though certain traits betrayed the owners' urban origins.

Eighteenth-century homes that are still standing were made of fieldstone, while later cottages were built of wood. These examples of domestic architecture found favour with the first summer residents perhaps because they represented the only type of construction possible in the region, given its isolated location. The typical summer resident's house was thus a single-storey, usually facing the river, with its exposed framework resting on a raised foundation to keep it clear of the ground. The central door opened

283 *An austere house* Built to a traditional plan, this rudimentary home has the picturesque atmosphere sought after by summer residents. The absence of a chimney gives the impression that it is exclusively for summer use.

onto one large room. Often two bedrooms were fitted into the ground floor, behind partitions of planks set vertically. Under the sloping roof, a spacious attic could be divided into little bedrooms lit by a few dormer windows.

Later, perhaps to preserve the tradition of vacations spent in a habitant's house, some summer residents got hold of an old house and fixed it up to suit their requirements. The Joseph Collard house, reckoned to be one of the oldest in Cap-à-l'Aigle, was rented out to the Reverend Fothergill starting in 1860. Both the exterior and the interior bespoke its age. Curiously, the simplicity of its shapes and spaces gave it a modern look, and from a practical point of view it was almost ideal. A short distance away, the ancestral home of the Savards was also used by summer residents. They

284 *Glen Cottage at Murray Bay, around 1860* New elements have been added to traditional architecture, for example, the extension to the gutter overhang, which serves as a roof over the veranda. Further examples are the geometric trellis-work of the balcony and the windows with their small panes and shutters. Here we see a diversity of influences; the symmetry of the whole points equally to the classic revival in vogue at the time and to the logical thinking of peasants.

made only a few modifications to add space. Sitting in the simple country landscape, the once humble dwelling took on the look of a small mansion.

The Bonner-Cabot family bought the Mount Murray seigneury at the beginning of the twentieth century. In 1933, on part of this land, Maud Cabot and her husband Patrick Morgan rebuilt stone by stone a house they had brought from Les Éboulements by schooner. The rebuilding was not done in slavish fashion; young Morgan, who had studied architecture at Harvard and Columbia, was at pains to make Chouette functional while retaining its former look. The chimneys at either end and the dormer windows show that this is the work of a master mason.

It was a different story with Clos des Lupins, on the ancestral land of the Villeneuves in Terrebonne at Pointe-au-Pic. In March 1893, François Villeneuve sold his farm to the widow Chamard and her son William. This simple wooden house, covered by a roof with wide overhanging eaves, had been used by the farmer as a dwelling place. After renovating the old part, the Chamards added a perpendicular wing and covered the whole place

285/286 *From rustic house to ornate cottage* Locally inspired seasonal architecture is an idealization of traditional architecture, which in its earliest form tended towards the cubical and closed-in. Later, the humble dwelling acquired decorative elements borrowed from the neo-Renaissance style in fashion in Canada from 1850 to 1875.

287 *The Aviary* The Collard house, built in the 1840s, served as a convalescent home for Canadian airmen during the First World War. For a short while it was known as The Aviary.

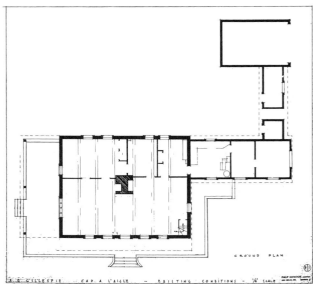

288 *Front and side elevations* The regularity of the lines, the balance of the St. Andrew's cross motif in the balcony, and the gentle slope of the roof combine to give this house a rustic character.

289 *Ground plan* Here interior space is divided up as in a traditional house. The entrance opens directly onto a big room that runs right across the width of the house and leads to other rooms. There is a staircase in one corner.

290 *The Collard house* The gentle slope of the roof extends into projecting eaves. The balcony runs the width of the house. The window-frames show the influence of the Regency style.

with rose-coloured bricks from Baie-St-Paul. The house then passed into the hands of a farmer, who kept it for twenty-four years and in 1931 sold it, in dilapidated condition, to the Thébauds of Washington. The new owners did not move in until 1940, after doing major restoration work. The hipped roof with its dormer windows was transformed into a truncated gable-end, and the whole place was roofed with metal sheets in the French Canadian manner. Madame Thébaud and her gardener, Alfred Villeneuve, took considerable care with the flower-beds, which were a symphony of different shades of blue.

This passion for the houses of Québec prompted some summer residents to engage an architect to reproduce authentic regional models. One traditional house in La Malbaie had particularly elegant lines; it was the source of inspiration for several modern houses, the first built by Charles Warren in 1917. Warren's structure is a graceful blend of the practical and the aesthetic.

291 *Romantic traditionalism* This property was sold in 1922 by Georges Savard of Cap-à-l'Aigle to Alfred E. Francis of Montréal. The new owner respected the original character of the farmer's house and limited himself to turning the fields that surrounded it into a huge English-style garden with a pond, some shady corners, and a green carpet of lawn.

292 (caption following page)

292/293/294 *Chouette* This abandoned house, originally near Les
Eboulements, was restored in 1933 by
the Morgans, who contributed so
much to raising the standard of popular arts in Charlevoix. American by
birth, they strove to recreate the traditional home of the local habitant as
part of their programme of "total
immersion" in the culture of the
region. With unshakeable faith in the
creative potential of the self-taught
artist, they encouraged all forms of
art—for example, by incorporating
a piece of sculpture by Roland Bouchard into the façade of their villa.

295 *Terrebonne* This is Clos des Lupins as it was in the 1930s, while restoration was going on. Its summer-resident owners named it after the rural road on which it stood.

296 *Clos des Lupins* This old farmhouse, built in 1847, carries its years well. The soft, porous local bricks and the gabled turret give it an uncommon distinction.

297 *Murray Village* This village scene in La Malbaie, taken by Notman, the well-known photographer from Montréal, conjures up the picturesque atmosphere so beloved at the turn of the century.

298 *Les Cerceaux* Although the architect can be charged with imitation here, Charles Warren's originality is quite clear. He shows perfect mastery not of style, but of the spirit of the traditional house—notwithstanding the French windows along the front, which betray this house's summer role.

When William Notman photographed his son sitting in a cart in a village street early in the century, he probably had no idea that he was about to immortalize the beautiful house to the side; it had a curved gutter overhang, the sweeping lines of which would be many times imitated in the future. The unpretentious, restrained feature is always compatible with architectural evolution; it can meet the needs of any period that calls for it. Rustic simplicity is ageless; in Charlevoix it has inspired many generations of summer residents to build modest homes in the style of their farmer neighbours. They love the rustic for its picturesqueness — but they choose sites for the view.

299 *La Folie Rose* The flared roof covers a terrace with a view that sweeps down to the river. A point of interest here is the curved underside of the eaves, more often found in south-shore architecture. The arrival of several families from the other side of the river explains the introduction of regional characteristics originally foreign to Charlevoix.

300 *Duncairn* Said to be the oldest
summer residence in Pointe-au-Pic,
this villa bears the stamp of its times.
The elegance of the scroll-work in
the balcony is typical of the 1870s.
This was the period when the complex and asymmetric plan first made
its appearance, contrasting with the
simplicity of the traditional house.
Duncairn, a Scottish name meaning
rocky slope, went by the name
La Rose au Bois before being
destroyed in 1989.

THE INFLUENCE OF SUBURBAN ARCHITECTURE

In reaction against the neo-classical, with its affectation and symmetry of
proportions imposing a certain rigidity on the country homes, the nineteenth century was swept by a passionate taste for the picturesque. England
slowly cast off styles that had become too rigid and adopted the mainly
rustic style known as domestic survival. In North America, the architectural
style that emerged was called the picturesque; it reclaimed the English
cottage and adapted it to suit the continent.

In Charlevoix, the traditional house met the needs of a simpler era. How
exactly could this architecture meet the expectations of summer residents
trying to find a new rapport with nature? In the search for its identity,
the summer cottage progressively acquired the features appropriate to
changing needs. The new architecture represented a plethora of styles.
Called the eclectic, it wedded the classical repertory with the more individu-
alized tastes of Victorian style.

One of its many considerations was that given to the natural landscape.
The well-known American horticulturist Andrew Jackson Downing was a
spirited defender of the principle that a building and its site must form
a harmonious whole. In many publications, beginning with *Landscape
Gardening* in 1841, Downing stressed that architectural style should depend
on location.[26] This idea gave birth to a suburban type of architecture that
slowly became the choice of the majority. Realizing that rusticity and the
countryside were inseparable, city dwellers anxious to get back to nature
chose, as a compromise, to establish themselves in suburbs. Detached
houses with their own gardens were affordable and so proliferated, the
majority of them modeled first on English houses, then on those of the
United States. It was thus the outlying districts of towns that benefited

from the generally improved architecture of the second houses of the rich.

In Québec the construction of villas—the rural version of town residences, often with Palladian lines—increased significantly after 1840.[27] In succeeding decades, the suburbs of Québec City became covered with cottages,[28] some quite modest, which drew their inspiration from English models.[29] This architecture, seasonal at first, grew more suitable to year-round residence as time went by.

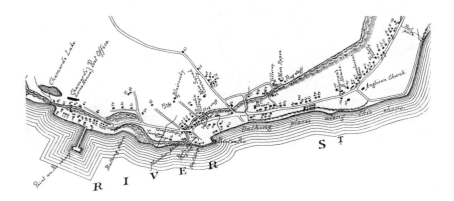

301 *The suburban phenomenon in the country* The development of Pointe-au-Pic at the end of the last century in certain respects echoed the fanning-out of suburbs.

302 *Blairvocky* After a period of classical austerity in architecture, there was a tendency to add ornamental details to the exterior framework. The chiseled decor of Blairvocky (a Gaelic name meaning bushy place), creates a theatrical effect.

303 *Regency style* This villa was a
meeting between the neo-classical
and the picturesque. The style was
fashionable from 1810 to 1840; it
often made use of a central belvedere
and a veranda running across the
façade.

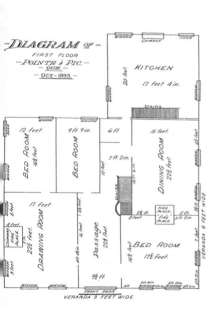

304 *A logical arrangement of interior
space* The arrangement of interior
space gives each room a precise
function.

The new structures clung to the slopes of the cliff at Pointe-au-Pic. One
inspirational model, Blairvocky, while it appeared somewhat traditional,
also expressed a taste for neo-classical order. Its four-paneled roof, with a
tall chimney at either end and the covered gallery running around it,
differentiated this villa from earlier ones; with its shape and size, it abandoned rustic values and prepared the way for an architecture better adapted
to summer residence.

The main body of the house was almost square, permitting a geometrical
division of the interior. The advantage of the neo-classical quadrangular
volume was that it allowed the best use to be made of interior space in a
relatively simple structure. The layout discarded the traditional central
chimney for a wide passage that gave access to each room. The kitchen
retreated, now forming an annex at the back of the main body of the
building. This reflected new preoccupations with hygiene and also the idea
that each room should have its own function. On the second floor five
bedrooms lay astride the central passage, with two other bedrooms for the
staff above the kitchen annex. The third floor served as an open storage
space. A staircase was built in the centre of the house. The house was
roomy enough to accommodate a big family; there was a welcoming air
about it, an air of serenity and dignity that came as much from its lines as
from the décor. This cottage, inspired by English architecture and built by
the Buchanans, showed surprisingly modern taste for a structure built in
1893.

A wooden château on the approaches to the cliff was a radical contrast
to the classical lines of Blairvocky. Indeed, the asymmetrical plan of Villa

305 *A Flemish villa* The absence of ornamentation accentuates the façade, which recalls the starkness and purity of classical lines. This house, the present owner of which is Belgian, is called "T'Vlaams Hof," The Flemish House.

306 *A more functional layout* The plan shows the main body of the house, where the entrance hall has been enlarged so that it forms a room by itself, a modern architectural feature.

307 *A small entrance hall* The hall has become a room with many functions; it enlarges the living-room and gives access to the other areas of the ground floor, while remaining the place for welcoming visitors.

Mon Repos, its silhouette crowned with gables and turrets, gave it the look of a fortress; with its crenellated tower and verticality, this building seemed to flaunt its individuality. Despite the eccentricity, the façade showed what an important part the overall view played. The walls were riddled with windows. Such features were decorative, not functional; they simply dramatized the spectacle the "châtelaine," Madame F.E. Roy, probably wanted in order to impress her distinguished guests — among them the Russian prince Grigor Galitzin, Sir Adolphe Chapleau, and man of letters Ernest Gagnon, whom she received one evening in July 1894.

The jurist Joseph Isaac Lavery of Québec, installed with his family within the bounds of Pointe-au-Pic, would almost certainly also have been visited by the Russian prince. For his home Lavery chose a typical suburban house, standing tall on the bank of the river. The style of Villa Bellevue is difficult to describe. It inspired respect by its height, which had something of the Victorian in it. The brick chimneys recalled English masonry. The sweep of the roof and the siding of cedar shingles looked oddly neo-colonial. The composition as a whole appeared to have influenced other local cottages, which retained the charm of suburban housing.

During the final decades of the nineteenth century, American suburbs were covered with cottages of all sorts: Swiss, Gothic, English, Italian, Norman, or Elizabethan. This variety of styles was first encouraged by Downing, Wheeler, and Gardner, whose writings started the notion that every decent citizen should own a personalized house.[30] Claiming that diversity is indispensable to life, they flooded the market with a multitude of plans for new forms of housing, the influence of which can still be felt today. In big-city suburbs, domestic architecture seemed at least to come into its own. Next came enterprising architects like Calvert Vaux and Samuel Sloan, who published books and models called pattern books, which had the effect of endlessly multiplying stylistic possibilities. Public response was so favourable that a mail-order campaign was aimed at the growing middle classes.[31] In this atmosphere of freedom, known as the age of innocence, the architecture of the countryside seemed like a tissue of inconsistency and incoherence. Reacting against the hotchpotch of styles, a wave of young university-trained architects returned to the past to study the models of the colonial period. From the outset, this move was badly

308 *A visitor from Moscow at Villa mon Repos* Of the Russian prince Galitzin's visit to Pointe-au-Pic it was nostalgically recorded: "Villa Mon Repos was ablaze with light when we called an hour later to visit the lady of the house. The Prince immediately showed his interest in the charming souvenirs from her travels spread about all over the drawing-room. Madame R., who had visited several European countries, and even some of the interesting parts of Africa, immediately hastened to open her albums and unlock her caskets, and answered the Prince's questions as he examined all these beautiful objects" (Ernest Gagnon, *Feuilles volantes et pages d'histoire*, [Québec 1910], 27).

309 *A wooden château* The silhouette, often only frontal, is used to create a gripping effect. This graceful French-inspired house was called Villa mon Repos.

received by the American public, who inevitably found the style foreign. No one dared imagine an American style — though such a thing had existed in the past.

310 *Villa Bellevue* The surprising thing about this building, which goes back to 1888, is the choice of vertical panels so close to the river. The abrupt rises, suburban in character, contrast with the vast horizon that faces the house. Villa Bellevue is an inn today, La Petite Marmite.

311 *Worthy of a smart neighbourhood* This villa, the home of the notary Fournier in the TV series *Le temps d'une paix*, meets all the standards of a smart suburban house. Its stone facing and high hipped roof inevitably give it a haughty look.

Erza McCagg did not remain indifferent to patriotic sentiments. This lawyer worked for Chicago's historical society and was aware of the steps being taken by young architects who sought inspiration from the old buildings of New England. Their efforts resulted in a more sober style, a purification of line and a feel for proportions. New ways appeared of approaching interior space and using building materials. Henceforth, stonework and shingles kept their natural look. Porches were covered by an enveloping roof, which resembled the gambrel or mansard roof of

312 *The Spinney* The mansard roof with two slopes and the porch with coping were widespread during the "archeological" renaissance. The economy of line recalls colonial buildings constructed before the American Revolution. The exterior, with its fairly simple geometric figures, displays a stripped-down texture with surfaces of white shingle. A spinney is a small wood or copse.

colonial architecture. The return to simplified forms reflected a taste for intimacy and increased comfort; in other words, planning emphasized the interior over the exterior. The front door opened onto a hall, where the central staircase formed the pivot around which internal traffic circulated. To meet the demands for space, room size showed little increase. Rooms, when moderation called for a more simple life-style, had to be considered in terms of the whole.

313 *Comfort by the fire* Carefully arranged interiors combined a variety of relaxing, decorative styles.

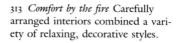

314 *Jardin Joyeux* In Dutch colonial houses, the ground floor was where one lived; crops were stored on the floor above. This explains the size of the roof. Here, the balcony is completely covered by the upper floor.

This new trend reduced the work of the architect to a sort of formal homogeneity based on elementary masses and a functional layout. Along the Hudson River in New York, models were found in the traditional houses of colonists from Holland. The Schenck family, of Dutch descent, could choose no better model for their summer cottage at Pointe-au-Pic. The lines of the house were conducive to comfort and simplicity. It was longer than it was wide, covered with a massive roof. The entrance was inviting; and inside, the low ceilings gave an impression of cosiness. The vivid and contrasting colours used for the outside marked a departure from the discreet grays and whites of the old houses of New England.

315 *An inviting entrance* These side benches are typical of Dutch farmhouses in New York and New Jersey.

316 *A later model* The lines of the Dutch farmhouse are slowly losing their original character and conforming to the taste of the day.

317 *Torwood* Built during the winter of 1903–4, this unpretentious house uses the two-sided roof in a functional way. The curved eaves and the overhang of the upper floor cover the balcony that runs around the house. The elimination of decorative features gives an air of restraint to the exterior, which however retains a certain distinction, thanks to its autumn colours.

This renaissance of indigenous styles rekindled an interest in Québec architecture. Apart from the increased property values that resulted, new types of housing came into being. The juxtaposition of diverse architectural elements created unusual lines; this was not in any way a backward-looking architecture. Though the façades might have appeared antiquated, behind them, modern functionalistic principles were brought into play. Henceforth, houses were built to look at the view — no longer merely to be looked at. The expert architect refused to copy styles that were considered historic, and had to show originality if he was to answer the demands of summer residents. Restraint was still called for in décor, but the modification of internal space improved circulation. Verticality, with its sometimes freakish effect, gave way to simpler, single-volume masses.

318 *Ground plan* The narrow hall on the ground floor helps circulation, while central chimneys give the house a feeling of life.

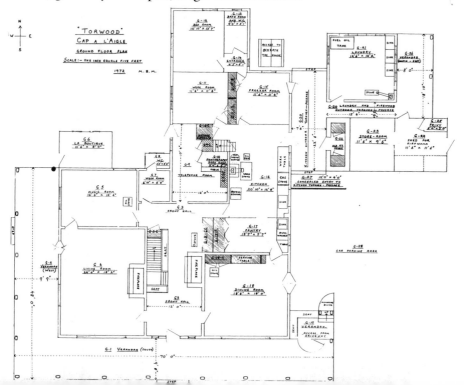

319 *The imposing profile of Porte-Bonheur* This house has been treated in grandiose fashion—monumental proportions given to traditional architecture.

320 *Le Cran* This building throws together elements of the Regency and classical revival styles, a veranda trellis with geometric motifs and traces of a gable-ended façade. The first-floor balconies are reminiscent of the French houses of Louisiana. Yet beyond its lines, its main entrance, placed at the side, proclaims the horizontality of the building, which would soon become a favourite feature of contemporary cottage architecture. "Cran" is a French Canadian word signifying cliff, or bare rock rising from the ground.

Despite sporadic attempts at innovation, summer architecture at Charlevoix retained its romantic feel; as always, the underlying idea was to make the house as natural as the landscape itself. Styles were diverse but picturesque; some houses flaunted a classic profile, while others displayed an affected silhouette. With the latter, the main objective was to achieve a theatrical effect. Most homes with "refined" lines were concentrated around Pointe-au-Pic, as suburban houses were grouped around a city.

A somewhat more restrained period followed, which saw the reintroduction of archaic characteristics such as interiors of natural wood and large stone chimneys. Influential in this development was the revival of interest in the colonial period, with its simpler lines.

The progression was from centralization to the opening up of space, without imitating or trying to give the effect of the picturesque. It took place around the turn of the century when architects started using latticed frameworks. This lighter method of construction allowed them to position walls more freely, thus giving more flexibility to the arrangement of internal spaces. Thus technological possibilities transformed interiors—a good example of how new forms are produced by successful responses to new demands.

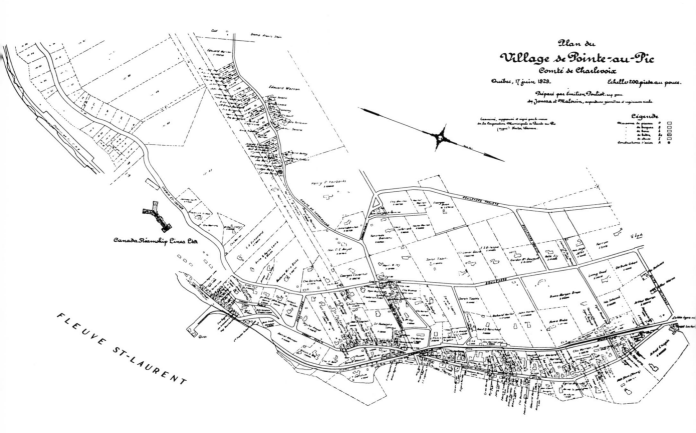

321 *Suburban planning* It is somewhat surprising to find that in 1929 the village of Pointe-au-Pic was divided into allotments like some well-to-do suburb in America. From an architectural point of view, such a variety of buildings represents an inestimable heritage for Charlevoix.

322 *Northern Lights* This villa, set high up, expresses the landscape of Charlevoix, namely, the large mountains and reassuring calm of the river. It is modern by virtue of the attention given to the living standards of its occupants. This is in no way mere surface architecture, for the whole composition is essentially directed at making the place comfortable.

BEYOND STYLES

The age of imitation finally passed; the time had come for integration of the house and the landscape. Against a background of rustic and picturesque architecture, a new style was born. The concept of the box, of such-and-such a cubic volume, gave way to the idea of space as freedom. Surfaces were stretched to form unusual geometric shapes, and interaction between interior and exterior zones became dynamic. This was a rational, open-minded approach which dependence on historic styles had never been able to achieve and which increased the stature of summer-cottage architecture. It now turned toward the exploration of space. Here, a home would spread out horizontally to take full advantage of its site; there, its spaces would crowd together in an asymmetric and seemingly disordered plan; yet again, it would exhibit a more homogeneous shape. The movement called for

323 *Bringing the outside in* The terrace, built into the façade, is an integral part of the design. Glass panels seek to do away with the barrier between indoors and out.

324 *Rochegrise* To make the most of its site, this house runs horizontally, with the service wing set at a different angle. It contains seventeen big rooms, including seven bedrooms with five bathrooms, and ten stone fireplaces.

architects to build peripherally, on the crests of the cliff, or in a wooded area, wherever nature demanded. There was a time when summer-cottage architecture made use of the most primitive of finery; only recently has it discarded this practice, in almost brutal fashion, and returned to its prime task—to offer communion with nature.

By her choice of a colonial house, Mabel Thorp Boardman managed to fit seventeen large rooms into a building that was anti-monumental in spirit. In 1920, she had a villa called Northern Lights built on one of the plateaus of the cliff at Pointe-au-Pic, located at such a height that it dominated the bay. The house was well proportioned. The layout of the rooms along its length made for easy movement indoors. The interaction of volumes and surfaces seemed to have been planned with the site always in mind; the combination of horizontal layout and picture windows gave a wide and continuous view of the outside. A perpendicular wing at one end

325 *Sur La Côte* This building, shaped like an extended H, expresses balance through symmetry. The roof, rounded and sweeping, is an impressive mass set atop the whole.

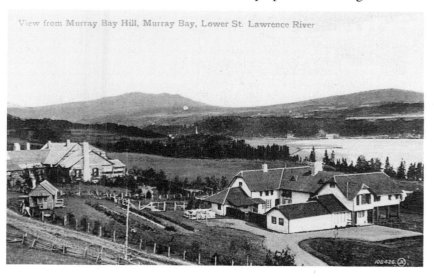

View from Murray Bay Hill, Murray Bay, Lower St. Lawrence River

326 *A shaggy façade* Built from the plans of Oscar B. Smith, jr, in 1921, this sturdy building has a rectangular body flanked by two jutting wings and topped by truncated gables.

of the main body of the house was reserved exclusively for guests; at the other end, a self-contained wing housed the servants.

This expanded U-plan turned out to be perfectly suited to summer residence. The oblong shape provided comfortable spaces; there had been no striving for symmetry in the façade, merely a determination to cover every aspect of good house planning. Mabel T. Boardman, who came from an aristocratic family from the American Midwest, had had the good taste to insist that her house not be noted for anything in particular—only that her guests, of whom there was always a great number, be as happy as possible.

Another great American lady, Elizabeth Hewlett Scudder Thébaud, who became a Binsse after her third marriage, made more or less the same choice for the general plan of her house, Sur La Côte. Its axis followed the same transverse plan with a perpendicular arm at each end. The arrangement of space inside, however, was different; traffic radiated from a single

327 *The Tibbits' house* This somewhat elongated building blends well with its site. Its pleasingly horizontal lines, emphasized by the flat part of the Japanese-style roofs, recall the American architect Frank Lloyd Wright's Oriental lines. On the front face, the loggia fits neatly into the general composition.

328 *Composite materials* The play of the revetment adds discerningly to the value of each level of this building. The volumes adjust automatically to changes in material.

329 *A summer drawing-room* This room epitomizes the prime task of cottage architecture, which is to bring the interior and the exterior together, with loving care.

central fireplace. Modern construction methods using a light framework were skilfully handled by Trefflé Bergeron, one of Charles Warren's competitors. This made it possible to build many narrow windows into the façade, providing the necessary light.

Improved technology permitted much freer planning, which now stressed the horizontal lines in which large glazed surfaces introduced light and improved the view. Even more than before, materials and shapes integrated the villa with its site. A good example was the Tibbits' house, which looked as though it had grown from the ground. The front was perfectly symmetrical and set firmly on its foundations. The dormer windows with their conical cables were a discreet reminder that the house was surrounded by conifers, and the flared slope of the trees harmonized with the obtuse angle of the roof. The overhanging eaves made an elegant cornice around the building, an effect enhanced by the rows of windows with their regularly spaced openings. The tall chimney alone interrupted the horizontal setting—and at the same time ennobled it. This mixture of disciplined order and freedom was based on a plan, still axial in this particular case, that gave the interior space a coherent and continuing space. Open rooms were placed athwart a simple line, prolonged by the solarium and verandas.

In some houses, asymmetrical shapes—if proper use were made of them—added space to surfaces. This was probably what prompted Murray Kennedy to choose a colonial construction in 1904. Perched on a plateau overlooking the course of the Murray Bay Golf Club, Ça Nous Va followed no particular style but rather expressed the function of each of its area masses. The length of the main body faced the landscape squarely, and the roof came sweeping down on both sides, concealing the entrances. The service wing formed a perpendicular attachment at the rear. Decorative elements were picked out in white: Doric columns on either side of the house, and carved ornamentation above the windows in the gabled wall, which added a colonial note. The slope of the all-enveloping roof was accentuated by the truncated gable atop the dormer window; here, the stubby roof of the gable repeated the same angle of descent as the main roof. On the other hand, the arrangement of the interior did not give the impression of movement that was so noticeable in the villas mentioned above; but the hall, with a brick hearth that welcomed each newcomer, and the big living-room, which continued onto a veranda, were inviting. The proportions of the dining-room toned down its importance; this modest note somehow imparted a feeling of modernity to the whole place.

330 *Ça Nous Va* Recourse to the simplicity of traditional lines sometimes produces interesting results. By prolonging its slope, the roof here is made to overhang the veranda. The unified effect of the building depends partly on lack of variation in texture.

Marshaling spaces in haphazard fashion with no regard to proportion — that was more or less the impression given by the houses of the Gibert sisters from New York. Their return to the sources of North American primitivism was part of the back-to-nature movement, but it was honoured more in the spirit than in the letter. Though these houses had all the modern conveniences, their every last detail was rustic. Strips of spruce covering the outside were left in their natural glory, with the rough bark showing. Tiles covering the roof were also untouched; time and the weather would give them their patina. Multiple chimneys, built with local fieldstone and a minimum of dressing, evoked the rough quality of the traditional log-house. Inside, heat was provided by the many fireplaces, which were the main feature in the principal rooms. Mid-sized windows preserved the interior from excessive drops in temperature. The general layout of Canaan and St Antoine cottages was specifically designed to meet the needs of summer residence.

The back-to-nature concept was reflected in the furniture of nearly every villa in Pointe-au-Pic and Cap-à-l'Aigle. As we have seen, Charles Warren left his personal mark on the interior architecture of his houses; and in all of them he devoted particular attention to his choice of furnishings. His clients brought him their models — often American colonial in style — and his cabinet-makers reproduced them carefully. Joseph Bouchard, the foreman of Warren's furniture shop, handled the business at Pointe-au-Pic on his own; two generations followed him, taking original models, updating them, and replacing them with new items as necessary. Over in Cap-à-l'Aigle, Joseph Riverin was doing the same thing; for more than thirty years he looked after the clients around his village, skilfully fulfilling every demand, however unusual.

331 *Canaan Cottage* The use of raw materials without ornamentation, this was the honest romanticism of the 1920s. Rejection of the haughty mannerisms appropriate to historic styles created an opposite mannerism that came to be known as the craftsman style.

332 *St Antoine Cottage* The architecture of simple life takes many forms. This cottage harmonizes with the natural landscaping.

333 *A suite of furniture signed Charles Warren* The architect-builder created most of his houses as a whole, and no detail escaped his keen eye. He designed furniture as part and parcel of the house; and the quality of his materials, left in their natural state, added an air of relaxed distinction.

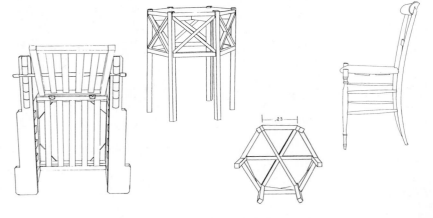

334 *Furniture in style* These reproductions are in the style of American colonial revival and English arts and crafts.

335 *American inspired* This corner chair, colonial in spirit, goes back to around 1740. It is known in New England as a roundabout chair. The reproduction is attributed to the cabinet-makers of Charles Warren's workshop at Pointe-au-Pic.

In 1930, Blowden Davies praised these craftsmen for the quality of their workmanship:

> In Murray Bay you will also find French Canadian cabinet makers busy in their little workshops by the roadside, making fine and beautiful furniture. They have inherited a gift for woodwork and today not only do they make native furniture but they can make beautiful copies as well. I have seen all sorts of things, from good copies of really beautiful old Chippendale chairs to pieces in the fashion of the Art Moderne. They are clever artisans, as they have always been, for I have seen pieces, made back in the French régime, in which native cabinetmakers had the magnificent courage to reproduce designs of the finest Louis Fourteenth tradition, and they did it extraordinarily well, in native woods.[32]

336 *British inspired* This armchair
with adjustable back was inspired
by the arts and crafts movement in
England, which William Morris
promoted in the nineteenth century.
The reproduction is attributed to
the cabinet-makers of Charles Warren's workshop at Pointe-au-Pic.

337 *Joseph Bouchard* This is the façade
of the former cabinet-makers' shop
where three generations of Bouchards
worked. One of the most popular
articles, produced by Clement-Joseph
Bouchard, was a lamp "à cremail-
lère," first created about 1910.

338 *The refined line of modern art* This
massive sideboard does not pretend
to be anything but what it is, which
explains the sparseness of its design.
It is attributed to the craftsman
Joseph Riverin of Cap-à-l'Aigle.

This enthusiasm for craftsmanship was shared by the artist Patrick Morgan, who stimulated and supported it in Charlevoix all his life. At the age
of seventy, he started building a house at the edge of a wood, still anxious
to renew his friendship with nature. In Cache-Cache, as he named the
house, the artist sought total integration of nature and art. He chose the
short curved lines of the Québec house, interpreting them freely. The
surface plan was well conceived, and the elevations and manner in which
various masses were combined made the cottage a masterpiece of synthesis,
a perfect summing-up of the essence of summer-residence architecture.

The cube shape of the modest wooden cabin was reintroduced here in
the juxtaposition of square and rectangular modules. A central chimney—
that appropriate mark of rustic simplicity—acted as a source of heat. The
façade showed a taste for order and regularity, and the exterior décor
emphasized the charming lines of the cottage's sharp contours. Recycled
materials were used, without compromising the integrity of the building.
Fortunately, irregular surface shapes prevented ossified formalism, which
would have been fatal to the interior dynamics. Finally, interplay between
the solid and hollow parts of the building opened it up—ample proof of
the studied consideration Morgan had given to the environment.

How beautiful a cottage is when artistically designed! The desire to
pursue a project beyond slavish imitation can lead to a new concept of
horizontality. Traditional lines meld with new spaces in a building integrated with its site. This is the lesson of summer-residence architecture,
which from its earliest days has tended toward functionalism; the remem-
brance of tradition in the designs of today—without, however, excluding
contributions from elsewhere—makes it an eminently realistic architecture.

In short, such architecture never achieves a state of permanency. It is
attuned to the rhythm of the times, reflects evolving techniques and tenden-
cies and tastes. It is a safe bet that in the near future we will see more little

châteaux springing up in Charlevoix, and more traditional houses, as well as modern villas, which would perfectly suit the Charlevoix landscape. This, then, is the architectural mix that forms Charlevoix's heritage; and it is indispensable to fulfillment of the vow made by Charles Warren to create a Laurentian architecture.

339 *Cache-Cache* By the lines he retained, Patrick Morgan went beyond imitation. This form of architecture, embellished with the fundamental virtues of its style, is a good example of proportion. With its somewhat naive charm it fits in spontaneously with the site.

340 *Front and side elevations* The free composition here bears witness to a mastery of traditional architecture without its paralyzing restriction.

341 *Ground plan* The handling of space at Cache-Cache, astonishingly modern, reminds one that the privacy of certain rooms is as vital to comfort as the sudden opening up of common areas.

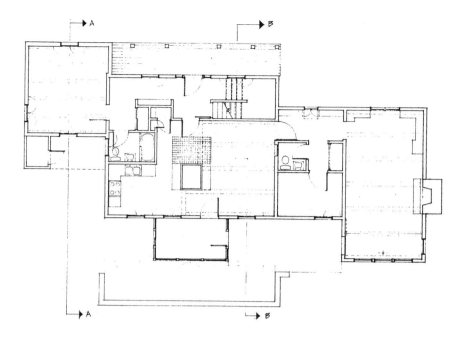

342 *At the edge of the sea* The boldness of American architects who built close to the water can be seen in Engineer Roger Warren's Roche Platte, built in 1978. Its cross-section, dominated by a solar roof set at an angle of fifty-five degrees, suggests some interesting solutions for the future.

LANDSCAPE ARCHITECTURE

The history of summer-residence architecture in Charlevoix teaches us that it cannot be defined by any one style, but that it can be identified by the way in which buildings occupy surfaces. We have passed from the "closed box" of early days to the open spaces of today, where the interior seems almost to burst from its shell toward the outside, instilling in the occupant a love of and knowledge of the landscape.

Midway between the architecture of the house and the natural beauty of its surroundings lies landscape gardening; it combines elements of both, and calls for solutions that can be extreme. In some places, leveled ground plans are laid out in regular shapes, flower-beds meticulously squared, plants arranged geometrically, and pools made either square or circular. In other places, irregularity is the rule: lawns with uneven slopes, wild flowers, shrubs, and woods, and water either in ponds or running free. These are the two opposing approaches; one is said to have come from Italy by way of France, and the other from England. In these artificial landscapes that we call gardens, a choice must be made between the two; either one must organize nature, or leave her to exert her charm more or less untouched.

As we have seen, the long period of infatuation with the past ended after the turn of the century. Its legacy was a taste for order. In horticulture as in painting, a keen desire to create new forms was now felt. What had been lost in grandeur and profusion was gained in refinement. Increasingly, landscape gardening sought a balance between architecture and nature. It was this new spirit that Patrick Morgan, painter and landscape gardener as well as architect, brought to his many landscaping projects.

For Morgan, nature was one huge garden. All that was needed to bring it to perfection, to glorify it, was to free it from the vegetable kingdom. He rejected regular, geometric flower-beds for deliberate disorder, in a composition that imitated nature. Having achieved that, he would immediately set about improving it. In his own wild garden at Bas-de-l'Anse, the arrangement of stones, water flow, and plants reproduced nature in all its dynamism. By sheer patience, the artist created an almost exact imitation of the natural life of the forest. For him, gardens were miniature landscapes brought to a kind of perfection — the quintessence of landscape, so to speak.

Morgan proved this again in the gardens of his nephew Francis H. Cabot, though in a different way. Some features of the gardens at Les Quatre Vents were based on his plans, embellishing the garden scheme laid out by Edward J. Matthews and added to in recent years by Francis H. Cabot. The ground was divided up scenically, each section with its own view and its own centre of interest; the scenes changed continually, in a harmonious pattern somewhat like that of a pastoral symphony, with different motifs for each moment of the day and different melodies for each period of the summer. There was no sparing of sudden transitions and contrasts of shape, colour, and shadow. The eye passed rapidly from restricted to broad views. And care had been taken to distribute masses of light across shadowed areas. The layout revealed a rare skill. Communication between each of its parts was by broad avenues, or narrow paths, or a Chinese bridge straddling a dyke, or a rope bridge like those in Nepal that spanned the wooded depths of the valley below.

Nature itself could be brought to order, too. Morgan tried in his own way to give another property, Les Falaises, a cheerful look. The garden, with its hedges trimmed like low stone walls, was intended to bring nature to heel by imposing a geometrical feature. Morgan countered this by

343 *Patrick Morgan (1904–82)* In June 1982, when friends and relatives were stunned by the sudden death of this kind and popular artist, Richard Lapointe, a farmer, had these words of comfort: "The good Lord needed a naturalist landscape architect — so he came and took the best."

344 *An English-style park for Les Quatre Vents* The park was designed by an artist who sought to reproduce nature in the raw; the pond had to look like an irregular-shaped lake.

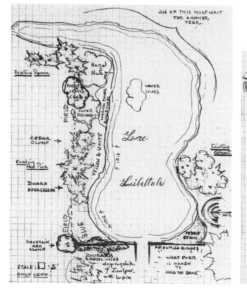

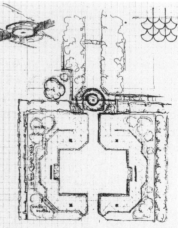

345 *Lake Libellule* Nature, rediscovered in this garden, creates near miracles.

346 *A French-style garden* This type of garden needs precise surroundings. Here, architecture steps in; its rational lines bring order and symmetry.

leaving some areas free and airy. In this arrangement, he seems to have considered the garden a prolongation of the house, a sort of sitting-room in the open air; the architectural rules governing lines, scale, and proportion applied to them both.

Morgan displayed an inventive skill in his blending of reason and emotion, nature and culture; one notable example is Cache-Cache, a beautifully built home. The free-ranging composition of its gardens showed considerable maturity, ranging from brightly lit spots to the most shaded nooks. The deployment of elements imparted a sort of rhythm to a garden stroll, interspersing closed and open views. The scale might have been a bit overwhelming in places, but the effect was always beautiful. Although the gardens had been carefully planned, there was always room to introduce some new idea. In this respect, they reflected the flexibility of the new architecture which united the traditional and the contemporary in graceful fashion.

348 *Rope bridge* In this valley of light and shade, many species foreign to the natural flora of Charlevoix can be found. They were introduced by Francis H. Cabot, who made several trips to Asia to satisfy his horticultural curiosity.

Before Cache-Cache and Les Quatre Vents were landscaped, there was an English-style garden at Cap-à-l'Aigle known as Twin Poplars, which had been planted in 1922 on a farm. With its well-conceived asymmetry the plan was curiously like the British ideal, which offers a degree of intimacy not found in the more theatrical French- or Italian-inspired gardens. The Anglo-Saxon style seeks to eliminate dividing lines between house and garden, and the major planning consideration is often economy, not beauty; the upkeep of a park is indeed less expensive than an avenue lined on either side with flower-beds. Anything that smacks of a formal garden, laid out in neat squares like a carpet, is studiously avoided. Thus one finds annuals planted at a lower level than the house solely for their colour effect. At Twin Poplars, the veranda was treated as an extension of the interior space, and the landscaped garden had a similar "decompartmentalized" effect. The pools and fountains, the tall flag-staff, the statues and busts,

349 *Flowers at Les Falaises* Patrick
Morgan managed to integrate perfectly the shapes of the garden and the
architecture of the house, designed
by J. Hampden Robb.

350 *Nature tamed* At the end of the
pathway, which plunged deeper as
it went, lay a vase of flowers on a
pedestal of classical line; this always
drew the attention of the lone stroller.

even the layout of the fish-pond—all helped charge the atmosphere with
the feeling of sobriety appropriate long solitary walks.

Summer-residence architecture integrated cottage and villa more closely
with environment, an achievement that owed more to choice of site than
to transformation of landscape. It was really a simple question of unity
between nature and architecture, obtained by the expression of simple
shapes and the use of natural materials.

The Torwood Estate, situated at Pointe-à-Gaz, at the edge of Cap-à-
l'Aigle, has its own story. George T. Bonner, who bought the vast seigneury
of Mount Murray in 1902, was from the start taken with the idea of

residential development for summer residents. He went into partnership with Archibald H. Campbell of Montréal, who acted as promotion agent. The Estate amounted to some 140 acres on the point and included a mile-long stretch along the bank of the St Lawrence. The site as a whole offered natural terraces, some of which lay as high as 325 feet above sea level. The landscape architect Frederick G. Todd of Montréal envisaged dividing the property into lots of about two acres.

351 *A mixed garden* Vegetables and flowers enclosed in terraced raised beds of spruce – saved from the ravages of the spruce bud worm – make for a pleasant stroll.

His plan suggested a practical type of sub-division in which the various lots, located mainly in sloping woodland, would form a big park with a meticulously planned network of seemingly unplanned roads. In the heart of the property houses would be built here and there, in an unregimented pattern, and reached by one of these roads. The expanse of leafy trees and conifers promised picturesque charm, grouped so that unexpected views would suddenly open up. Pines were green throughout the year, while in the fall deciduous trees underwent spectacular colour changes. However, there being no supply of potable water, Bonner and Campbell's project never got beyond the first rough draft; and a quarter of a century later Campbell's original cottage is the sole monument to his grand plan. The concept originated in suburban planning. The garden city was the logical outcome of the movement toward urban parks that was in full swing at the turn of the century. Frederick G. Todd was the first Canadian active in this field; an American by birth, he had completed his apprenticeship with the firm of Olmsted and Eliot, which was responsible for the Mount Royal Park in Montréal. In 1900 Todd set up his own practice in Canada, where he completed several prestigious architectural landscaping projects, among them the magnificent plan for the Champs de Bataille Park in Québec City.

352 *A garden on the sea* The rectilinear design of the quickset hedge, which is set at an angle, creates a beautiful effect. This landscaping arrangement of 1936 still shows traces of the handiwork of Edward J. Mathews, who produced the original plan for Les Quatre Vents.

Earlier the well-known Olmsted brothers had completed a project at Pointe-au-Pic for Mrs. T.D. McCagg of Chicago. They were carrying on the business of their father, Frederick Law Olmsted, who as mentioned previously was internationally known for having designed seventeen urban parks in America, among them New York's Central Park. The sons of this visionary pioneer of architectural landscaping, John Charles and Frederick Olmsted, Jr., did not restrict themselves to urban projects. Demands like Mrs. McCagg's kept rolling into their office; it was a time when everyone was praising "landscapism" for its therapeutic effects. This society lady had no doubt been impressed by the general harmony of the site of the world's fair in Chicago in 1893, for as she wrote to the creators of that exhibition about her own proposed summer residence at Pointe-au-Pic, "I wish to have the place, plain as it is, so far as may be, at once harmonious, pleasing and unpretending, and I know you can combine all three."[33]

The Olmsteds and their associates championed the idea that a landscaped garden or park should confine itself to improving on nature. The architects planned McCagg's house, The Spinney, and its environs as integrated parts

353 *Twin Poplars* The solitude that reigns over this pool could serve as background to English dreams. Among the statues and old columns, Queen Victoria's bust looms authoritatively.

354 *Angels in our lands* In the layout of this body of water, nothing spoils the impression of comfort.

355 *Water scenery at Tamarack Top* This water-garden, adopted by domestic ducks, gives the general landscaping more than just a simple decorative look. Distinctive vegetation—rushes, osmunds, and giant ferns—surrounds the pool.

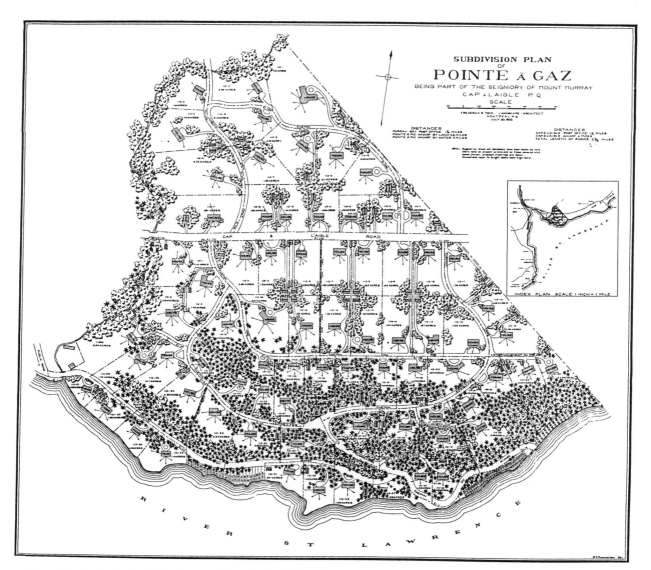

356 *A garden-city in Charlevoix* In this suburban-type development, the landscape architect Todd envisaged more than seventy lots. Broad avenues crossed open spaces and led to houses skilfully oriented toward the sun.

of a whole. The design was relatively simple. The garden was a lawn dappled with light and shadow stretched out to the edge of the wood, which was left alone. The only formal note was an area south of the house, a patterned flower walk that had the effect of prolonging the spacious verandas and terrace. The whole was pleasantly set off by the wooded area, in which various species of trees grew and a mixture of leafy trees and pines ensured balance of volume. The garden did not exist primarily for visitors; its main purpose was to give pleasure to the residents. The effect of the garden, as of the asymmetrical house, was generally informal; it could produce surprises, having eliminated the usual division between house and garden.

Such principles, which smacked of the romantic, would not have affected the writer Henry Dwight Sedgwick, a connoisseur of the classical. With a touch of the philosophical, he treated gardening as perfect recreation:

> Among my chief pleasures at Murray Bay has been the little garden in our curtilage. The young prefer active pleasures. Not until twenty-seven does one appreciate Wordsworth, at thirty-five Thomas à Kempis, at forty Mme. de Sévigné's letters, and at forty-five, on returning home, one goes to the garden before entering the house. But it is in the sixth and seventh decades of a man's pilgrimage through this Valley of Illusion, if it be such, that he begins to understand what a marvellous creation the vegetable world is and that the Creator's most plausible claim to goodness is that He created flowers and mankind with the faculties to enjoy them.[34]

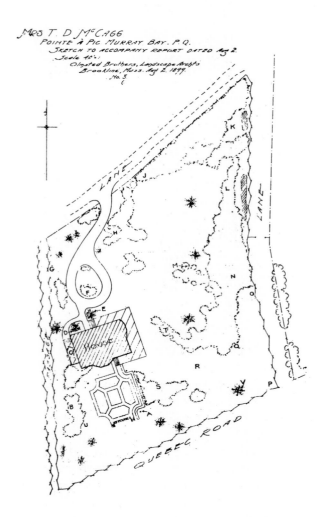

357 *"Mrs T.D. McCagg, Pointe à Pic, Murray Bay, P.Q."* This house is tucked away on the higher part of a clearing. The grassy meadow surrounding it facilitates free circulation through the landscaped layout.

358/359 *At the edge of the wood* This little forest of scattered trees encourages the spread of wild flora. Among the hardy perennials sheltering in the shade of hardwood trees are columbines, foxgloves, and ferns.

Where the bee strays diligent, and with extracted balm
Of fragrant woodbine loads his little thigh.

Wild garden.

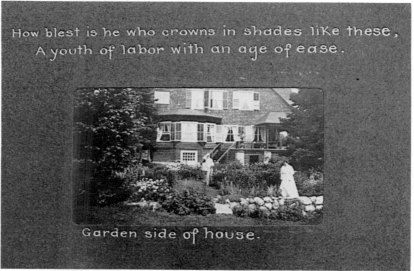

How blest is he who crowns in shades like these,
A youth of labor with an age of ease.

Garden side of house.

360 *One of the attractions at The Spinney* Except for the informal garden along the façade, the cedar backdrop that rose up like obelisks formed the oldest part of the Olmsted brothers' landscaping. The function of this sort of natural screen was to shield the central, flat portion of the design.

Sedgwick talked to his plants as though they were friends. On daily visits to his garden the writer maintained a close relationship with his vegetable world, which he ruled exactly as he pleased, to suit his whim and sense of setting. His approach to gardening, as to his spheres of activity, was theatrical, in the sense that he affirmed man's supremacy over nature rather than concentrating on the strict beauty of woods and meadows. It was man's works that preoccupied and interested him; everything else seemed to him futile and subordinate.

This view of the world was also faithfully displayed in the garden next to Sedgwick's which belonged to his brother-in-law Robert B. Minturn. The strictly ordered compass of flower-beds made for a spectacular effect, the brilliant display of blossoms shouted for attention. Of course, round flower-beds of this type are out of date now — it costs far too much to keep them up nowadays. Today's preference is for a conveniently placed lawn where one can take one's ease and enjoy.

Also in the family of highly formal aesthetic effects was the circular pool designed by Stanford White. It had a sculptured fountain that can be attributed to the artist Janet Scudder, who produced numerous decorative ornaments for the celebrated architect. His delicate little body of water contrasted oddly with the immense river in the background and showed how ridiculously mannered such refinement, used unwisely, could look. The incompatability of the classical piece and the natural back-drop detracted from both.

The intimacy that existed between the immense kitchen garden of the Gibert sisters and its familiar surroundings depended on diametrically opposed attitudes. On the one hand, there was the desire to break free from the rural by a display of extreme affectation; on the other, there was the determination to "go rustic" by transforming an estate into a veritable produce garden. The contrast bore witness to a certain uneasiness in the

361 *Henry Dwight Sedgwick (1861–1957)* When he wore his gardening clothes, Sedgwick liked to describe himself as an amateur. He came from wealth and went to the best colleges and universities in the United States without ever taking his lessons seriously. However, after a change in the family fortune he had to work as a lawyer; later he was able to earn a living as a writer. He gardened much as he wrote — with considerable humour, in conformity with the precepts of his master, Epicurus.

362 *At Robert B. Minturn's* The geometry of this flat design is well suited to the symmetrical layout of the surface. In the centre, the sundial gives balance to the whole. Note the dry-wall enclosing part of this elegant area.

363 *The garden as an oasis* This dreamy little pool is dappled where the sun pierces the shady screen of umbrella pines close around it.

364 *The Giberts' vast kitchen-garden* This market garden—slightly surprising in the context of our subject—is worthy of being classed among the finest examples of its type. The Gibert sisters and their neighbour, Mme Binsse, grew vegetables, herbs, and fruits of rare beauty, which they enjoyed serving to their numerous guests.

face of a nature that had only recently been tamed. Several decades earlier, when the first summer residents were discovering Charlevoix, the most common reaction was that of the timid spectator trying anxiously to find serenity in a panorama that had astonished the earliest settlers.

Between the informal garden and the formal geometric garden lies a whole range of approaches to landscaping. But such categories pale next to the majesty of Charlevoix's natural setting, which reigns supreme and imposes its law. In early days, the garden was a private, shut-in place; with the passage of years it opened up and became receptive to the natural grandeur of the area. Evolving into something more akin to a glade, it now interacts with the surrounding landscape. The background of mountains,

365 *A belvedere* This little kiosk, one of the first of its kind, gave visitors a feel for "environmental consciousness."

with their greens and blues, grey and mauves, and the river cutting its way through the land like an arm of the sea—these are excuse for boldness.

Landscaping expresses the natural beauty of a site. The creation, at La Malbaie, of the fourth golf course in North America was the first example in Charlevoix of this use of the dynamics of space and probably set the fashion for projects that followed. Today, Charlevoix is a mosaic of private gardens, parks, golf courses, fields, and meadows—oases of greenery that, for sheer diversity, are unequaled anywhere else. Without them, the region would not be what it uncontestably is, The Land of Landscapes.

366 *The force of panorama* Scholarly theory alone cannot account for the relationship between architecture and landscape. Only a firm sense of the countryside can produce a villa or garden that joins this beautiful landscape in eternal union.

SUCH a graceful picture I
meant to paint ... and all
I've done is dabble!

Arthur Buies,
Chroniques, humeurs et caprices

It is true that "tradition," as
distinct from consciously
received "influence," might be
defined as those influences
which are so pervasive in any
historical situation that the
human beings who are
involved in them are not
consciously aware of them at
all. It is the ultimate model of
reality through which the
human brain works in every
generation.

Vincent Scully,
*The Shingle Style Today, or the
Historian's Revenge*

Conclusion

CHARLEVOIX is now a popular place for tourists and summer residents. This is the result neither of a well-handled public-relations campaign nor of fashion but rather of a time-honoured tradition of hospitality. Charlevoix's shores have been visited by a continuous stream of explorers, settlers, and vacationers looking for new places. The saga of Charlevoix and its visitors would never have unfolded as it did without the happy cooperation of two Scottish officers. In 1762, officers of the Regiment of Fraser Highlanders began developing their seigneuries of Murray Bay and Mount Murray, aided by the courage and determination of colonists both French and Scottish. Even in those early days, people came from far-off Scotland to pass the summer months in a region already renowned for its beauty. Once the traveller had ventured beyond the stretch lying between the Saguenay and Cape Tourmente, he came upon grand mountains running sheer down to the river. Intimate harmony between the ever-present water and enormous masses of rock and earth gives the region an impression of virginity that summarizes perfectly its charm.

Later, the St Lawrence River was the "royal road" for travellers who came by turns to explore. With the advent of steamships, those floating palaces, the number of trips to La Malbaie increased and the small inns grew. At first lodging was improvised; visitors stayed with families who lived around Pointe-au-Pic, which was close to the dock. Between the time of the modest little inn and the later Victorian grand hotel, Charlevoix became the mecca of North American tourists, who took pride in staying there. Being so far from urban centres, the region satisfied a growing need to escape to a place where time seemed to have stopped.

Vacationers introduced not only modern comforts to the isolated area but also a wide range of sports activities. When golf appeared in 1876, it seemed almost ridiculous to tie up a whole meadow just to hit a little white ball. The event marked the meeting point of two opposing modes of life, the urban search for leisure and the rural struggle for subsistence. Intrusions into the peaceful life of the countryside did not stop fruitful exchange between the two cultures; each profited from the presence of the other, in an atmosphere of tolerance and friendship. One of the sports both groups shared was angling in the fish-laden waters of the hinterland. All felt humble in the presence of nature—generous, but so proud and implacable.

Distance was no hindrance; families like the Tafts came from regions as far away as Ohio. One Taft, William Howard, the twenty-seventh president of the United States, called Murray Bay a "state of mind" over which none of the world's presidents could wield their power. The Blakes, a famous family of magistrates and politicians, came from Toronto to find peace and quiet. One of them, William Hume Blake, used his literary talents to immortalize the beauty of the region and enriched English-language literature with his translation of Louis Hémon's *Maria Chapdelaine*. Charlevoix has the wonderful attribute of inspiring the traveller to create poems, songs, and paintings. Artists, from the British water-colourist George Heriot to the painter Jean-Paul Lemieux, have been unanimous in their praise.

As well as nature's opulence, the immediate surroundings of La Malbaie offer the best examples of summer residence architecture. Most cottages were built in the early years of this century, and most are modern in the sense that they interact intimately with nature's panorama. The two horns of the natural amphitheatre linking Cap-à-l'Aigle to Pointe-au-Pic, that indefinable junction of mountains and sea, are magnificent, as the very first visitors remarked.

To the ethnographer, Charlevoix offered the purity of a traditional life; to the tourist, a magnificent site for exploration. Both visitors projected an image of the region to outsiders. From the sixteenth century on we have had many guides: the first discoverers, the early travellers, the adventurers, and finally the tourists. Their testimonies are worthy of attention because they are the only remnants of Charlevoix's past. They have often idealized the countryside, without representing the concerns of those who pioneered the area and those who live there now. The projected image, however, also affects local inhabitants; it encourages discussion among them about the proper way to present an accurate picture of their home. It is difficult to draw the line between the idealized and the true, for "man's dream is to escape his surroundings, and find others better suited to his transient expectations."[1]

Thus the romanticism of travellers seeking peace, and rest, and the hope of a better world in an isolated countryside, has resulted in an image of a bucolic society apparently without problems. This image, fed back to the local inhabitant, has gradually given him an identity, that of the "ethnic personality"—which implies a sense of both rejection and acceptance by the outside world. The habitant is different; as the father of Québec ethnology remarked, "Just like myself, strangers in the country of Charlevoix are not slow to notice characteristics which are found hardly anywhere else—for example, expressions of speech, woven material, vegetables such as horse beans, and also a particular way of building cowsheds, which they refer to as lean-tos."[2]

Other admirers have attributed a spiritual dimension to the ancestral land; thus Félix-Antoine Savard spoke of Charlevoix as a "metaphysical country,"[3] and Léonce Boivin wrote, "At Ruisseau Clair, between the mountain and the river, far from all noise, in a solitary lair visited only by the Sun of God, I dream in memory of the Creator's marvels."[4] From the exaltations of the first Scottish vacationer to the candid account in *Temps d'une paix*, such words have announced to the world that Charlevoix is a place to visit.

Notes

INTRODUCTION

1 Murray Bay is not an alteration of La Malbaie, and there is no semantic relationship between the two names. Murray Bay was given to part of the former seigneury of La Malbaie, granted in 1762; it was only later that tourists applied the name to the whole of the region comprising Pointe-au-Pic, Cap-à-l'Aigle, and La Malbaie. As for me, when I have to use a general name for the territory of La Malbaie and its environs – the object of the present study – I prefer to use Charlevoix; but I always remember that it is commonly applied to a much larger region, defined arbitrarily as a cultural zone, and cut up into legal parcels by official administrative order.

2 For the purposes of this study, the word *tourism* may be taken temporarily to imply summer residence, which may be defined as sedentary tourism. I do not wish here to fudge the terminological nuances, but rather to apply them in a broader sense. On this subject, see my article "Faire l'histoire du pays visité: Charlevoix," *Loisir et Société/Society and Leisure* 6, no. 1 (spring 1983): 211–28.

3 Newport, on the coast of Rhode Island, halfway between New York and Boston, was the fashionable rendezvous for the richest Americans in the nineteenth century.

4 When I started my research, the only bibliographical collection about the region contained about a hundred titles, listed on 53–5 of *Charlevoix Communautaire* (now out of print), published in 1975 by the Economic Council of Charlevoix Region. Nowadays, researchers have at their disposal a working tool containing 1,810 bibliographical references published in 1984 by the Institut qué-

bécois de recherche sur la culture as *Bibliographie de Charlevoix*.

5 I focused on local periodicals such as *L'Écho des Laurentides* (1884–7), *Le Touriste* (1885–7), *The Murray Bay Habitant* (1907–22), and *The Colony Life* (1953–65), and fashionable illustrated magazines like *L'Opinion publique* (1869–83), *Canadian Illustrated News* (1869–83), and *Dominion Illustrated News* (1888–95).

6 The most eloquent of these academics is still Roger Brière, who wrote *Géographie du tourisme au Québec* as his doctoral thesis at Université de Montréal in 1967.

7 George M. Wrong, *A Canadian Manor and Its Seigneurs* (Toronto 1908), 240.

8 For more information on the Fraser family of Mount Murray – now Cap-à-l'Aigle – see the first three chapters of Burt Brown Barker, *The McLoughlin Empire and Its Rulers* (Glendale 1959), 15–79.

9 F.-X. Eugène Frenette, *Notes historiques sur la paroisse Saint-Étienne de la Malbaie (Charlevoix)* (Chicoutimi: Médéric Parent 1952), 94 p.

10 Roger Lemoine, *La Malbaie esquisse historique* (La Malbaie: Imprimerie de Charlevoix 1972), 12 p.

11 France Gagnon-Pratte, *L'architecture et la nature à Québec au dix-neuvième siècle: les villas* (Québec 1980), 162 p.

12 Here is a thought-provoking passage from Jacques le Goff: "Unlike realism, which in literature as in art is not a photograph of

reality, but a visual presentation of the world and of society, the history of everyday life is an authentic vision of history, for it is one of the last approaches to global history, in which each actor and each element in historical reality is given a part in the functioning of the systems which permit the deciphering of the whole" ("L'histoire du quotidien," *Magazine littéraire* 164 [Sept. 1980]: 41).

13 On this subject, see Jean-Claude Dupont, ed., *Mélanges en l'honneur de Luc Lacoursière* (Montréal: Leméac 1978) 485 p.

14 The expression archeo-civilization is taken from Pierre Erny, *Ethnologie de l'éducation* (Paris: PUF 1981), 25.

15 Jean Poirier, *Ethnologie générale* (Paris: Gallimard 1968), 1907 p.

16 A classic in the field is Sister Marie-Ursule, *Civilisation traditionnelle des Lavallois* (Québec: Les Archives de folklore 5–6, PUL 1951), 403 p.

17 After consulting Roger Nadeau's "Présentation d'une methodologie de recherche en tourisme: le cas du tourisme en Estrie," *Bulletin de Recherche* [Department of Geography, University of Sherbrooke], no. 33 (May

1977): 52, I realized that his approach dealt exclusively with contemporary tourists' behaviour, collecting quantifiable data to determine the causes of a phenomenon. My more inductive approach was completely different; it involved working up from the facts to the general law — that is, by the collection and compilation of multiple facts or variants thereof, I found myself drawn towards a general proposition. On this subject, see my research note "L'hospitalité comme fait historique," *Théoros* 1, no. 2 (2e trimestre 1982): 28.

18 Léonce Boivin, *Dans nos montagnes* (Les Éboulements 1945), 219.

19 James M. Lemoine, *L'Album du touriste* (Quebec 1872), 358–9.

20 I leave this idea from the Abbé Tessier to the discretion of the reader; it seems to echo the excess of imitation against which we are also warned: "First and foremost, tourism must be for us a means of strengthening our ethnic personality. This is the only condition in which it will remain alive. When we have become unsuccessful copies of Americans, we shall be of no interest any longer" (Les valeurs nationales et économiques du tourisme," *Pour survivre* 5, no. 5 [Nov. 1943]: 51).

A COUNTRY

1 *The Voyages of Jacques Cartier*, APC XI (1924): 117.

2 *Oeuvres de Champlain* 2nd ed., vol. 2, book 5 (Québec: Geo.-E Desbarats 1870), 790. I refer to Laverdière's edition, which suggested in a footnote, a corrected version differing from that published in 1613. Furthermore, I could not ignore the interpretative work of H.P. Biggar, published in 1922 under the title *The Works of Samuel De Champlain*, which adopts — this time in the text — the correction suggested in Laverdière.

3 Roger Lemoine, a professor at the University of Ottawa, wrote *La Malbaie: esquisse historique* on the occasion of La Malbaie's tricentenary (1672–1972). In nine pages he established a precise chronology of events during the period of New France. A later publication, *La région de La Malbaie, 1535–1760*, gave him the opportunity of listing the sources on which was based the development of the region under the French régime.

4 Deed of grant of the seigneury of La Malbaie to Jean Bourdon by Jean de Lauson, 21

Dec. 1653. Office of the notary Gilles Rageot.

5 Deed of grant by Jean Talon, bailiff of New France to Philippe Gaultier, sieur of Comporté, 7 Nov. 1672. Mentioned in the deed of sale from Gaultier de Comporté to François Hazeur on 15 Oct. 1687.

6 Deed of sale by Philippe Gaultier de Comporté and Marie Bazire, his wife, to François Hazeur and Pierre Soumande, sieur de L'Orme, 15 Oct. 1687. Office of the notary Gilles Rageot.

7 Contract between François Hazeur and Jean-Baptiste Côté, 18 Nov. 1701. Office of the notary Louis Chambalon.

8 Deed of sale of the seigneury of La Malbaie and its outbuildings by Messrs Thierry Hazeur, canon and grand penitentiary of Québec Cathedral, and Pierre Hazeur de L'Orme, canon and precentor, to Monsieur Bégon, bailiff acting in the name of His Majesty, 29 Oct. 1724. Office of the notary Florent de La Cetière.

9 Inventory and description of all the

goods, furnishings, livestock, and other implements whatsoever to be found in the location of La Malbaie, 25 Sept. 1724. Office of the notary François Rageot.

10   In all probability, the name of Saint-Étienne as patron saint of the parish of La Malbaie was inspired by the role played there by François-Étienne Cugnet, who handled the affairs of the Western Estate from his arrival in the country in 1719 till his death in 1751.

11   See on this subject *The Jesuit Relations* covering the years 1656 to 1750, in Reuben Gold Thwaites, *The Jesuit Relations and Allied Documents* (New York 1959), 42: 248–52; 48: 48–9; 50: 78–9; 63: 250; 69: 14–17, 80–95, 122–35, 289–90.

12   Journal of a voyage made in the country of Tadoussac by Sieur Louis Aubert de la Chesnaye in 1731. Quoted in "Une folle aventure en Amérique: la Nouvelle-France," *La documentation photographique* (special edition 1977): doc. 11.

13   Inventory and valuation of houses, buildings, furnishings, and implements, 5 June 1733. Office of the notary Jacques-Nicholas Pinguet Vaucour. After this inventory, Gilles Hocquart, bailiff of New France from 1731 to 1748, gave an account of progress made on the land and in the seigneury of La Malbaie from 1725 to 1732, in a report written at Québec on the administration of the Western Estate in Canada ("Memorandum on all aspects of the Administration of the Western Estate in Canada," *MG1* 59, series C11A [1733]: 391–635, in the National Archives of Canada [Ottawa].) In his examination of this short period of agricultural production on this estate, he criticized certain aspects of the plan of development of Claude-Thomas Dupuy, his predecessor as bailiff.

14   Decree by Gilles Hocquart, bailiff of New France, permitting Pierre Denis, called Quimper, to enter the seigneury of La Malbaie appertaining to the king, 10 Jan. 1736. In Pierre-Georges Roy, *Inventaire des ordonnances des intendants de la Nouvelle-France . . .* , vol. 2 (Beauceville 1919), 194.

15   Memorandum by Father Claude-Godefroy Coquart on the posts in the king's estate, 5 Apr. 1750, in Reuben Gold Thwaites, *The Jesuit Relations and Allied Documents*, vol. 69: (New York 1959): 80. A copy of Coquart's memorandum addressed to François Bigot may be found in the collection of manuscripts MG18, C-5, National Archives of Canada. The Jesuit father Claude-Godefroy Coquart was a missionary at Tadoussac for the posts in the king's estate from 1746 to 1757.

16   Thwaites, *The Jesuit Relations*, 80.

17   Ibid., 122–3.

18   In my reconstruction of the life of the Nairnes, I was largely inspired by George M. Wrong's monograph, *A Canadian Manor and Its Seigneurs: The Story of a Hundred Years, 1761–1861*. This history professor at the University of Toronto spent many summers at Murray Bay in the early part of the century and produced a remarkable study on the life of a seigneur under the English régime. The text is based on rigorous documentary research carried out in the archives of the manor during his vacations.

19   James Murray, "Grant of land lying on the North Side of the river St. Lawrence from the Cap aux Oyes, limit of the parish of Eboulemens, to the south side of the river of Malbaie, and for three leagues back," 27 Apr. 1762, *Collection John and Thomas Nairne*, MG23 GIII 23, vol. 5 (National Archives of Canada).

20   Letter from John Nairne to Robert Hepburn, Murray Bay, 1798, in ibid., vol. 3: 414.

21   Letter from Alexander Gilchrist to Captain John Nairne, Things Wells near Aberdeen, 28 Jan. 1775, in ibid., vol. 3: 51.

22   Letter from Alexander Gilchrist to Captain John Nairne, Castle Fraser, 6 May 1775, in ibid., vol. 3: 57.

23   James Thompson, *Journal, 1779–1781* P 254-0002: 67 (La Malbaie, 13 May 1780, Archives nationales du Québec [Québec]). The following passage is taken from Thompson's journal:

> When we lay broadside on in the bay, the first thing that met our eyes was Major Nairne's manor, with its imposing 50-foot frontage, its rooms lying in depth, its two storeys. Built by English hands! Magnificently situated, on high ground. At high tide, the St. Lawrence bathes the foot of the promontory, in front of the manor. From the west coast of the bay, several cottages can be seen. On the east side lies the River Malbaie, 750 feet wide, and enormously rich in fish of various kinds, especially salmon and trout said to be the most delicious in the province. The

river divides the two seigneuries, Fraser's and Nairne's; both of them were formerly in the 78th Regiment.

24   Letter from John Nairne to Lieutenant John Nairne (Jr), Hill Head, 22 Jun. 1795, p. 4 in *Collection John Nairne* 1: 170–1.

25   These two drawings, clearly dated 7 Oct. and 3 Nov. 1764, were the object of an exhaustive search on my part in the Collections of Plans of the Surveyors-General deposited in the Archives of the Ministère de l'Energie et des Ressources du Québec; but I could not verify their existence. A more extensive search would entail my going to London, where many original documents of the British colonial era are preserved.

26   Letter from John Nairne to Richard Dobie, Murray Bay, 5 Nov. 1799, p. 2 in *Collection John Nairne*, 3: 449–50.

27   For a publication of the Northwest Historical Series 5, Burt Brown Barker wrote "The McLoughlin Empire and Its Rulers." This monograph on one of the founding families of the State of Oregon, whose roots went back to the Frasers of the seigneury of Rivière-du-Loup (Fraserville), deals in its first three chapters with the history of the seigneur of Mount Murray and his heirs. Nearer our own day, Louis-Philippe Lizotte has put together, in the second part of *La vieille Rivière-du-Loup, ses vieilles gens, ses vieilles choses*, a biography of the Fraser family who settled on the south shore, with some twenty-five pages dealing with the seigneur of Mount Murray and his descendants. Unlike Wrong's study of the Nairnes, the two works mentioned above suffer from faulty documentation, which unfortunately I was unable to remedy.

28   Malcolm Fraser, "Extract from a manuscript journal relating to the operations before Quebec in 1759, kept by Colonel Malcolm Fraser," *Manuscripts Relating to the Early History of Canada*, (Québec, Québec Literary and Historical Society 1868), 37 p.

29   Grant of a seigneury on the north shore of the River St. Lawrence between the River Malbaie and the Rivière Noire by the Honourable James Murray Esquire, governor of Québec, to Lieutenant Malcolm Fraser of the 78th Regiment of Foot, 17 Apr. 1762, *Collection Fraser*, box 30, 5: 103 (Archives nationales du Québec).

30   James Thompson, *Journal*, P 254–0002: 67 (La Malbaie 13 May 1780, Archives nationales du Québec). "The river divides the two seigneuries, Fraser's and Nairne's; both of them were formerly in the 78th Regiment. Fraser owned an elegant farm, with a pleasant house, a barn, stables, and considerable livestock which I was told had spent the previous winter outdoors until March, which is unusual because of our climate. Fraser's farmer pays only 20 pounds a year, but is obliged to sell his butter to the seigneur at 6 pence on demand. This is the only farm yet settled here."

31   Letter from John Nairne to Robert Hepburn, Murray Bay, 1798, p. 5, *Collection John Nairne* 3: 411–12.

32   Isidore Lebrun, *Tableau statistique et politique des Deux Canadas* (Paris 1833), 287.

33   Charles-Henri-Philippe Gauldrée Boilleau, "Paysan de Saint-Irénée," *Les ouvriers des deux mondes* 5, no. 39 (1875): 53. From information gathered on the spot in 1861 and 1862.

34   Lebrun, *Tableau*, 282–3.

35   Joseph Bouchette, *Description topographique de la province du Bas-Canada* (London 1815), 582.

36   George Heriot, *Travels through the Canadas* (London 1807), 53.

37   Ibid., 267.

38   Francis Hall, *Travels in Canada and the United States in 1816 and 1817* (Boston 1818), 60.

39   Ibid., 64.

40   John J. Bigsby, *The Shoe and Canoe* (London 1850), 1: 226.

41   Ibid., 235–6.

42   Lt. F. Henry Baddeley, "On the geognosy of a part of the Saguenay Country," *Transactions of the Literary and Historical Society* (1829): 141.

43   Nich. Andrews, *Rapport des Commissaires nommés pour l'exploration du pays* (Québec 1831), 16.

44   Walter Henry, *Events of a Military Life* (London 1843), 159.

45   Ibid., 164.

46   Ibid., 165.

47   France Gagnon-Pratte, *L'architecture et la nature à Québec au dix-neuvième siècle: les villas* (Québec 1980), 49–53.

48 [Madame Daniel Macpherson née Charlotte Holt Gethings], *Mes mémoirs: ce que j'ai vu et entendu* (Montréal, about 1890), 47–9. These memoirs were first published in their original English version under the title *Reminiscences of Old Quebec* (Montréal, John Lovell 1890), 128 p.

49 Anonymous, *The Quebec Guide Comprising an Historical Tour and Descriptive Account of the City and Every Place of Note in the Vicinity* (Québec 1844), 182–3.

50 Anonymous, *The Canadian Guide Book* (Montréal 1849), 97.

51 *Acte pour amender l'Acte de la représentation parlementaire de 1853*, passed on 19 May 1855, chap. 76, art. 11: 274.

HOLIDAYS

1 Theodore Dwight, Jr., *The Northern Traveller, Containing the Routes to the Springs, Niagara, Quebec and the Coal Mines* (New York 1841), 121.

2 W. Norman, *The Quebec Guide, Being a Concise Account of All the Places of Interest* (Point Levi 1857), 34.

3 Anonymous, "The Saguenay," *Harper's New Monthly Magazine* (July 1859): 147.

4 J.M.G., *Excursions to Murray Bay, River Du Loup, Kakouna and the Far-Famed River Saguenay with a Map of the Route* (Québec 1856), 16.

5 Anonymous, "The Saguenay," 158.

6 J.M. Lemoine, *L'album du touriste* (Québec 1872), 355.

7 Arthur Buies, *Petites chroniques pour 1877* (Québec 1878), 45.

8 Ibid., 46–7.

9 Ibid., 48–9.

10 Meyer Auerbach, *Description of Leve's First Personally Conducted Excursion from New York, August 1877* (New York 1877), 21, 22.

11 Ibid., 28.

12 J.G.A. Creighton, "The Lower St. Lawrence and the Saguenay," *Picturesque Canada* (Toronto 1882), 702.

13 William D. Howells, *Une rencontre, roman de deux touristes sur le Saint-Laurent et le Saguenay* (Montréal 1893), 11.

14 Arthur Buies, *Petites chroniques*, 91.

15 Laurent-Olivier David, "Murray Bay, le 19 juillet 1870," *L'Opinion publique* (28 July 1870): 239.

16 Laurent-Olivier David, "Malbaie, 26 juillet 1871," *L'Opinion publique* (3 Aug. 1871): 377.

17 Arthur Buies, *Chroniques, humeurs et caprices* (Québec 1873), 173.

18 The Tourist, "Murray Bay: The Beach and the Village," *Canadian Illustrated News* (12 Aug. 1871): 98.

19 Buies, *Petites chroniques*, 68.

20 A.D. Decelles, "À La Malbaie," *L'Opinion publique* (15 Sept. 1881): 434.

21 Buies, *Petites chroniques*, 63–5.

22 James M. Lemoine, *Chronicles of the St. Lawrence* (Montréal 1878), 236.

23 Creighton, "The Lower St. Lawrence," 702.

24 A.B. Routhier, *En Canot* (Québec 1881), 10.

25 François Tremblay and Richard Dubé have put forward a thesis showing that the effervescence of the popular arts in Charlevoix is closely connected with the phenomenon of summer residence in Charlevoix. See *Peindre un pays. Charlevoix et ses peintures populaires* (Montréal: Editions Broquer, 1989), 160 p.

26 Napoléon Legendre, *Échos de Québec* (Québec 1877), 64–5.

27 Arthur G. Bradley, *Le Canada. Empire des bois et des blés* (Paris 1922), 52.

28 Anonymous, *Forest, Stream and Seashore*, s. l. (1905): 28.

29 It would be useful to consult the list of memoirs and accounts of events between 1854 and 1968 in the bibliography. This catalogue, arranged in chronological order of the authors' visits, comprises all the sources on which part 2 of this book is based.

30 Lemoine, *L'album du touriste*, 359.

31 Annie Howells Frechette, "Summer

Resorts on the St. Lawrence," *Harper's New Monthly Magazine* (July 1884): 200.

32   Henry Dwight Sedgwick, *Memoirs of an Epicurean* (New York 1942), 222–3.

33   This little summer parish, more than a hundred years old, was the subject of two studies published respectively in 1950 and 1972: Maud M. Pope, *Historical Sketch: Church of St. Peter-on-the-Rock, Cap-à-l'Aigle, Quebec* (Cap-à-l'Aigle 1950), 17 p, and Esther W. Kerry, *Church of St. Peter-on-the-Rock: What the Records Tell Us* (Montréal 1972), 28 p.

VILLAS ON THE CLIFF

1   See on this subject France Gagnon-Pratte's study, *L'architecture et la nature à Québec au dix-neuvième siècle: les villas* (Québec 1980), 334 p.

2   Th. Bentzon, "Saint-Laurent et Saguenay," *Revue des deux mondes* (1898): 523.

3   Shingle refers to the cedar shingles widely used in the nineteenth century for covering roofs in the American north-east. The shingle style was so called by Vincent J. Scully, author of an incisive book that first appeared in 1955, whose theories made their mark on the history of architecture: *The Shingle Style and the Stick Style* (New Haven 1971), 184 p.

4   The elements of this short biography came from interviews with Charles Warren's descendants. To establish the basis of the builder's life story, particular attention was paid to the statements of his eldest daughter, Charlotte, and to those of his son Murray, who had quite a reputation as an amateur historian. These were made in 1981 and 1982, before they died, one after the other, the following year. The more general references dealing with the Warren family as a whole were mostly suggested by Louis R. Pelletier, biographer of the Warrens of Pointe-au-Pic, and by Louis Warren, one of the builder's grandsons. I mention them here with gratitude.

5   In a manuscript letter in the form of a poem, preserved in Seigneur Nairne's archives, James Stevenson sings "Jock" Warren's praises with lyricism appropriate for retired military men. See George M. Wrong, *A Canadian Manor and Its Seigneurs* (Toronto 1908), 119–20.

6   Extract from a manuscript letter from Jean-Charles Warren in Cleveland written to his brother James in Montréal, 3 Aug. 1893, pp. 3–4, *Collection Louise Piller-Tahy*.

7   This American technique, known as balloon frame, was first used in the Chicago area around 1835; it spread rapidly through North America because of the obvious advantages of its light structure as compared with the heavy traditional framework constructed horizontally (layer by layer).

8   Jean M. Donald, *Quebec Patchwork* (Toronto 1940), 187.

9   Anonymous, "A Clapboard Cottage at Cap à l'Aigle," *Canadian Homes and Gardens* (May 1928): 48.

10   Anonymous, "In the Manner of a Normandy Farmhouse," *Canadian Homes and Gardens* (May 1928): 25–28.

11   In the early 1920s, Charles J. Livingood had developed the "garden suburb" Mariemont, financed by The Thomas J. Emery Memorial, of which he was president. This garden-city project, twenty minutes from downtown Cincinnati, had been designed by the town-planning partnership of Jean Nolen and Philip W. Foster of Cambridge, Massachusetts.

12   The University of Toronto did not offer a course in architecture until 1890. As for McGill University in Montréal, it had no programme of training in this field before the turn of the century.

13   Newport had since 1850 been the fashionable watering place of the wealthiest Americans, who built palaces all along the cliff to parade their riches. "Money shouts" they said at Newport; at Murray Bay, it was "money whispers." This neatly points up the contrasting styles adopted by these two societies, and the significance of their respective types of architecture. Paul Bourget of the Académie française, summed up his impressions of this society of millionaires in *Outre-Mer: notes sur l'Amérique* (1906).

14   This idea of purity and realism has been propagated at different times by cultural movements that more or less reject foreign influences.

15   Gagnon-Pratte, *L'architecture*, 202–3.

16   Luc Noppen and Marc Grignon, *L'art de l'architecte, trois siècles de dessin d'architecture à Québec* (Québec 1983), 262.

17 Anonymous, "Sea Side News," *Le Touriste* (3 July 1885): 2.

18 *Stanford White Correspondence*, Avery Library, Columbia University (New York), copy books 18, 20, 22–6.

19 Isaac N.P. Stokes, *Random Recollections of a Happy Life* (New York 1941), 108.

20 The Académie française was founded in 1648 to define the canons of beauty in accordance with the rigid principles of classicism and to raise the level of French art. In 1816, the institution started pursuing its ideal in cooperation with the Académie des Beaux-Arts. This in due course became Paris's École des Beaux-Arts, the precepts of which were to serve as the model for most of the architectural programmes in North America. This school's courses in architectural theory recommended adherence to French traditions inherited from Italy in the fifteenth century.

21 Harold D. Kalman, *The Railway Hotels and the Development of the Chateau Style in Canada* (Victoria 1968), 47 p.

22 Pierre-Georges Roy, *Vieux manoirs, vieilles maisons* (Québec 1927), 241.

23 Ramsay Traquair, *The Old Architecture of Quebec* (Toronto 1947), 324 p. Of Scottish origin, this professor Emeritus of architecture at McGill University was a pioneer in the field of preservation of the architectural heritage of Québec.

24 Letter from Philip MacKenzie to Philippe Dubé, August 1984, p. 1, Collection Musée régional Laure-Conan (La Malbaie).

25 To arrive at a better definition of summer-residence architecture, I feel it essential here to review its development—although without adhering to any precise chronology, for I consider classification by periods somewhat haphazard. In fact, traditions in the sphere of housing are long-lasting; changes take place slowly, and there is no great hurry to adopt new ideas. However, to make it easier to understand the phenomenon, I have arranged my material so that it will give a historic perspective to these "second" houses, from their origins up to their latest examples.

The object of this exercise is not to present a summary of the stylistic evolution of the villa, but rather to draw the reader's attention to the permanent characteristics of this seasonal architecture.

26 Andrew Jackson Downing, *A Treatise on the Theory and Practice of Landscape Gardening*, revision of the 1844 ed. (New York 1967), 576 p. Andrew Jackson Downing (1815–52), author of several books on landscaping, had a considerable influence on his contemporaries. Among his highly successful publications was *Cottage Residences*, which went into some twenty editions. One of Downing's followers was Frederick Law Olmsted, the father of American landscape architecture.

27 Gagnon-Pratte, *L'architecture*, 49–80.

28 Janet Wright, *L'architecture pittoresque au Canada*, (Ottawa 1984), 105–137.

29 Michael McMordie, "The Cottage Idea," *RACAR* 1 (1979): 17–27.

30 The following works on the subject may be read with profit: Andrew Jackson Downing, *The Architecture of Country Houses* (New York, 1850), 484 p.; Gervase Wheeler, *Homes for the People in Suburb and Country: The Villa, the Mansion, and the Cottage* (New York 1855), 443 p., and *Rural Homes, or Sketches of Houses Suited to American Country Life* (Auburn and Rochester 1855), 298 p., and Eugene Clarence Gardner, *Illustrated Homes: A Series of Papers Describing Real Houses and Real People* (Boston 1875), 287 p.

31 James L. Garvin, "Mail-Order House Plans and American Victorian Architecture," *Winterthur Portfolio* (winter 1981): 309–34.

32 Blodwen Davies, *Saguenay "Saginawa," The River of Deep Waters* (Toronto 1930): 90–1.

33 Letter from E.B. McCagg, Chicago, to Mr. Olmsted, Brookline (Massachusetts), 29 Dec. 1903, p. 2., *Olmsted Associates*, job file 348, Manuscript Division, Library of Congress, Washington, D.C.

34 Henry Dwight Sedgwick, *Memoirs of an Epicurean* (New York 1942), 228.

CONCLUSION

1 Luc Bureau, *Entre l'Éden et l'utopie* (Montréal 1984), 192.

2 Marius Barbeau, *Au cœur de Québec* (Montréal 1934), 53.

3 In collaboration, "Félix-Antoine Savard," *Lecture '66*, 12, no. 6–7 (Feb.–Mar. 1966): 177.

4 Léonce Boivin, *Les odes mystiques* (Les Éboulements Mar. 1946), 9, prelims.

Bibliography

To facilitate use of the bibliography, I have divided it into three parts — A Country, Holidays, and Villas on the Cliff — corresponding to the divisions in the text. Each section includes references to archival material, maps, and audio-visual presentations as well as to printed material. Sections on secondary sources begin with more general studies to allow the reader to place the history of Charlevoix in a wider context and continue with references to studies which concern specific aspects of the long chain of events, actions, and daily activities which make up the history of this area.

The following abbreviations are used in the bibliography:

B.R.H.	Bulletin des recherches historiques
D.B.C.	Dictionnaire biographique du Canada
M.R.L.C.	Musée régional Laure-Conan
R.A.P.Q.	Rapport de l'Archiviste de la province de Québec
S.H.S.	Société historique du Saguenay
T.L.H.S.	Transactions of the Literary and Historical Society

List of public organizations holding archives and audiovisuel records, that have been of direct use in this study.

Archives de l'Université Laval (Québec)
Archives du Séminaire de Québec (Québec)
Archives nationales du Canada (Ottawa)
Archives nationales du Québec à Chicoutimi
Archives nationales du Québec à Montréal
Archives nationales du Québec à Québec
Art Gallery of Ontario (Toronto)
Bibliothèque de la législature (Québec)
Bibliothèque nationale du Québec (Montréal)
Boston Public Library (Boston)
Canadien National (Montréal)
Club de golf de Murray Bay (La Malbaie)
Columbia University Libraries (New York)
Frederick Law Olmsted National Historic Site (Brookline, Mass.)
Groupe CSL Inc. [Canada Steamship Lines] (Montréal)
Inventaire des biens culturels du Québec (Québec)
Le Soleil (Québec)
Library of Congress (Washington)

Manoir Richelieu (Pointe-au-Pic)
Mariners Museum (Newport News, Virg.)
Massachusetts Historical Society (Boston)
McGill Rare Books Collection (Montréal)
Metropolitan Museum of Art (New York)
Metropolitan Toronto Library (Toronto)
Municipalités de La Malbaie, de Pointe-au-Pic et de Cap-à l'Aigle (Charlevoix)
Musée des Beaux-Arts du Canada (Ottawa)
Musée du Québec (Québec)
Musée du Saguenay-Lac-St-Jean (Chicoutimi)
Musée maritime Bernier (L'Islet)
Musée McCord (Montréal)
Musée militaire et maritime de Montréal (Montréal)
Musée national de l'Homme (Ottawa)
Musée régional Laure-Conan (La Malbaie)
Musées nationaux du Canada (Ottawa)
Mystic Seaport Museum (Mystic, Conn.)
New York Historical Society (New York)
New York Public Library (New York)
Ontario Archives (Toronto)
Parcs Canada [Inventaire des bâtiments historiques du Canada] (Hull)
Quebec Literary and Historical Society (Québec)
Queen's University Archives (Kingston)
Railway and Locomotive Historical Society (Boston)
Royal Ontario Museum (Toronto)
Société canadienne du microfilm (Montréal)
Société historique du lac Saint-Louis (Montréal)
Steamship Historical Society of America (Providence, R.I.)
Sterling Memorial Library [Yale University] (New Haven, Conn.)
Toronto Historical Board (Toronto)
University of Toronto (Toronto)
Vancouver Art Gallery (Vancouver)
Westmount Public Library (Montréal)
Widener Library [Harvard University] (Boston)

List of notaries whose records are deposited in the Archives nationales du Québec; prior to 1890, these records dealt with the region of La Malbaie:

Amyot, Joseph	1812–1816	Huot, C.-Louis-Napoléon	1847–1852
Chiniquy, Charles	1809–1821	Huot, Charles-Pierre	1817–1865
Cimon, Cléophe	1843–1888	Kane, John	1836–1875
Clément, Léon-Charles	1839–1882	Lavoye, Michel	1737–1772
Clément, Ovide-André	1849–1885	Lévesque, Isidore	1806–1853
Duberger, Charles Louis	1827–1831	Néron, Jean	1768–1798
Duperré, Adolphe-Frédéric	1834–1836	Sasseville, François	1799–1828
Gagné, Jean	1831–1872	Simard, J.-Alfred	1830–1866
Gauvreau, C.-Herménégilde	1815–1839	Tremblay, Édouard	1830–1867
Hudon-Beaulieu, Héli	1840–1869		

List of notaries whose records are preserved in regional judiciary archives or deposited with notary-assignees in La Malbaie:

Angers, Élie	1859–1918	Kane, John-A.-Joseph	1863–1903
Boulianne, Louis-Adjutor	1888–1951	Perron, Joseph	1859–98
Fortin, Télesphore	1843–1900	Warren, J.-Rolland	1914–57
Gagné, J.-Élias	1930–56		

A COUNTRY

The first part of the bibliography deals with the historical evolution of the region of La Malbaie from its discovery in 1535 to its official designation as the county of Charlevoix in 1855. My survey of this early period relies on material listed in the section on primary sources, which includes manuscripts, maps and plans, and, finally, published materials. Other works which cover this period of Charlevoix's history are grouped under secondary sources. This section lists general works on the voyages of the discoverers, the seigneurial regime, the missions, military history, rural life, and colonization. It also includes writings, this time more specialized, which contributed directly to my research on the history of this summer colony, whether the first developments at La Malbaie under the French regime, the scottish seigneurs, or the physical and human development of the county of Charlevoix.

I. Primary Sources

A. MANUSCRIPTS

1. Public Archives
a) Deeds

Acte de Concession en fief et seigneurie de la Malbaie à Jean Bourdon par Jean de Lauson.
    21 décembre 1653, Greffe du notaire Gilles Rageot. Coll. Archives nationales du Québec (Québec).
Acte de Concession en fief et seigneurie de la Malbaie de Jean Talon, intendant de Nouvelle-France, à Philippe Gaultier, sieur de Comporté.
    7 novembre 1672. Tel que mentionné dans l'Acte de vente de Gaultier de Comporté à François Hazeur du 15 octobre 1687. Greffe du notaire Gilles Rageot. Coll. Archives nationales du Québec (Québec).
Acte de vente de Philippe Gaultier de Comporté et de Marie Bazire, son épouse, à François Hazeur et Pierre Soumande, sieur de l'Orme.
    15 octobre 1687. Greffe du notaire Gilles Rageot. Coll. Archives nationales du Québec (Québec).
Marché, François Lavergne — François Hazeur.
    26 septembre 1688. Greffe du notaire Gilles Rageot. Coll. Archives nationales du Québec (Québec).
Marché d'engagement, Guillaume Pagé dit Carsy — François Hazeur.
    16 avril 1692. Greffe du notaire Louis Chambalon. Coll. Archives nationales du Québec (Québec).
Acte de vente de messire Louis Soumande, chanoine de l'église cathédrale de Québec, tant en son nom comme frère aîné habile à se dire et porter seul et unique héritier quant aux fiefs de défunt Pierre Soumande, sieur de l'Orme, vivant capitaine sur les vaisseaux du roi, au sieur François Hazeur de ses intérêts dans le fief et seigneurie de la Malbaie.
    28 mai 1700. Greffe du notaire Louis Chambalon. Coll. Archives nationales du Québec (Québec).
Contrat entre François Hazeur et Jean-Baptiste Côté.
    18 novembre 1701. Greffe du notaire Louis Chambalon. Coll. Archives nationales du Québec (Québec).
Inventaire et description de tous les biens, meubles, bestiaux et autres ustencils generallement quelconques qui se sont trouvés sur le dit lieu de la Malbaye.
    25 septembre 1724. Greffe du notaire François Rageot. Coll. Archives nationales du Québec (Québec).
Acte de vente de la seigneurie de La Malbaie et de ses dépendances par MM. Thierry Hazeur, chanoine et grand pénitencier de la cathédrale de Québec, et Pierre Hazeur de Lorme, chanoine et grand chantre, à monsieur Bégon, intendant agissant au nom de sa Majesté.
    29 octobre 1724. Greffe du notaire Florent de La Cetière. Coll. Archives nationales du Québec (Québec).

Journal d'un voyage fait dans le pays de Tadoussac par le Sieur Louis Aubert de la Chesnaye en 1731 de Québec au pays de Tadoussac et retour à Québec.
  1731. Coll. Archives nationales de France (Paris).
Inventaire et estimation des maisons, bâtiments, meubles et ustancils.
  5 juin 1733. Greffe du notaire Jacques-Nicholas Pinguet de Vaucour. Coll. Archives nationales du Québec (Québec).
Ordonnance de Gilles Hocquart, intendant de la Nouvelle-France qui permet à Pierre Denis dit Quimper d'aller sur la seigneurie de la Malbaie dépendante du Roi.
  10 janvier 1736: 2. Ordonnance des Intendants (NF2, 24). Coll. Archives nationales du Québec (Québec).
Volumes of the Acts of Civil Status, 1770–1812.
  8 vol. Coll. St. Andrew's Church (Québec).
Conveyance John F. Reeve to George T. Bonner.
  20 septembre 1902 (n° 10710). Greffe du notaire Joseph G. Couture. Coll. Archives nationales du Québec (Québec).

b) *Collections*

Thomas Ainslie CPA, SIA. «Copy of a Letter from Mr Ainslie to the Inspector General in Answer to his Letter of the 5th Instant August 1786», 5 p. Coll. Archives nationales du Canada (Ottawa).
Archives des colonies, France. MG1, série C11A. «Mémoire de Gilles Hocquart, intendant de la Nouvelle-France, sur toutes les parties de la région du Domaine d'Occident en Canada». 1er «septembre 1733, vol. 59: 581–598. Coll. Archives nationales du Canada (Ottawa).
Warren Baker «Lettre de Malcolm Fraser à James Kerr», Murray Bay, 22 janvier 1803, 5 p. Coll. Musée régional Laure-Conan (La Malbaie).
Francis H. Cabot Titre de concessions et correspondance de Malcolm Fraser. Coll. Musée régional Laure-Conan (La Malbaie).
Domaine du Roi MG18, C5. «Mémoire daté 5 avril 1750 sur l'état des postes au Domaine du Roi adressé à François Bigot, intendant, par le père Claude-Godefroy Coquart de la compagnie de Jésus». 29 p. Coll. Archives nationales du Canada (Ottawa).
Famille Fraser P 0081 et P 0297. Coll. Archives nationales du Québec (Québec).
Malcolm Fraser MG23, K1. Coll. Archives nationales du Canada (Ottawa).
Haldimand Papers B 183. «Papers and Correspondence relating to Rebel Prisoners, 1778–1783»: 51. Coll. Archives nationales du Canada (Ottawa).
Thomas et John Nairne MG23, G III, 23. «Instrument de recherche n° 573», 20 p. Coll. Archives nationales du Canada (Ottawa).
James Thompson P 254, 0001 à 0014. «Journal 1779–1781», vol. 0002. Coll. Archives nationales du Québec (Québec).
William S. Wallace MS 37. Coll. University of Toronto (Toronto).
Henry James Warre MG24, F71. Coll. Archives nationales du Canada (Ottawa).
George M. Wrong MS 36. Coll. University of Toronto (Toronto).

c) *Dossiers*

Dossier 166 pièce 1 «Notes de M. Édouard Tremblay, notaire de La Malbaie de 1830 à 1867». 6 p. Coll. Société historique du Saguenay (Chicoutimi).
Dossier 166 pièce 2 «Les rangs de La Malbaie». Coll. Société historique du Saguenay (Chicoutimi).
Dossier 166 pièce 4 «Dévastations des Anglais». Coll. Société historique du Saguenay (Chicoutimi).
Dossier 166 pièce 5 «Le moulin de Hazeur». Coll. Société historique du Saguenay (Chicoutimi).
Dossier 166 pièce 14 «Extrait du contrat de ventre entre Monsieur M.E. Duggan Gray, Vancouver, C.B. et Monsieur Alfred Savard, La Malbaie». (Réf.: lots 575 & 575-8). Coll. Société historique du Saguenay (Chicoutimi).
Dossier 166 pièce 15 «Lettre de Victor Tremblay au Père Urbain-Marie, concernant le nom de La Malbaie». Coll. Société historique du Saguenay (Chicoutimi).
Dossier 292 pièce 33 «Bettez, Bouliane, McCullock, etc.» Coll. Société historique du Saguenay (Chicoutimi).

B. MAPS AND PLANS

Bellin, Jacques-Nicholas. *Carte du cours du Fleuve de Saint-Laurent Depuis la Mer jusqu'à Québec en Deux Feuilles*, s. 1. Dressée au Dépost des Cartes de la Marine pour le service des vaisseaux français, 1761. Échelle de Lieues Marines de France et d'Angleterre de Vingt au Degré. Coll. Mr and Mrs Thomas C. Hoopes.

Bellin, Jacques-Nicholas. *Carte du cours de la rivière du Saguenay appelée par les Sauvages Pitchitouichetz*, s. 1 Dressée sur les manuscrits du dépost des Cartes et Plans de la Marine, 1744. Échelle de Lieues Communes de France de 282 toises. Coll. Archives nationales du Canada (Ottawa), H3 310 1744.

Bouchette, Joseph. *Carte topographique de la province du Bas-Canada sur laquelle sont indiquées les limites des districts, des comtés, des seigneuries et des cantons ainsi que les terres de la Couronne et celles du clergé, etc.*, London, W. Faden, 1815 (rééditée par les Éditions Élysées en 1980), s. éch. Coll. Archives nationales du Québec (Montréal).

Bouchette, Joseph. *To His Most Excellent Majesty King William IV this Topographical Map of the Districts of Québec, Three Rivers, St. Francis and Gaspé. . .* , London, James Wyld, 1831. [Échelle: environ 1:170 000.] Coll. Archives nationales du Québec (Montréal).

Bouchette, Joseph. *Topographical Map of the Province of Lower Canada, showing its Division into Districts, Countries, Seigniories and Townships with all the Land Reserved Both for the Crown and the Clergy. . .* , London, W. Faden, 1815. [Échelle; environ 1:170 000.] Coll. Archives nationales du Québec (Montréal).

Chaperon, Ls. H. *Plan of Part of the Domain Seigniory of Murray Bay, Property of W.E. Duggan, Esq.*, s. 1., s. éd., 1884–1894. Échelle: 1" = 2 chaînes. Coll. Musée régional Laure-Conan (La Malbaie).

Duberger, Jean-Baptiste. *Plan designating the Lines of Division Between the Seigniory of Mount-Murray and the Waste Land of the Crown*, Québec, Crown Land Department, 25 janvier 1853. Échelle: 28 arpents au pouce. Coll. Ministère Énergie et Ressources du Québec (Québec), M-10.

Duberger, Jean-Baptiste. *Plan figuratif de la propriété de Sieur A. Bélair situé en la paroisse. St-Étienne de Mount-Murray désignant le chemin actuel ainsi que le proposé avec Pont et Pontage sur icelle*, Malbaie, s. éd., 29 novembre 1820. Échelle 1" = 60' – 0". Coll. Archives nationales du Québec (Québec), N-1274 206.

Laure, Pierre-Michel. *Carte du Domaine en Canada dédiée à Monseigneur le Dauphin*, s. 1., s. éd., 23 août 1731, s. éch. Coll. Archives nationales du Canada (Ottawa), PH 900, 1731.

Vondenvelden, William. *A New Topographical Map of the Province of Lower Canada, Compiled from all the Former as well as the Latest Surveys, Taken by Order of the Provincial Government. . . ,* London, W. Faden, 1803. [Échelle: environ 1:500 000.] Coll. Archives nationales du Québec (Montréal).

Anonymous. *La Malbaie* (copie de J.-Antoine Pelletier), s. 1., s. éd., 1798, s. éch. Coll. Archives nationales du Canada (Ottawa), F 325.

Anonymous. *Mount Murray* (copie de J.-Antoine Pelletier), s. 1., s. éd., 1792, s. éch. Coll. Archives nationales du Canada (Ottawa) F 325, C 113323.

Anonymous. *Plan of Murray Bay, plan for Cultivating the Farm at Murray Bay, Beginning in the Year 1787*, s. 1., s. éd., s. d. Échelle: 3" = 21 arpents. Coll. Archives nationales du Canada (Ottawa), MG 23, GIII 23, vol. 5.

Anonymous. *Seigneurie Mount Murray*, s. 1., s. éd., 1835. Échelle: 16 arpents au pouce. Coll. Archives nationales du Canada (Ottawa), H2 325.

C. PUBLISHED MATERIALS

1. Reference

Bellin, Jacques-Nicholas. *Remarques sur la carte de l'Amérique Septentrionale comprise entre le 28ᵉ et le 72ᵉ degré de latitude avec une description géographique de ces parties par M. Bellin. . . ,* Paris Imprimrie de Didot, 1760, 131 p.

Blaeu, Johan. *The Third Centenary Edition of Johan Blaeu, le Grand Atlas ou Cosmographie blaviane: Amsterdam 1663*, Amsterdam, Theatrum Orbis Terrarum, Copyright 1967–1968, Fac-similé, vol. 12.

Blouin, Amédée. *Canada, ses villes et ses villages*, Manuscrit déposé à la Bibliothèque nationale du Québec (Montréal), 1960, 5 vol., MS S108.

Bouchette, Joseph. *The British Dominions in*

North America: or Topographical and Statistical Description of the Provinces of Lower and Upper Canada, London, Longman, Rees, Orme, Brown, Green and Longman, 1832, 2. vol.

Bouchette, Joseph. *A Topographical Dictionary of the Province Lower Canada*, London, Longman, Rees, Orme, Brown, Green and Longman, 1832, 358 p.

En collaboration. «Une folle aventure en Amérique: la Nouvelle-France», *La documentation photographique* [Paris], Hors Série, 1977, 70 p.

En collaboration. *Bibliographie de Charlevoix*, Québec, Institut québécois de recherche sur la culture, «Documents de recherche nº 3», 1984, 316 p.

Harper, J. Russel. *Early Painters and Engravers in Canada*, Toronto, University of Toronto Press, 1970, 370 p.

Hawkins, Alfred. *The Quebec Directory and Stranger's Guide to the City and Environs*, Québec, W. Cowan and Son, 1844, 252 p.

Langelier, J.C. *Liste des terrains concédés par la Couronne dans la province de Québec de 1763 au 31 décembre 1890*, Québec, C.F. Langlois (Imprimeur de la Reine), 1891, 1 921 p.

Lebrun, Isidore. *Tableau statistique et politique des deux Canadas*, Paris, Treuttel et Würtz, 1833, 558 p.

Le Moine, Roger. *La région de La Malbaie 1535–1760, (textes et documents présentés par Roger Le Moine)*, La Malbaie, M.R.L.C., Coll. L'accessible 1, 1983, 212 p.

Mackay, Robert W.S. *The Canada Directory Containing the Names of the Professional and Businessmen of Every Description in the Cities, Towns, and Principal Villages of Canada*, Montréal, John Lovell, 1851, 692 p.

Magnan, Hormisdas. *Dictionnaire historique et géographique des Paroisses, Missions et Municipalités de la Province de Québec*, Arthabaska, s. éd., [Imprimerie d'Arthabaska], 1925, 738 p.

McGregor, John. *British America*. London, T. Codell, Strand, Edinburgh, William Blackwood, 1832, 2 vol.

Québec, (Gouv.) *Rapport de l'Archiviste de la province de Québec*, Québec, Imprimeur de Sa Majesté, (1920–1921): 11, 12, 30; (1921–1922): 46, 379; (1941–1942): 186; (1943–1944): 86–90; (1947–1948): 143–183.

Québec (Gouv.) *Cadastres abrégés des sei-gneuries du district de Québec et publiés sous l'autorité des commissaires*, (Commission sous l'Acte seigneurial de 1854 amendé), Québec, Imprimeur de la Reine, 1863, 2 vol.

Richard, Édouard. *Supplément du Rapport du Dr Brymner sur les Archives Canadiennes (1899)*, Ottawa, Imprimeur du Roi, 1901: 87, 435, 513.

Roy, Antoine. «Bibliographie des monographies et histoires de paroisses», *R.A.P.Q.*, (1937–1938): 254–364.

Roy, Pierre-Georges. *Inventaire des Ordonnances des Intendants de la Nouvelle-France conservées aux Archives Provinciales de Québec*, Beauceville, L'Éclaireur Ltée, 1919, 4 vol.

Roy, Pierre-Georges. *Inventaire des Procès-Verbaux des Grands Voyers conservés aux Archives de la Province de Québec*, Beauceville, L'Éclaireur Ltée, 1923–1932, 6 vol.

Roy, Pierre-Georges. *Inventaire des Concessions en fief et seigneurie, Fois et Hommages et Aveux et dénombrements conservés aux Archives de la Province de Québec*, Beauceville, L'Éclaireur Ltée, 1927–1932, 6 vol.

Saugrain, Cl. *Dictionnaire Universel de la France ancienne et moderne et de la Nouvelle-France*, Paris, Veuve Saugrain, 1726, 3 vol.

Shortt, Adam. *Documents relatifs à la Monnaie, au change et aux finances du Canada sous le Régime français*, Ottawa, Bureau des publications historiques (Archives Canada), 1925, 2 vol.

Thwaites, Reuben Gold. *The Jesuit Relations and Allied Documents*, New York, Pageant Book, 1959, vol. 42: 248–252; vol. 48: 48, 49; vol. 50: 78, 79; vol. 63: 250; vol. 69: 14–17, 80–95, 122–135, 289, 290.

Wallace, William S. *The Dictionary of Canadian Biography*, Toronto, The MacMillan Company of Canada, 1945, 2 vol.

Anonymous. *Almanach de Québec pour l'année 1792*, [incluant des notes manuscrites de Malcolm Fraser—Coll. M.R.L.C.], Québec, Chez Samuel Neilson, 1792, 168 p.

Anonymous. *Almanach ecclésiastique et civil de Québec pour 1846*, Québec, J.B. Fréchette, 1846, 172 p.

Anonymous. *The Quebec Almanack and British American Royal Calendar for the year 1827, Being the Third After Leap Year*, Québec, Neilson and Cowan, 1827, 284 p.

2. Guidebooks

1839 Anonymous. *The North American Tourist*, New York, A.T. Goodrich, 1839, 506 p.

1844 Holley, O.L. *The Picturesque Tourist: Being a Guide Through the Northern and Eastern States and Canada. . .*, New York, J. Disturnell, 1844, 336 p.

1844 Anonymous. *The Quebec Guide, Comprising an Historical and Descriptive Account of the City and Every Place of Note in the Vicinity*, Québec, W. Cowan and Son, 1844, 198 p.

1849 Anonymous. *The Canadian Guide Book with a Map of the Province*, Montréal, Armour and Ramsay, 1849, 153 p.

1850 Burr, William. *Descriptive and Historical View of Burr's Moving Mirror of the Lakes, the Niagara, St. Lawrence and Saguenay Rivers. . .*, New York, George F. Bunce, 1850, 48 p.

1851 Sinclair, P. *The New Guide to Quebec and its Environs*, Québec, Armour and Ramsay, 1851, 76 p.

1853 Van Cleve, J. *The Ontario and St. Lawrence Steamboat Company's Hand-Book for Travellers to Niagara Falls, Montreal and Quebec, and Through Lake Champlain to Saratoga Springs*, Buffalo, Jewett, Thomas and Co., 1853, 174 p.

1854 Mackay, Robert W. Stuart. *The Stranger's Guide to the Cities and Principal Towns of Canada. . .*, Montréal, C. Bryson, 1854, 168 p.

1854 Perham, Josiah. *Descriptive and Historical View of the Seven Mile Mirror of the Lakes, Niagara, St. Lawrence and Saguenay Rivers. . .*, New York, Baker, Godwin and Co., 1854, 48 p.

1855 Anonyme. *Springs, Water-Falls, Sea-Bathing, Resorts and Mountain Scenery of the United States and Canada. . .*, New York, J. Disturnell, 1855, 227 p.

3. Memoires and Narratives*

1535 Cartier, Jacques. *The Voyages of Jacques Cartier*. Published from the Originals with Translation notes and Appendices by H.P. Biggar, Ottawa, Publications APC XI, 1924, 330 p. — In spite of the mystery which continues to surround the authorship of texts attributed to Jacques Cartier, I decided to refer to the original work, which was published by H.P. Biggar.

1608 Champlain, Samuel de. *Œuvres de Champlain*. This edition of six books (in two volumes) was published in 1870 (second edition), with the support of l'Université Laval, by Father C.H. Laverdière from the original, *Les Voyages de la Nouvelle-France occidentale, dicte Canada, faits par le Sr de Champlain Xainctongeois, Capitaine pour le Roy en la Marine du Ponan, & toutes les Descouvertes qu'il a faites en ce pais depuis l'an 1603 jusques en l'an 1629*, Paris, Louis Sevestre, 1632.

1720 à 1730 Laure, Pierre-Michel. *Mission du Saguenay. Relation inédite du R.P. Pierre Laure s.j.*, Montréal, Archives du Collège Sainte-Marie, 1889, 72 p. — The preface of this rare document, edited by Arthur Edouard Jones, contains biographical notes on the Jesuit missionary.

1759 [Fraser, Malcolm] *Manuscripts Relating to the Early History of Canada*, «Extract from a manuscript journal relating to the operations before Quebec in 1759, kept by Colonel Malcolm Fraser», Québec, Quebec. Literary and Historical Society, 1868, 37 p.

1760 à 1830 Bennett, Ethel Hume. *A Treasure Ship of Old Quebec*, Toronto, The MacMillan Company of Canada, 1936, 226 p.

1760 à 1815 Connor, Ralph (pseud. de Charles W. Gordon) *The Rock and the River, a Romance of Quebec*, Toronto, The McClelland and Stewart Ltd, 1931, 377 p.

Circa 1790 Aubert de Gaspé, Philippe. *Mémoires*, Québec, N.S. Hardy, 1885, 563 p.

1791 et 1792 Campbell, Patrick. *Travels in the interior inhabited Parts of North America in the Years 1791 and 1792*, Toronto, The Champlain Society (vol. 23), 1937, 326 p.

1807 Heriot, George. *Travels Through the Canadas*, London, R. Phillips, 1807, 2. vol.

1815 Bouchette, Joseph. *Description topographique de la province du Bas-Canada avec des remarques sur le Haut-Canada, et sur les relations des deux provinces. . .*, Montréal, Éditions Élysées, 1978 (réédition de Faden, 1815), 664 p.

1816–1817 Hall, Lᵗ Francis. *Travels in Canada*

*Dates in italics correspond to the year the author visited La Malbaie; others, to the year the edition was published.

and the United States, in 1816 and 1817, Boston, Wells and Lilly, 1818 (republished from the London Edition), 332 p.

1823 Bigsby, John J. The Shoe and Canoe or Pictures of Travel in the Canadas, London, Chapman and Hall, 1850, 2 vol.

1825 Talbot, Edward Allen. Cinq années de séjour au Canada, Paris, Boulland, 1825, 2 vol.

1829 Baddeley, Lt F. Henry. «On the Geognosy of a Part of the Saguenay Country», T.L.H.S., vol. 1 (1829): 79–166.

1830 Andrews, Nich. Rapport des commissaires nommés pour l'exploration du pays, borné par les rivières Saguenay, Saint-Maurice et Saint-Laurent, Québec, Ordonné pour impression par la Chambre de l'Assemblée, 1831, 50 p.

Circa 1835 Macpherson, Mrs Daniel (née Charlotte Holt Gethings) Reminiscences of Old Quebec, Montréal, John Lovell and Son, 1890, 128 p.

Circa 1835 Macpherson, Mrs Daniel (née Charlotte Holt Gethings). Mes Mémoires. Ce que j'ai vu et entendu en traversant le long chemin de la vie depuis l'année 1835 et ce qui m'a conduit à la Sainte Église Catholique, Montréal, L'Auteur, s. d., 17 p.

1839 Henry, Walter. Trifles from my port-folio or Recollections of Scenes and small Adventures During Twenty-Nine Year's of Military Service. . . , Québec, W. Neilson, 1839, 2 vol.

1840 Warre, Henry James. Sketches in North America and the Oregon Territory, Barre (Mass.), Imprint Society, 1970, (rééd. de 1848), 26 p., 71 pl.

1841 Bonnycastle, Sir Richard H. The Canadas in 1841, London, Henry Colburn, 1841, 2 vol.

1843 Henry, Walter. Events of a Military Life: Being Recollections After Service in the Peninsular War, Invasion of France, The East Indies, St. Helene, Canada and Elsewhere, London, William Pickering, 1843, 2 vol.

1849 Logan, William-Edmond. Exploration géologique du Canada. Rapport de progrès pour l'année 1849–1850, Toronto, Imprimé par ordre de l'Assemblée législative, 1850, 120 p.

II. Secondary Sources

A. GENERAL

Amusart, Joseph (pseud. of Benjamin Sulte) Causons du pays et de la colonisation, Montréal, Granger Frères, 1891, 250 p.

Boswell, Hazel. French Canada: Pictures and Stories of Old Quebec, New York, Atheneum, 1967, 76 p.

Browne, James. A History of the Highlands and of the Highland Clans, Glasgow, A. Fullarton & Co., 1838, 4 vol.

Bruchési, Jean. «George Heriot, peintre, historien et maître de poste», Les Cahiers des Dix, no 10 (1945): 191–205.

Campbell, Wilfred. The Scotsman in Canada, Toronto. The Muson Books Co., s. d., vol. I, 432 p.

Caron, Ivanhoé. La colonisation du Canada sous la domination française, [précis historique], Québec, s. éd., 1916, 90 p.

Caron, Ivanhoé. «Historique de la voirie dans la Province de Québec (suite et fin)», B.R.H., vol. 39 no 8 (1933): 463–482.

Coates, Hazel A. A Quebec Mosaic, a Story of Quebec and its Crafts, Granby, Simms printing Co., 1967, 92 p.

Desjardins, Alphonse. «The Abolition of the Seigneurial Tenure», Canada: an Encyclopedia of the Country, J. Castell Hopkins, édit, vol. III (1898): 124–135.

Daniel, Abbé François. Histoire des grandes familles françaises du Canada, Montréal, Eusèbe Sénécal, 1867, 610 p.

Drapeau, Stanislas. Études sur les développements de la colonisation du Bas-Canada depuis dix ans: (1851–1861), Québec, Léger Brousseau, 1863, 593 p.

Dufebrvre, B. (pseud. of Émile Castonguay) Cinq femmes et nous, Québec, Belisle, 1950, 289 p.

Fauteux, Joseph-Noël. Essai sur l'industrie au Canada sous le Régime français, Québec, Ls.-A. Proulx, 1927, 2 vol.

Finley, Gerald E. George Heriot 1759–1839, Ottawa, Galerie nationale du Canada. Coll. Artistes canadiens no 5, 1979, 81 p.

Fraser, Alexander. «Dealing with the Settlements of the Eighteenth Century», Fraser's Scottish Annual, vol. 3 (1902): 17–25.

Fraser, Alexander. The Clan Fraser in Canada. Souvenir of Firsh Annual Gathering, Toronto, May 5th, 1894, Toronto, Mail Job Printing Co., 1895, 112 p.

Gale, George. Quebec Twixt Old and New, Québec, The Telegraph Printing Co., 1915, 296 p.

Gariépy-Smale, Ruth. «Notice préliminaire sur le régime seigneurial», *Rapport des Archives nationales du Québec* (tome 53), Québec, Ministère des Affaires culturelles, 1976, p. 268–275.

Gauthier, Raymonde. *Les manoirs du Québec*, Québec, Éditeur officiel du Québec/Fides, 1976, 244 p.

Gregg, William. *History of the Presbyterian Church in the Dominion of Canada*, Toronto, Presbyterian Printing and Publishing Co., 1885, 646 p.

Hale, Katherine (pseud. of Amelia Beers Garvin). *Historic Houses of Canada*, Toronto, The Ryerson Press, 1952, 152 p.

Hale, Katherine (pseud. of Amelia Beers Garvin). *Canadian Houses of Romance*, Toronto, The MacMillan Company of Canada Limited, 1926, 213 p.

Hatch, Robert McConnell. *Trust for Canada. The American Attempt on Quebec in 1775–76*, Boston, Houghton Mifflin Company, 1979, 295 p.

Heidenreich, Conrad E. «Mapping the Great Lakes; the Period of Imperial Rivalries, 1700–1860», *Cartographica*, vol. 18 no 3 (1981): 74–109.

Keltie, John S. *A History of the Scottish Highlands, Highland Clans and Highland Regiments With an Account of the Gaelic Language, Literature and Music*, Edinburgh, Thomas C. Jack, 1883, 2 vol.

Maclean, J.P. *An Historical Account of the Settlements of Scotch Highlanders in America Prior to the Peace of 1783 Together With Notices of Highland Regiments and Biographical Sketches*, Cleveland, The Helman-Taylor Company, 1900, 459 p.

McIan, R.R. and James Logan. *The Clans of the Scottish Highlands, The Costumes of the Clans*, London and Sydney, Pan Books, 1980 (réédition de 1845 en un volume), 206 p.

Macdonald, Norman. *Canada, 1763–1841: Immigration and Settlement, the Administration of the Imperial Land Regulations*, London, Longman's, Green and Co., 1939, 576 p.

Maheux, Arthur. *Ton histoire est une épopée, nos débuts sous le Régime anglais*, Québec, s. éd., 1941, 212 p.

Michel, F.-Xavier dit Francisque. *Les Écossais en France. Les Français en Écosse*, London, Trübner et Cie, 1862, 2 vol.

Morisset, Gérard. *La peinture traditionnelle au Canada français*, Ottawa, Le Cercle du Livre de France, 1960, 216 p.

Ouellet, Fernand. *Histoire économique et sociale du Québec, 1760–1850, structure et conjoncture*, Montréal, Fides, 1966, 639 p.

Pilon, Henri. «Baddeley, Frederick Henry», *D.B.C.*, vol. 10 (1871–1880): 31, 32.

Rasporich, Anthony W. «Bigsby, John Jeremiah», *D.B.C.*, vol. 11 (1881–1891): 79–81.

Reid, Stanford W. et coll. *La tradition écossaise au Canada*, Ottawa, Centre d'édition du gouvernement du Canada, 1980, 401 p.

Roberts, Kenneth Lewis. *March to Quebec: Journals of the Members of Arnold's Expedition*, New York, Doubleday, Doran & Co., 1938, 657 p.

Roche-Monteix, Camille de. *Les Jésuites et la Nouvelle-France au XVIIIe siècle d'après des documents inédits*, Paris, Alphonse Picard et Fils, 1906, 2 vol.

Roy, Pierre-Georges. «Le choléra asiatique de Québec,» *B.R.H.*, vol. 12 no 3 (1906): 88–92.

Roy, Pierre-Georges. *Les noms géographiques de la province de Québec*, Lévis, s. éd., 1906, 514 p.

Roy, Pierre-Georges. *Les petites choses de notre histoire*, Lévis, s. éd., 1919, 300 p.

Roy, Pierre-Georges. «Les Ordonnances des six premiers intendants de la Nouvelle-France», *B.R.H.*, vol. 25 no 6 (1919): 161–174; vol. 25 no 7 (1919): 193–205.

Roy, Pierre-Georges. *Vieux manoirs, vieilles maisons*, Québec, Commission des monuments historiques de la province de Québec, 1927, 376 p.

Roy, Pierre-Georges. *À travers les Mémoires de Philippe Aubert de Gaspé*, Montréal, G. Ducharme, 1943, 279 p.

Roy, Pierre-Georges. *Toutes petites choses du Régime anglais*, Québec, Garneau, 1946, 2 vol.

Séguin, Maurice. *La nation «canadienne» et l'agriculture (1760–1850)*, Trois-Rivières, Les Éditions Boréal Express, 1970, 279 p.

Spendlove, F. St. George. *The Face of Early Canada*, Toronto, The Ryerson Press, 1958, 162 p.

Stewart, Col. David. *Sketches of the Character, Manners and Present State of the Highlanders* of Scotland: with Details of the Military Service of the Highland Regiments, Edinburgh, Archibald Constable and Co., 1822, 2 vol.

Stephens, Mary Hilda. The Old Gentlemen Stood to Pray, Tales of Remembrances of and by the People of St. Andrew's Presbyterian Church, Quebec City, Québec, s. éd., 1980, 142 p.

Sulte, Benjamin. «The Seigneurial Tenure in Lower Canada», Canada: An Encyclopedia of the Country, J. Castell Hopkins, édit., vol. III (1898): 119–123.

Summers, Jack L. and René Chartrand. L'uniforme militaire au Canada 1665–1970, Ottawa, Musées nationaux du Canada (Publication d'histoire militaire n° 16), 1981, 187 p.

Taché, Joseph Charles. De la tenure seigneuriale en Canada et projet de commutation, Québec, Lovell et Lamoureux, 1854, 63 p., xix p.

Tessier, Albert. «La vie rurale vers 1800», Les Cahiers des Dix, n° 10 (1945): 169–189.

Tessier, Albert. «Les voyages vers 1800», Les Cahiers des Dix, n° 6 (1941): 83–108.

Thompson, Don W. L'homme et les méridiens: histoire de l'arpentage et de la cartographie au Canada, Ottawa, Imprimeur de la Reine, 1966, 2 vol.

Tremblay, Victor et coll. Histoire du Saguenay depuis les origines jusqu'à 1870 (S.H.S. n° 21), Chicoutimi, La Librairie régionale, 1968, 465 p.

Trudel, Marcel. Initiation à la Nouvelle-France, histoire et institutions, Montréal, Holt, Rinehart et Wilson, 1968, 323 p.

Trudel, Marcel. Le Régime seigneurial, Ottawa, Les brochures de la Société historique du Canada, n° 6, 1971, 21 p.

Trudel, Marcel. Le terrier du Saint-Laurent en 1663, Ottawa, Cahiers du Centre de recherche en civilisation canadienne-française n° 6, Université d'Ottawa, 1973, 618 p.

Wade, Mason. Les Canadiens français de 1760 à nos jours, Ottawa, Le Cercle du Livre de France, 1963, 685 p.

Winder, Gordon C. «Logan, William Emond». D.B.C., vol. 10 (1871–1880): 486–492.

B. SPECIFIC

Barbeau, Marius. The Kingdom of Saguenay, Toronto, The MacMillan Company of Canada, 1936, 167 p.

Barbeau, Marius. «Pile ou face pour une seigneurie», Le Canada français, vol. 27 n° 4 (décembre 1939): 294–308.

Barbeau, Marius. Le Saguenay légendaire, Montréal, Librairie Beauchemin, 1967, 147 p.

Barker, Burt Brown. The Dr John McLoughlin House, A National Historic Site, Oregon City, The McLoughlin Memorial Association, 1949, 44 p.

Barker, Burt Brown. The McLoughlin Empire and its Rulers, Glendale (California), The Arthur H. Clark Company, 1959, 370 p.

Boily, Raymond. Le Guide du voyageur à la Baie-Saint-Paul au XVIIIᵉ siècle, Montréal, Leméac, 1979, 133 p.

Boivin, Léonce. Dans nos montagnes (Charlevoix), Les Éboulements, s. éd., 1941, 254 p.

Bourassa, Marcel. «Le clocher du colombier est tombé mais on espère encore sauver le beau manoir Nairne», Le Soleil (12 mars 1960): 13, 20.

Brassard, François J. «Mémoires d'un vieillard», Archives de Folklore, vol. 4 (1949): 151–154.

Caron, Ivanohé. «Le Chemin des Caps», B.R.H., vol. 32 n° 1 (1926): 23–41.

Conan, Laure (pseud. of Félicité Angers). «Comment on voyageait de Québec à La Malbaie», Le Monde illustré, vol. 12 n° 593 (14 septembre 1895): 283.

Conan, Laure (pseud. of Félicité Angers). Philippe Gaultier de Comporté, premier seigneur de La Malbaie, Québec, L'Action Sociale Ltée, 1917, 13 p.

Cossette, Joseph. «Coquart, Claude-Godefroy», D.B.C., vol. 3 (1741–1770): 147, 148.

Culver, R.C. «Malbaie», The Murray Bay Habitant, vol. 1 n° 3 (1907): 3.

Decelles, A.D. «Histoire d'une paroisse canadienne par M. le professeur Wrong», La Presse (31 octobre 1908): 30.

Desloges, Yvon. «Fraser, Malcolm», D.B.C., vol. 5 (1801–1820): 362, 363.

Fraser, Charles Ian. The Clan Fraser of Lovat, Edinburgh and London, Johnston & Bacon Publishers, 1952, 32 p.

Frenette, Chanoine F. X.-Eug. Une enfant volée à La Malbaie en 1849, Chicoutimi, s. éd., 1951 (2ᵉ éd.), 11 p.

Frenette, Chanoine F. X.-Eug. Notes historiques sur la paroisse St-Étienne de La Malbaie (Charlevoix), Chicoutimi, Médéric Parent, 1952, 94 p.

Galloway, Strome. «Death of a Family — The End of the Nairnes of Murray's Bay», Families, vol. 19 n° 2 (1980): 66–77.

Gauldrée-Boilleau, Charles-Henri-Philippe. «Paysan de St-Irénée» [d'après les renseignements recueillis sur les lieux en 1861 et 1862], Les ouvriers des deux mondes, tome 5 n° 39 (1875): 51–108.

Gérin, Léon. Le type économique et social des Canadiens, milieux agricoles de tradition française, Montréal, Éditions de l'ACF, 1938, 218 p.

Hamelin, Jean. «Bourdon, Jean», D.B.C., vol. 1 (1000–1700): 115–117.

Harper, Col. J. Ralph. The Fighting Frasers in Canada. A Short History of the Old 78th Regiment of Fraser's Highlanders 1757–1763, Montréal, DEV-SCO Publications Ltd. 1966, 98 p.

Harper, Col. J. Ralph. «Notre vieux tartan du 78e, l'avons-nous retrouvé?», Bulletin du Musée militaire et maritime de Montréal, vol. 1 n° 4 (mai 1976): 1, 2.

Harper, Col. J. Ralph. The Fraser Highlanders, Montréal, La Société du Musée militaire et maritime de Montréal, 1979, 203 p.

Knott, Leonard L. «An Ancient Seigneury at Murray Bay», Canadian Homes and Gardens, vol. 9 n° 4 (1932): 19, 40, 42.

Knott, Leonard L. «The Old Seigneury at Murray Bay», Canadian Homes and Gardens, vol. 12 n°s 6–7 (1935): 27.

Langton, H.H. «A Canadian Manor and its Seigneurs», The Canadian Historical Review, vol. 7 (1926): 336, 337.

Latulippe, Lucien. «Une allumette dans un cendrier aurait mis le feu au manoir Mont-Murray», Le Soleil, (10 juin 1975): A-16.

Legendre, J.-Thérèse. «150 ans d'histoire s'envole en fumée avec l'incendie du manoir Mont-Murray», Le Soleil (9 juin 1975): A-16.

Lemoine, James Macpherson. «Fraser's Highlanders», Morning Chronicle (17 October 1867): 1.

Lemoine, James Macpherson. The Scot in New France: an Ethnological Study, Montréal, Dawson, Bros., 1881, 83 p.

Lemoine, James Macpherson. Monographies

et esquisses, s. l., s. éd., 1885, 478 p.

Lemoine, Roger. La Malbaie, esquisse historique, La Malbaie, [Imprimerie de Charlevoix], 1972, 12 p.

Lighthall, W.D. «English Settlement in Quebec», tiré de Shortt, Adam et Arthur G. Doughty, Canada and its Provinces. A History of the Canadian People and Their Institutions by One Hundred Associates, Toronto, Glasgow, Brook and Co., vol. 15 (1914): 121–164.

Lizotte, Louis-Philippe. La vieille Rivière-du-Loup, ses vieilles gens, ses vieilles choses, (1673–1916), Québec, Éditions Garneau, 1967, 175 p.

Macmillan, Helen. John Nairne, s. l., [manuscript kindly loaned by the author], (circa 1978), 184 p.

Massicotte, É.-Z. «Deux personnages du comté de Terrebonne», B.R.H., vol. 38 n° 11 (1932): 703, 704.

Monet, J. «Gaultier De Comporté, Philippe», D.B.C., vol. 1 (1000–1700): 335.

Munro, William Bennett. «A Canadian Manor and its Seigneurs», Review of Historical Publications Relating to Canada, vol. 13 (1908): 85, 86.

Nish, Cameron. «Cugnet, François-Étienne», D.B.C., vol. 3 (1741–1770): 162–165.

Roy, Jacqueline. «Nairne, John», D.B.C., vol. 5 (1801–1820): 683–685.

Roy, James. Lieutenant-General Simon Fraser, Son of Lord Lovat of the '45, Edinburg, [manuscript, originally from the Library of Scotland, loaned by the Musées nationaux du Canada], 111 p.

Roy, Pierre-Georges. «Saint-Étienne de la Malbaie», B.R.H., vol. 1 n° 1 (1895): 123, 124.

Roy, Pierre-Georges. «Les Postes du Roy», B.R.H., vol. 2 n° 12 (1896): 187, 188.

Roy, Pierre-Georges. «Prévot de la maréchaussée en la Nouvelle-France», B.R.H., vol. 7 n° 12 (1901): 368, 369.

Roy, Pierre-Georges. «Notes sur François Hazeur», B.R.H., vol. 32 n° 12 (1926): 705–711.

Roy, Pierre-Georges. «Les concessions en fief et seigneurie sous le Régime anglais», B.R.H., vol. 34 n° 6 (1928): 321, 322.

Roy, Pierre-Georges. «La famille Gaultier de Comporté», B.R.H., vol. 40 n° 6 (1934): 321–352.

Roy, Pierre-Georges. «La famille Hazeur», *B.R.H.*, vol. 41 nº 6 (1935): 321–349.

Simard, Hidalla. «Les seigneuries du district de Saguenay», *Le Progrès du Saguenay*, vol. 30 nº 49 (8 juin 1916): 3; vol. 30 nº 51 (22 juin 1916): 3; vol. 31 nº 2 (13 juillet 1916): 9, 10.

Sulte, Benjamin. «Les Écossais au Canada», *La Revue des deux Frances*, vol. 2 nº 11 (août 1898): 119–121.

Therrien, Armand. «Regard sur le passé de Charlevoix», *Le Confident de la rive nord,* vol. 5 nº 16 (19 août 1964): 6; vol. 5 nº 17 (2 septembre 1964): 5; vol. 5 nº 19 (7 octobre 1964): 22; vol. 5 nº 20 (21 octobre 1964): 15; vol. 5 nº 21 (4 novembre 1964): 6, 7; vol. 5 nº 22 (18 novembre 1964): 14; vol. 5 nº 24 (16 décembre 1964): 7.

Tremblay, Victor. ‹Laure, Pierre-Michel›, *D.B.C.*, vol. 2 (1701–1740): 372–374.

Wallace, W.S. «Notes on the Family of Malcolm Fraser of Murray Bay», *B.R.H.*, vol. 39 nº 5 (1933): 267–271; vol. 39 nº 6 (1933): 349, 350.

Wallace, W.S. «Some Notes of Fraser's Highlanders», *Canadian Historical Review*, vol. 18 nº 2 (1937): 131–140.

Wallace, W.S. «The Footprints of Fraser's Highlanders on the Sands of Time», *Culture*, vol. 9 nº 1 (March 1948): 29–31.

Wrong, George MacKinnon. *A Canadian Manor and its Seigneurs*, Toronto, The MacMillan Co., 1908, 295 p.

Yeigh, Frank. «Two Fine Historic Quebec manor Houses», *The Globe*, [Toronto], (6 September 1911): 6.

Zoltvany, Yves F. «Hazeur, François», *D.B.C.*, vol. 2 (1700–1740): 285–287.

Anonymous. «Le colonel Malcolm Fraser», *B.R.H.*, vol. 46 nº 10 (1940): 306.

Anonymous. «Les seigneuries de Jean Bourdon», *B.R.H.*, vol. 42 nº 6 (1936): 336–338.

Anonymous. «Lettre(s) de Josette (Josephte) Murray à Malcolm Fraser», *B.R.H.*, vol. 45 nº 1 (1939): 27, 29, 29.

Anonymous. «Lieu de sépulture de Malcolm Fraser», *B.R.H.*, vol. 60 nº 1 (1954): 45.

Anonymous. «The Journal of Sergeant James Thompson 1758–1830», *T.L.H.S*, nº 22 (1898): 53–56.

Anonymous. «Vieux manoir de La Malbaie, bientôt démoli pour faire place à une maison privée», *Le Soleil* (9 mars 1960): 24.

HOLIDAYS

In this second part of the bibliography, the section on primary sources includes a series of memoirs and journals which I have listed, as in the first part, in chronological order according to the date of the visit or, when that was unavailable, by edition. This body of recollections, which often haunt the gardens of literature, forms the warp on which I have woven this work. In addition to these personal narratives I have listed travel books, including brochures, which, taken together, cover the period from 1853 to 1982. The local newspapers, which are intimately linked with the summer colonies and provide a record of daily activities, have allowed me to determine how frequently visitors came to Charlevoix. Interviews also provided important information on the history of the oldest families, several generations of which have spent their vacations at Murray Bay. Several films provided documentary evidence for my research. As well, a large number of short essays, listed under secondary sources, have helped me to see more clearly the elusive phenomenon of population movement. The general works have assisted my efforts at synthesis, as I wished to provide a global context, while the specific works have helped me to understand more clearly the multiple facets which make up the history of a summer colony.

I. Primary Sources

A. MANUSCRIPTS
1. Public Archives
a) Collections

C.H.A. Armstrong George M. Wrong. «Murray Bay Revisited», 1918, 32 p. Coll. Musée régional Laure-Conan (la Malbaie).

Brian Buchanan Harry Lorin Binsse. «The Lorne», s. d., 5 p. Coll. Musée régional Laure-Conan (La Malbaie).

Francis H. Cabot Claudie L. W. Walker. «Bonner Family History», 1937–1938, 80 p. Coll. Musée régional Laure-Conan (La Malbaie).

Canada Steamship Lines General archives of the Canada Steamship Lines from its beginning to the present. Coll. Le Groupe C.S.L. Inc. (Montréal). Management of the Canada Steamship Lines. Coll. Queen's University (Kingston).

John B. Dempsey John B. Dempsey II. «Memorandum», ‹Manoir Richelieu], 1982, 16 p. Coll. Musée régional Laure-Conan (La Malbaie).

Thomas C. Hoopes W.H. Blake. «Petit Lac Malbaie and Lac à Muraille or better Lac Emmuraillé», 1911–1923, 62 p. Coll. Musée régional Laure-Conan (La Malbaie).

John Nairne MG 23 G III, 23, vol. 5. Coll. Archives nationales du Canada (Ottawa).

Donald B. Mackay A.B. Mackay. «Fishing Records 1880–1894», 20 p. Coll. Musée régional Laure-Conan (La Malbaie).

Philip Mackenzie Famille Blake. «Diary Mille Roches 1884», 1884, 58 p.
   W.H. Blake. «Cooking Recipes», novembre 1913, 198 p.
   W.H. Blake. «His Book de Piscibus», s. d., 114 p.
   W.H. Blake. «Log of the Galliotte», 1879, 12 p.
   W.H. Blake. «The Anna of Quebec», s. d., 15 p.
   Coll. Musée régional Laure-Conan (La Malbaie).

Murray Bay Golf Club Management. Minutes and annual reports of the club from 1876 to the present. Coll. Murray Bay Golf Club (La Malbaie).

Sedgwick Correspondance, 1896–1900. Coll. Massachusetts Historical Society (Boston).

Lynn Stewart Manuscript and printed sources. Coll. Canadian Golf Museum and Historical Institute (Ottawa).

Taft Helen Taft Manning. «History of the Tafts in Murray Bay», 12 p. Coll. Musée régional Laure-Conan (La Malbaie).

b) Dossiers

Dossier 166 pièce 11 «Lettre manuscrite de Victor Tremblay à André Bouchard, Chicoutimi, le 5 décembre 1956». Coll. Société historique du Saguenay (Chicoutimi).

Dossier 624 pièce 13 «Le tour du Saguenay». Coll. Société historique du Saguenay (Chicoutimi).

2. Private Archives

Edward Francis Blake Coll. Elizabeth Bacque.
William Hume Blake Coll. Philip Mackenzie.
Harry L. Binsse Coll. Brian Buchanan.
Donald Guay Coll. Donald Guay.
Thomas C. Hoopes Coll. Thomas et Ann Hoopes.
George M. Wrong Coll. Mrs. C.H.A. Armstrong.
Minutes of Garden Club of Charlevoix Pointe-au-Pic, P.Q. (1949–1960), 46 p. Coll. Mme Jean De Roussel Warren.

B. MAPS AND PLANS

Baillargé, G.F. [*Charlevoix and Chicoutimi Counties Roads], Remarques au sujet des principales lignes de Chemins*, s. l., s. éd., 1982, s. éch. Coll. Archives nationales du Canada (Ottawa), H3 320.

Duberger, C.C. *Murray Bay Atlas and Maps of it's Environs*. Murray Bay, Alfred Cimon & Co., 1895. (12 cartes: 11 planches et 1 plan index). Échelle: 1″ = 600′-0″. Coll. Musée régional Laure-Conan (La Malbaie).

Duberger, J.B. *Plan Désignant le bornage du terrain de Dame Anne Atkinson, épouse de D.C. Thomson et situé à la Pte au Pic, exécuté pour accompagner le procès-verbal ci-annexé*, Murray Bay, s. éd., 1er septembre 1865. Échelle: 1″ = 120′-0″. Coll. Ministère Énergie et Ressources du Québec, Québec, M-10.

Du Tremblay, Pamphile P.V. *Plan officiel du village de la Pointe-au-Pic, comté de Charlevoix*, Saint-Anne-de-la-Pérade, Bureau du cadastre, 18 novembre 1877. Échelle: 1 arpent au pouce. Coll. Bureau d'enregistrement (La Malbaie).

Hall, W.C. *Parc national des Laurentides. (La rivière Malbaie et environs)*, Québec, s. éd., 22 octobre 1902. Échelle: 1″ = 40 chaines [ou ¹/₂ mille]. Coll. Archives nationales du Québec (Québec), D-310.

Roy, Ch.-F. *Cap-à-l'Aigle, P.Q., plan showing Soundings and Sections of Proposed Pier*, s. l., s. éd., 1880. Échelle: 1″ = 100′-0″. Coll. Archives nationales du Canada (Ottawa), H-11-340.

Trudeau, L.E. *Cap-à-l'Aigle, Charlevoix County, P.Q.*, s. l., Public Works of Canada [projet du quai de Cap-à-'Aigle], 1874. Échelle: 1″ = 5500′-0″. Coll. Archives nationales du Canada (Ottawa), F-340.

Warren, Hector. *Plan montrant les propriétés acquises par madame Jean Warren née Eliza-beth Duchesne, par ses fils Hector, Lucien, Eugène et Jules, propriétés situées dans le village de Pointe-au-Pic, Québec*. Pointe-au-Pic, s. éd., 20 décembre 1932. Échelle: 1″ = 50′-0″. Coll. Archives nationales du Canada (Ottawa), RG-11M 77803/22, 351.

Anonymous. [*Charlevoix*], s. l., s. éd., 1850. Échelle: 1″ = 18 milles. Coll. Archives nationales du Canada (Ottawa), H12 320.

Anonymous. *Chasse et pêche de Baie St-Paul à Saint-Siméon*, s. l., s. éd., s. d. Échelle: 1″ = 1 mille. Coll. Archives nationales du Québec (Québec), D-320.

Anonymous. *Insurance Plan of the Towns of St. Etienne de La Malbaie and Pointe-au-Pic, P.Q.*, La Malbaie, Underwriter's Survey Bureau Ltd., 1953. (18 cartes). Échelle: 1″ = 1000′-0″. Coll. Archives nationales du Canada (Ottawa), 1P PA-340.

Anonymous. *Landing Pier, Murray Bay. Grande-Débarquement Point-au-Pic*, s. l. Office of Public Works of Quebec, 1852. Échelle: 1″ = 20′-0″. Coll. Archives nationales du Québec (Québec), C-335.

Anonymous. *Plan détaillé démontrant une partie du village de Pointe-au-Pic, à partir du Couvent (Commission scolaire) jusqu'à la route de Terrebonne (chemin de Québec)*, s. l., s. éd., 1937. Échelle: 1″ = 50′-0″. Coll. Archives nationales du Canada (Ottawa), RG-11M-77803/22, 355.

Anonymous. *Plan officiel de la paroisse de La Malbaie, Comté de Charlevoix (Première division d'enregistrement de Charlevoix)*. Sainte-Anne-de-la-Pérade. Bureau du cadastre, 18 novembre 1877. Échelle: 5 arpents au pouce. Coll. Bureau d'enregistrement (La Malbaie).

Anonymous. *Pointe-au-Pic—Qué.*, s. l., s. éd., [vers 1920], s. éch. Coll. Archives nationales du Canada (Ottawa) RG-11M-77803/22, 330.

Anonymous. *Pointe-au-Pic (Murray Bay)*, s. l., s. éd., s. d. Échelle: 1″ = 100′-0″. Coll. Archives nationales du Canada (Ottawa), F-340.

Anonymous. *St. Paul's Bay, Éboulements, St.*

Irénée, Murray Bay, Charlevoix, Co., P.Q., s. l., Public Works of Canada, 1880. Échelle: 1″ = 5400′-0″. Coll. Archives nationales du Canada (Ottawa), F-320.

C. AUDIOVISUAL MATERIALS

1. Interviews

Bancroft, Sydney Cap-à-l'Aigle, 1981, 30 min. Coll. Musée régional Laure-Conan (La Malbaie).

Boosey, Margaret Cap-à-l'Aigle, 1980, 30 min. Coll. Musée régional Laure-Conan (La Malbaie).

Campbell-Robertson, Joan Cap-à-l'Aigle, s. d., 90 min. Coll. Musée régional Laure-Conan (La Malbaie).

Kyle, George A. Cap-à-l'Aigle, 1980, 30 min. Coll. Musée régional Laure-Conan (La Malbaie).

Mackay, Donald B. Cap-à-l'Aigle (Mount Murray), 1980, 30 min. Coll. Musée régional Laure-Conan (La Malbaie).

Naylor, Mary B. Cap-à-l'Aigle, 1980, 30 min. Coll. Musée régional Laure-Conan (La Malbaie).

Robb, Philip H. Cap-à-l'Aigle, 1980, 30 min. Coll. Musée régional Laure-Conan (La Malbaie).

Sévigny-Giguère, Madeleine. Québec, 1982, 90 min. Coll. Musée régional Laure-Conan (La Malbaie).

2. Records

Choquette, Michel. *Sur la côte, sur la côte, Songs of Murray Bay*. 33 tours, Montréal, 21 novembre 1959. Coll. Mr and Mrs F. Victor Elkin.

3. Films

70th Birthday Celebration of William H. Taft, Murray Bay in 1927, 1927, 25 min, 16 mm, noir et blanc. Copie d'un film de la famille Taft. Coll. Musée régional Laure-Conan (La Malbaie).

Charlevoix, 1966, 14 min, 16 mm, couleur. Office national du film. Coll. Archives nationales du Canada (Ottawa).

Charlevoix, pays du huitème jour, 1980, 58 min, 16 mm, couleur. Imagidée. Réalisé par Richard Geoffrion. Coll. Archives nationales du Canada (Ottawa).

Les jardins de La Malbaie, 1981, 20 min. super 8 mm, couleur. Réalisé par Denison Hatch (Standford, Conn.). Coll. Mr and Mrs Francis H. Cabot.

Murray Bay, 1928, 625 pieds, 35 mm, noir et blanc. Associated Screen News. Coll. Archives nationales du Canada (Ottawa), ANF 75 12 72 à 74.

Murray Bay, Pointe-au-Pic, P.Q., 1928–1960, 1 200 pieds, 35 mm, noir et blanc et couleur. Collage de plusieurs films sur la famille Dempsey en vacances dans Charlevoix. Coll. Mr and Mrs John B. Dempsey II.

Richelieu Canada, 1925, 80 min, 35 mm, noir et blanc. Coll. Archives nationales du Canada (Ottawa), 2190, 2191, 2192.

Tadoussac, 1928, 6 min 11 s, 35 mm, noir et blanc. Associated Screen News. Coll. Archives nationales du Canada (Ottawa), ANF 7908 664.

D. PUBLISHED MATERIALS

1. Reference

Armstrong, G.H. *The Origin and Meaning of Place Names in Canada*, Toronto. The MacMillan Company of Canada Limited at St. Martin's House, 1930, 312 p.

Beaulieu, André et Jean Hamelin. *Les journaux du Québec de 1764 à 1964*, Québec, Les Presses de l'Université Laval, 1965, 329 p.

Canada (Gouv.) *Liste des navires publiée par le ministère de la Marine et des Pêcheries ou liste des navires inscrits sur les registres maritimes du Canada au 31 décembre 1929*, Ottawa, Imprimeur de la Reine, 1930, 155 p.

Deschamps, C.E. *Liste des municipalités dans la province de Québec*, Lévis, Mercier et Cie éditeurs, 1866, 816 p.

Godenrath, Percy F. *Catalogue of the Manoir Richelieu Collection of Canadiana*, [Montréal], Canada Steamship Lines, 1930, 73 p.

Godenrath, Percy F. *Supplementary Catalogue of the Manoir Richelieu, Murray Bay, P.Q., Historical Collection of Canadiana*,

[Montréal], Canada Steamship Lines, 1931, 13 p.

Godenrath, Percy F. *Supplementary Catalogue and an Abridged Index of the Manoir Richelieu, Murray Bay, P.Q., Historical Collection of Canadiana*, [Montréal], Canada Steamship Lines, 1939, 46 p.

Guay, Donald. *Bibliographie québécoise sur l'activité physique (1850–1973)*, Québec, Éditions du Pélican, 1974, 316 p.

Hamelin, Jean et coll. *Brochures québécoises*, Québec, Ministère des Communications du Québec, 1981, 598 p.

Hudon, M.P. *Catalogue de la Bibliothèque paroissiale de La Malbaie*, Québec, Imp. La Libre Parole, 1910, 47 p.

Irwin, W.H. *Directory of the City of Quebec, Levis, St. Sauveur, Three Rivers, Sorel, Berthier, Rimouski, Fraserville, St. Anne's La Pocatière, Montmagny, Murray Bay, etc. etc. for 1875–76*, Québec, W.H. Irwin and Co., 1875, 383 p.

Mackay, Robert W.S. *The Canada Directory Containing the Names of the Professional and Business Men of Every Description in the Cities, Towns. . .*, Montréal, John Lovell, 1851, 692 p.

Mills, John M. *Canadian Coastal and Inland Steam Vessels, 1809–1930*, Providence, The Steamship Historical Society of America, 1979, 135 p.

Piché, Odessa. *Index des municipalités et paroisses de la province de Québec de 1896 à 1924*, Québec, Ministère de la Colonisation, des Mines et des Pêcheries, 1924, 498 p.

Québec (Gouv.) *Inventaire des ressources naturelles et industrielles. Comté municipal de Charlevoix*, Québec, Office de recherches économiques du ministère de l'Industrie et du Commerce, 1942, 233 p.

Rose, George MacLean. *A Cyclopedia of Canadian Biography, Being Chiefly Men of the Time*, Toronto, Rose, 1886–1888, 2 vol.

Rouillard, Eugène. *Dictionnaire des rivières et des lacs de la Province de Québec*, Québec, Département des Terres et Forêts, 1914, 432 p.

Roy, Pierre-Georges. *Les juges de la province de Québec*, Québec, Imprimeur de Sa Majesté le Roi, 1933, 588 p.

Wood, Col. William et coll. *The Storied Province of Quebec Past and Present*, Toronto, The Dominion Publishing Co., 1931, 5 vol.

Anonymous. *The British American Guide-Book: Being a Condensed Gazetteer, Directory and Guide to Canada, the Western States and Principal Cities on the Seaboard*, New York, H. Bailliere, 1859, 4 vol.

Anonymous. *The Canada Directory for 1857–58: Containing Names of Professional and Businessmen, and of Principal Inhabitants in the Cities, Towns and Villages. . .*, Montréal, John Lovell, 1858, 1 544 p.

Anonymous. *Catalogue of the First Annual Exhibition of Canadian Arts, Manoir Richelieu, Murray Bay, Qué.*, Montréal, Canada Steamship Lines, 1930, 24 p.

Anonymous. *Consolidation of the Act of Incorporation of 1857 with the Amendments Thereof up to 1899 of the Richelieu and Ontario Navigation Co.*, Montréal, C.O. Beauchemin, 1899, 24 p.

Anonymous. *Lovell's Business and Professional Directory of the Province of Quebec for 1890–91. . .*, Montréal, John Lovell and Son, 1890, 1 032 p.

Anonymous. *Lovell's Business, Professional Directory of the Province of Quebec for 1902–03. . .*, Montréal, John Lovell and Son, 1902, 1 362 p.

Anonymous. *Lovell's Canadian Dominion Directory for 1871: Containing Names of Professional and Business Men and Other Inhabitants, in the Cities, Towns and Villages. . .*, Montréal, John Lovell, 1871, 2 563 p.

Anonymous. *Manoir Richelieu Collection of Canadiana, Murray Bay, Quebec, Pictorial History of The «Siège of Quebec» 1759 (located in the Murray Room Main Lobby)*, [Montréal], Canada Steamship Lines, s. d., 39 p.

2. Periodicals

Annual Report of Cap-à-l'Aigle Church Season 1889 and Season 1892. Coll. Musée régional Laure-Conan (La Malbaie).

Annual Report of the Convalescent Home, Murray Bay From the first issue in 1874 up to the forty-eighth in 1922. Complete series. Coll. McGill University (Montreal).

By-Water Magazine Vol. 1 n° 1 (March 1916) to vol. 4 n° 2 (April 1919). Coll. Canada Steamship Lines (Montréal).

C.S.L. Chart Publié par Canada Steamship Lines Ltd (Montréal). Vol. 1 n° 1 (2 mai 1927) à vol. 3 n° 12 (avril-mai 1930). Coll. Musée régional Laure-Conan (La Malbaie).

Le Canadien Vol. 43 n° 41 (11 juillet 1873) à vol. 54 n° 56 (9 août 1884). Between these dates, summer editions of this tri-weekly Québec publication contained notices advertising excursions to Malbaie.

L'Écho des Laurentides Weekly newspaper published in La Malbaie. Vol. 1, no. 1 (13 juin 1884) to vol. 4, no. 20 (27 octobre 1887). Coll. Musée régional Laure-Conan (La Malbaie).

The Manoir and Colony Life Magazines Vol. 1 n° 1 (1953) à vol. 15 n° 1 (1966). Complete series. Coll. Musée régional Laure-Conan (La Malbaie). Gift of Mr and Mrs John B. Dempsey II.

The Murray Bay Habitant Vol. 1 n° 1 (July 1907) to vol. 14 n° 2 (August 1922). Coll. Musée régional Laure-Conan (La Malbaie).

Le Touriste A bilingual journal, published in July and August from 1885 to 1887. To my knowledge, only a single copy of the first edition still exists — vol. 1, no. 1 (23 juillet 1885): 4 pp. Archives nationales du Canada (Ottawa).

3. Guidebooks

1853 Beckett, Sylvester B. *Guide Book of the Atlantic and St. Lawrence, and St. Lawrence and Atlantic Rail Roads. . . ,* Portland, Sanborn & Carter and H.J. Little & Co., 1853, 180 p.

1856 Anonymous. *The Canadian Tourist,* Montréal, New Ramsay, 1856, 211 p.

1856 J.M.G. *Excursions to Murray Bay, River du Loup, Kakouna and the Far-Famed River Saguenay, with Map on the Route,* Québec, Middleton and Dawson, 1856, 25 p.

1857 Hunter, William S. *Hunter's Panoramic Guide from Niagara Falls to Quebec,* Boston, John P. Jewett and Co. and Cleveland (Ohio), Henry P. Jewett, 1857, 66 p.

1857 Norman, W. *The Quebec Guide, Being a Concise Account of All the Places of Interest in and About the City and Country Adjacent,* Point-Levi, Victoria Hotel, 1857, 48 p.

1857 Anonymous. *A trip Through the Lakes of North America; Embracing a Full Description of the St. Lawrence River, Together with All the Principal Places on its Banks. . . ,* New York, John Disturnell, 1857, 366 p.

1858 Anonymous. *Panorama of the River St. Lawrence Being an Illustrated and Descriptive Guide From Niagara to Quebec,* New York, Alex Harthill and Co., 1858, 70 p.

1862 Cary, George T. *The Lower St. Lawrence or Quebec to Halifax via Gaspe and Pictou. . . ,* Québec, Mercury Office, 1862, 122 p.

1862 Kelso, Samuel J. *Notes of the Saguenay for Tourists and Others,* Québec, At the Office of the «Morning Chronicle», 1862, 31 p.

1864 Disturnell, John. *The Traveler's Guide to the Hudson River, Saratoga Springs, Lake George, Falls of Niagara and Thousand Islands: Montreal, Quebec, and the Saguenay River. . . ,* New York, American News Co., 1864, 324 p.

1864 O'Brien Godfrey S. *The Tourist's Guide to Quebec,* Québec, Hunter, Rose and Co., 1864, 70 p.

1867 Small, Henry Beaumont. *The Canadian Handbook and Tourist's Guide. . . ,* Montréal, M. Longmoore and Co., 1867, 196 p.

1867 Roger, Chas (pseud. of Willis Russell) *Quebec: As it was, and as it is, or a brief History of the Oldest City in Canada. . . ,* Québec, L'Auteur, 1867, 138 p.

1869 Anonymous. *The All-Round Route Guide,* Montréal, Montreal Printing and Publishing Co., 1869, 86 p.

1870 Lemoine, James Macpherson. *The Tourist's Note-Book for Quebec, Cacouna, Saguenay River and the Lower St. Lawrence. . . ,* Québec, Middleton & Dawson, 1870, 28 p.

1870 Anonymous. *Chisholm's All Round and Panoramic Guide of the St. Lawrence. . . ,* Montréal, Chisholm & Co., 1870, 126 p.

Circa 1870 Anonymous. *Holiwell's New Guide to the City of Quebec and Environs with two New Maps of the City and District,* Québec, C.E. Holiwell, s. d., 117 p.

1872 Anderson, Dr. W.J. *The Lower St. Lawrence its Scenery, Navigation and Complete Tourist's Guide,* Québec, At the Office of the «Morning Chronicle», 1872, 49 p.

1872 Cary, George T.. *The Lower St. Lawrence or Quebec to Halifax via Gaspe and Pictou. . .*, Québec, Mercury, 1872, 143 p.

1872 Saint-Maurice, J. Faucher de. *Quebec and Montreal Travellers Free Guide. . .*, Montréal, Eusèbe Sénécal, 1872, 128 p.

1872 Pecher, J.E. *Flood's Guide Book of the Ottawa, St. Lawrence and Saguenay Rivers, also Montreal and Quebec*, Montréal, John Lovell, 1872, 48 p.

1873 Anonymous. *Chisholm's All Round Route and Panoramic Guide of the St. Lawrence. . .*, Montréal, Chisholm & Co., 1873, 146 p.

1874 Burt, Henry M. *Burt's Guide Through the Connecticut Valley to the White Mountains and the River Saguenay*, Springfield (Mass.), New England Publishing Co., 1874, 298 p.

1874 Anonymous. *Chisholm's All Round Route and Panoramic Guide of the St. Lawrence. . .*, Montréal, C.R. Chisholm and Co., 1874, 176 p.

1874 Anonymous. *Keyes' Hand-Book of Northern Pleasure Travel: to the White and Franconia Mountains, The Northern Lakes and Rivers, Montreal, Quebec and the St. Lawrence and Saguenay Rivers*, Boston, Geo. L. Keyes, 1874, 240 p.

1874 Anonymous. *The Hotel Guests' Guide for the City of Monteal 1874*, Montréal, The Railway and Newspaper Adversing Co. Ltd., 1874, 89 p.

1874 Anonymous. *The St. Lawrence Hall Guide from Niagara Falls to the Saguenay*, Montréal, F. Geriken, 1874, 64 p.

1875 [Langelier, J.C.]. *The Quebec and Lower St. Lawrence Tourist's Guide*, Québec, A. Côté & Co., 1875, 169 p.

1875 Sweetser, M.F. *The Maritimes Provinces: a Handbook for Travellers*, Boston, James R. Osgood and Co., 1875, 336 p.

1875 Anonymous. *The Montreal House Guide from Niagara Falls to the Saguenay*, Montréal, Decker, Stearns & Murray, 1875, 64 p.

Circa 1875 An Eminent Historian [J.M. Lemoine] *Guide to Historic Quebec and its Principal Business Houses*, s. i., s. éd., s. d., non paginé.

Circa 1875 Anonymous. *The St. Lawrence River and Tourist Guide from Niagara to the Saguenay*, Montréal, Mutual News Co. Ltd. s. d., 132 p.

1876 Anonymous. *Dominion of Canada Route Book. . .*, Montréal, W.H. Tapson & Co., 1876, 64 p.

1876 Anonymous. *Snow's Handbook of Northern Pleasure Travel to the White and Franconia Mountains, the Northern Lakes and Rivers, Montreal and Quebec, and the St. Lawrence and Saguenay Rivers. . .*, Worcester, Noyes & Snow, 1876, 256 p.

1879 Oliver, Thomas J. *Guide to Quebec City and Localities in Connection with it*, Montréal, Witness Establishment, 1879, 78 p.

1879 Anonymous. *Phelan Bros. St. Lawrence Traveller a Complete Hand Book and Guide to Northern Summer Resorts. . .*, Montréal, Phelan Bros., 1879, 152 p.

1879 Anonymous. *St. Lawrence Hall Tourists Guide*, Montréal, T.E. Foster, 1879, 120 p.

1880 Anonymous. *Chisholm's All-Round Route and Panoramic Guide of the St. Lawrence. . .*, Montréal, C.R. Chisholm & Co., 1880, 556 p.

1881 Anonymous. *Appleton's General Guide to the United States and Canada with Railway Maps, plans of Cities, and illustrations, Part I, New England and Middle States and Canada*, New York, D. Appleton and Company, 1881, 271 p.

1881 Anonymous. *Chisholm's All-Round Route and Panoramic Guide to St. Lawrence River and Western Tourist's Guide*, Montréal, C.R. Chisholm and Co., 1881, 458 p.

1882 Anonymous. *Guide to Quebec and the Lower St. Lawrence*, Québec, s. éd., 1882, 178 p.

1883 Anonymous. *All-Round Route and Panoramic Guide of the St. Lawrence. . .*, Montréal, Canada Railway News Co., 1883, 400 p.

1883 Anonymous. *Pleasant Places by the Shore and in the Forests of Quebec and the Maritime Provinces, via the Intercolonial Railway*, Toronto, A.H. Dixon, 1883, 65 p.

1884 Dawson, S.E. *Hand-Book for the Dominion of Canada. . .*, Montréal, Dawson Brothers, 1884, 335 p.

1887 Anonymous. *The Maritime Provinces: a Hand Book for Travellers*, Boston, Ticknor and Company, 1887, 336 p.

1891 Roberts, Charles G.D. *The Canadian Guide-Book. The Tourist's and Sportsman's Guide to Eastern Canada and Newfoundland,*

New York, D. Appleton and Co., 1891, 270 p.

1892 Anonymous. *Guide to Historic Quebec and Lower St. Lawrence*, Québec, H.H. Wright, 1892, 138 p.

1894 Baedeker, Karl. *The Dominion of Canada with Newfoundland and an Excursion to Alaska. Handbook for Travellers*, Leipzig, L'Auteur, 1894, 254 p.

1894 Taintor, Charles Newhall. *The Hudson River Route. New York to West Point, Catskill Mountains, Albany, Saratoga Springs, Lake George...*, New York, Taintor Brothers, 1894, 118 p.

1895 Anonymous. *Pen and Sunlight Sketches of Scenery Reached by the Grand Trunk Railway and Connections...*, s. 1., The Grand Trunk Railway Co., 1895, 112 p.

1895 Anonymous. *The Beauty Spots of Canada — From Niagara to the Sea*, Montréal, Richelieu and Ontario Navigation Co., 1895, 156 p.

1896 Canada (Gouv.). *A Souvenir for Tourists, Sportsmen and Invalids, a Souvenir of the Intercolonial Railway, the Popular and Scenic Route of Canada*, Ottawa, Government Printing Bureau, 1896, 85 p.

1896 Chambers, E.T.D. *The Guide to Quebec*, Québec, Quebec Morning Chronicle, 1896, 129 p.

1896 Phelan, F.E. *All-Round Route and Panoramic Guide of the St. Lawrence...*, Montréal, International Railway Publishing Co., Ltd. 1896, 308 p.

1896 Anonymous. *From Niagara to the Sea*, Montréal, Richelieu and Ontario Navigation Co., 1896, 176 p.

1897 Roberts, Charles G.D. *The Canadian Guide-Book Complete in one Volume. A Guide to Eastern Canada and Newfoundland...*, New York, D. Appleton and Co., 1897, 327 p.

1900 Baedeker, Karl. *Baedeker's Canada*, Leipzig, L'Auteur, 1900, 268 p.

Circa 1900 Anonymous. *Souvenir of Quebec, the Lower St. Lawrence, The Saguenay River, Roberval and Lake St. John*, Grand Rapids (Mich.), The James Bayne Co., s. d., non paginé.

1901 to 1914 Anonymous. *From Niagara to the Sea*, Montréal, Richelieu & Ontario Navigation Co., 1901, 1902, 1903, 1904, 1905, 1906, 1907, 1908, 1909, 1910, 1911, 1912, 1913, 1914, 146 p.

1903 Anonymous. *Tours to Summer Haunts*, Montréal, The Intercolonial Railway Co., 1903, 93 p.

1904 Bryce, P.H. *Climates and Health Resorts of Canada*, Montréal, Canadian Pacific Railway Co., 1904, 48 p.

1905 Anonymous. *Forest, Stream and Seashore*, Montréal, Intercolonial Railway Co. and Prince Edward Island Railway of Canada, 1905, 184 p.

Circa 1905 Anonymous. *The Lower St. Lawrence and the Saguenay*, Montréal, Richelieu and Ontario Nav. Co., s. d., n.p., [10 p.].

Circa 1908 Anonymous. *The Manoir Richelieu, Murray Bay, P.Q., cottages and golf course*, s. 1., Manoir Richelieu, s. d., 15 p.

Circa 1908 Anonymous. *The Manoir Richelieu and Cottages*, s. 1., s. éd., s. d., 16 p.

Circa 1910 Anonymous. *Souvenir of Lake St. John and Saguenay River*, Grand Rapids (Mich.), The James Bayne Co., s. d., n.p.

Circa 1912 Anonymous. *Guide and View Book of Murray Bay and Pointe-au-Pic*, Québec, Frank Carrel, s. d., 33 p.

1913 Callender, Romaine. *Summer Provinces by the Sea...*, Moncton (N.-B.), Intercolonial Railway of Canada, 1913, 310 p.

1914 Anonymous. *Niagara to the Sea*. Montréal, Canada Steamship Lines Ltd., 1914, 144 p.

1915 Agassiz, Garnault. *Niagara to the Sea*, Montréal, Canada Steamship Lines Ltd., 1915, 132 p.

1916 Anonymous. *All-Round Route and Panoramic Guide of the St. Lawrence...*, Montréal, Intercolonial Railway Publishing Co., 1916, 323 p.

1919 Anonymous. *Guide to the City of Quebec descriptive and illustrated with map...*, Québec, Frank Carrel, 1919, 212 p.

Circa 1920 Agassiz, Garnault. *Lake Superior to the Sea...*, Montréal, Canada Steamship Lines Ltd., s. d., 96 p.

1926 Québec (Gouv.). *Quebec, the French-Canadian Province. A Harmony of Beauty, History and Progress,* Québec, Ministère de la Voirie (Bureau provincial du tourisme), 1926, 87 p.

1929 Québec (Gouv.). *Sur les routes de Québec, guide du touriste*, Québec, Ministère de la Voirie et des Mines (Bureau provincial du tourisme), 1929, 874 p.

1929 Québec (Gouv.). *4, 5 and 6 Days in Quebec, Canada*, Québec Ministère de la Voirie (Bureau provincial du tourisme), 1929, 63 p.

1932 Anonymous. *Niagara to the Sea, The Finest Trip on the Finest Steamer on Inland Waters*, s. 1., Canada Steamship Lines, 1932, 38 p.

1932 Québec (Gouv.). *Quebec Ready Reference*, Toronto, Central Bureau in Canada, 1932, 73 p.

1934 Anonymous. *The Manoir Richelieu at Murray Bay, Canada*, Montréal, Canada Steamship Lines, 1934, 16 p.

1934 Anonymous. *Murray Bay and Vicinity, guide touristique de Charlevoix-Est*, s. 1., s. éd., 1934, 48 p.

1935 Anonymous. *Murray Bay and Vicinity, guide touristique de Charlevoix-Est*, s. 1., s. éd., 1935, 32 p.

1936 Québec (Gouv.). *Charlevoix, Chicoutimi, Lake St. Jean*, Québec, Bureau provincial du tourisme, 1936, 24 p.

1940 Québec (Gouv.). *Hunting and Fishing in La Province de Québec*, Québec, Bureau provincial du tourisme, 1940 (6ᵉ éd.), 65 p.

1948 Steel, Bryon. *Let's Visit Canada*, New York, Robert M. McBride and Co., 1948, 496 p.

1955 Québec (Gouv.). *Province de Québec «Paradis du Touriste»*, Montréal, Société nouvelle de publicité incorporée, 1955 (2ᵉ éd.), 735 p.

1955 Anonymous. *The Nagel Travel Guide Series Canada*, Genève, Nagel Pub., 1955, 485 p.

1960 Binsse, Harry Lorin. *Holiday in Canada, province of Quebec*, Montréal, Travel Publications Limited, 1960, 199 p.

1967 Québec (Gouv.). *Côte de Beaupré, Charlevoix, Côte Nord (route 15)*, Québec, Ministère du Tourisme, de la Chasse et de la Pêche, 1967, 56 p.

1971 Québec (Gouv.). *Beaupré, Charlevoix, Côte Nord*, Québec, Ministère du Tourisme, de la Chasse et de la Pêche, 1971, 71 p.

1982 Guetta, Pauline. *Inns and Manoirs of Quebec*, Ottawa, Denson, s.d., 241 p.

4. Memoirs and Narratives*

1854 Lanman, Charles. *Adventures in the Wild of the North America*, London, Longman, Brown, Green and Longmans, 1854, 300 p.

1856 Sangster, Charles. *The St. Lawrence and the Saguenay and other Poems*, Kingston, John Creighton and John Duff, 1856, 262 p.

1857 Trudelle, abbé [Charles]. *Trois souvenirs*, Québec, Imprimerie de Léger Brousseau, 1878, 172 p.

1859 Anonymous. «The Saguenay», *Harper's New Montly Magazine*, vol. 19 nᵒ 110 (July 1859): 145–160.

1868 Gérard, A.G. *Itinéraire de Québec à Chicago*, Montréal, C.O. Beauchemin et Valois, 1868, 178 p.

1870 David, Laurent-Olivier. «Murray Bay, 19 juillet 1870», *L'Opinion publique*, vol. 1 nᵒ 30 (28 juillet 1870): 239; «Murray Bay, 28 juillet 1870», vol. 1 nᵒ 31 (4 août 1870): 246; «Correspondance, Malbaie août 1870», vol. 1 nᵒ 32 (11 août 1870): 250, 251.

1870 David, Laurent-Olivier. *Mélanges historiques et littéraires*, Montréal, Librairie Beauchemin Ltée, 1917, 338 p.

1870–1871 Buckley, Rev. M.B. *Diary of a Tour in America. A Special Missionnary in North America and Canada in 1870 and 1871*, Dublin, Sealy, Bryers & Walker, 1886, 384 p.

1871 Buies, Arthur. *Chroniques, humeurs et caprices*, Québec, C. Darveau, 1873, 2 vol.

1871 Buies, Arthur. *Chroniques canadiennes, humeurs et caprices*, vol. I, Montréal, Eusèbe Senécal & Fils imprimeurs, 1884, 446 p.

1871 David, Laurent-Olivier. «Correspondance éditoriale, Malbaie, 26 juillet 1871», *L'Opinion publique*, vol. 2 nᵒ 8 (3 août 1871): 377.

1871 Lemoine, James Macpherson. «Causerie historique», *Revue canadienne*, tome huitième (1871): 659–663.

1871 Tourist. «Murray Bay, the Beach and the Village», *Canadian Illustrated News*, vol. 4 nᵒ 7 (12 August 1871): 98, 99.

*Dates in italics correspond to the year the author visited La Malbaie; others, to the year the edition was published.

1871 Tourist. «The Watering Places of the Lower St. Lawrence», *Canadian Illustrated News*, vol. 4 n° 9 (26 August 1871): 129–131; vol. 4 n° 11 (9 September 1871): 162; vol. 4 n° 12 (16 September 1871): 178, 179.

1872 Génand, J.A. *Notes de voyage, le golfe et les provinces maritimes*, Montréal, Eusèbe Senécal, 1872, 34 p.

1872 Lemoine, James Macpherson. *L'album du touriste*, Québec, Augustin Côté, 1872, 385 p.

1872 Viator. «Courrier des eaux», *L'Opinion publique*, vol. 3 n° 29 (18 juillet 1872): 337, 338; vol. 3 n° 30 (25 juillet 1872): 350, 351; vol. 3 n° 32 (8 août 1872): 373.

1872–1878 Dufferin and Ava. *My Canadian Journal (1872–1878)*, London, John Murray, 1891, 422 p.

1873 Howells, William Dean. *Une rencontre, roman de deux touristes sur le Saint-Laurent et le Saguenay* [translation of «A Change Acquaintance» by Louis Fréchette], Montréal, Société des Publications Françaises, 1893, 132 p.

1873 R.E.X. *Trip to Gaspe and Back in the Yacht «Oriole» July 1873*, Montréal, Canadian Illustrated News Steam Printing House, 1873, 23 p.

1877 Auerbach, Meyer. *Description of Leve's First Personnally Conducted Excursion From New York, August 1877, (A Glimpse of Canada)*, New York, G. Leve, 1877, 38 p.

1877 Buies, Arthur. *Petites chroniques pour 1877*, Québec, Darveau, 1878, 162 p.

1877 Legendre, Napoléon. *Échos de Québec*, Québec, Augustin Côté, 1877, 2 vol.

1878 Lemoine, James Macpherson. *The Chronicles of the St. Lawrence*, Québec, Dawson & Co., 1878, 380 p.

1881 Captain Mac (pseud. of J.T. Macadam) *Canada: from the Lakes to the Gulf: the Country, its People, Religions, Politics, Rulers, and its Apparent Future. . .*, Montreal, Printed for the Author, 1881, 208 p.

1881 Decelles, A.D. «À La Malbaie», *L'Opinion publique*, vol. 12 n° 37 (15 septembre 1881): 433, 434.

1881 Routhier, Adolphe Basile. *En canot, petit voyage au Lac St-Jean*, Québec, O. Fréchette, 1881, 202 p.

1882 Creighton, J.G.A. «The Lower St. Lawrence and the Saguenay», *Picturesque Canada: the Country as it was and is*, vol. 2 (George Monroe Grant, édit.), Toronto, Belden Bros. (1882): 697–740.

1882 Lemoine, James Macpherson. *Picturesque Quebec: a Sequel to Quebec Past and Present*, Montréal, Dawson Bros., 1882, 535 p.

1882 Routhier, Adolphe Basile. *Les Échos*, Québec, Delisle, 1882, 287 p.

1882 Anonymous. «A Trip to the Saguenay», *Canadian Illustrated News*, vol. 26 n° 8 (19 August 1882): 115, 121.

1884 Fréchette, Annie Howells. «Summer Resorts on the St. Lawrence», *Harper's New Montly Magazine*, vol. 69 n° 410 (July 1884): 197–209.

1884 Taylor, Frank H. *Glimpses of St. Lawrence Summer Life among the Islands, Down the Rapids, and in Canadian Cities*, New York, Leve & Alden's Publication Department, 1884, 14 p.

1885 Clapin, Sylva. *La France transatlantique. Le Canada*, Paris, Plon, Nourrit et Cie, 1885, 262 p.

1886 Brière, L. de la *L'Autre France, voyage au Canada*, Paris, Dentu, 1886, 144 p.

1886 Gregory, J.U. *En racontant. Récits de voyages en Floride, au Labrador et sur le fleuve Saint-Laurent*, Québec, C. Darveau, 1886, 244 p.

1889 Lemoine, James Macpherson. *Historical and Sporting Notes on Quebec, Montmorency Falls, its Environs and Lake St. John and our Trout Lakes*, Québec, Demers, 1889, 135 p.

1889 Roy, J. Edmond. *Au royaume du Saguenay, voyage au pays de Tadoussac*, Québec. A. Côté, 1889, 234 p.

1890 Gutteridge, Rev. John A. *Summer Days in America*, Newark (N.J.), Printed for the Author, W.L. Brice and Co., 1890, 240 p.

1890 Blake, Samuel Verschoye. *The Camp Les Érables 1890*, s. l., Les Auteurs (printed by Warwick and Sons), 1891, 79 p.

1891 Chevillard, Valbert. *Paysages canadiens*, Paris, A. Lemere, 1891, 225 p.

1891 Cimon, abbé Henri. *Impressions de voyage. Première partie: de Québec à Rome. . .*, Québec, Léger Brousseau, 1895, 156 p.

1891–1892 Cimon, abbé Henri. *Aux vieux pays (impressions et souvenirs)*. Montréal, Librairie Beauchemin Ltée, 1917 (3e édit.), 341 p.

1893–1894 Françoise (pseud. of Robertine Barry). *Chroniques du lundi*, s. i., s. éd., s. d., 325 p.

1894 Gagnon, Ernest. *Feuilles volantes et pages d'histoire*, Québec, Laflamme et Proulx, 1910, 361 p.

1894 Gagnon, Ernest. *Pages choisies*, Québec, J.P. Garneau, 1917, 338 p.

1895 Gourmont, Remy de. *Les Canadiens de France*, Paris, Librairie de Firmin-Didot, 1895, 256 p.

Circa 1895 Sedgwick, Henry Dwight. *Memoirs of an Epicurean*, New York, The Bobbs-Merrill Co., 1942, 275 p.

1896 Bockoven, Geo. H. *Travel and Adventure. Experienced in Crossing the Continent (...). Supplemented by a Pleasure Tour of the St. Lawrence, Ottawa and Saguenay Rivers. . .*, Palmyra (N.Y.), F.G. Grandall, 1896, 57 p.

Circa 1896 Comeau, Napoléon-Alex. *Life and Sport of the North Shore of the Lower St. Lawrence and Gulf*, Québec, Daily Telegraph Printing House, 1909, 440 p.

Circa 1896 Comeau, Napoléon-Alex. *La vie et le sport sur la côte nord du bas Saint-Laurent et du golfe. . .*, (traduit de l'anglais par Nazaire LeVasseur), Québec, E. Garneau, 1945, 372 p.

1897 Huard, abbé V.-A. *Labrador et Anticosti, journal de voyage, histoire, topographie, pêcheurs canadiens et acadiens, indiens montagnais*, Montréal, C.O. Beauchemin, 1897, 505 p.

1898 Bentzon, Th. «Saint-Laurent et Saguenay», *Revue des deux mondes*, vol. 8 n° 146 (1898): 507–543.

1898 Bentzon, Th. *Nouvelle-France et Nouvelle-Angleterre. Notes de voyages*, Paris, Calmann Lévy, 1899, 320 p.

1898 Lemoine, James Macpherson. *The Legends of the St. Lawrence Told During a Cruise of the Yatch «Hirondelle»*, Québec, C.E. Holiwell, 1898, 203 p.

Circa 1900 Blake, William Hume. «Laurentides National Park», *The University Magazine*, vol. ii (February 1912): 41–60.

Circa 1900 Blake, William Hume. *Brown Waters and Other Sketches*, Toronto, The MacMillan Co., 1915, 264 p.

Circa 1900 Blake, William Hume. *In a Fishing Country*, Toronto, The MacMillan Co., 1922, 263 p.

Circa 1900 Blake, William Hume. *A Fisherman's Creed*, Toronto, The MacMillan Co., 1923, 40 p.

Circa 1900 Oliver, John Rathbone. *Rock and Sand*, New York, The MacMillan Co., 1930, 524 p.

1901 Durham, major J. H. et coll. *A Trip from Buffalo to Chicoutimi, during the Pan American Exposition at Buffalo, N.Y . . .*, (vol. II of the Thousand Island Library), Grand Rapids (Mich.), The James Bayne Co., 1901, 163 p.

1901 Gard, Anson A. *The Yankee in Quebec*, New York, The Emerson Press, 1901, 262 p.

1902 Chase, Eliza B. *In Quest of the Quaint*, Philadelphia, Ferres & Leach, 1902, 253 p.

1902 Gard, Anson A. *The Wandering Yankee or the Fun of Seeing Canada*, New York, The Emerson Press, 1902, 349 p.

1904 Bradley, Arthur G. «The Humours of a Canadian Watering-Place», *MacMillan's Magazine*, vol. 9 (May-October 1904): 424–430.

Circa 1904 Casgrain, Thérèse-F. *Une femme chez les hommes*, Montréal, Les Éditions du Jour, 1971, 296 p.

1905 Browne, George Waldo. *The St. Lawrence River, Historical, Legendary, Picturesque*, New York, Putnam's Son, 1905, 365 p.

1905 Townsend, Reginald T. *God Packed my Picnic Basket, Reminiscences of the Golden Age of Newport and New York*, New York, The New England Society in the City of New York, 1970, 94 p.

1906 Leclaire, Alphonse. *Le Saint-Laurent, historique, légendaire et topographique*, Montréal, Revue canadienne, 1906, 254 p.

1907 Fairchild, G.M. jr. *From my Quebec Scrap-Book*, Québec, Frank Carrel, 1907, 316 p.

1908 Fairchild, G.M. jr. *Gleanings from Quebec*, Québec, Frank Carrel, 1908, 216 p.

1910 Johnson, Clifton. *The Picturesque St. Lawrence*, New York, The MacMillan Co., 1910, 253 p.

1913 Hopkins, John Castell. *French Canada and the St. Lawrence, Historic, Picturesque and Descriptive*, Toronto, Bell and Cockburn, 1913, 431 p.

1913 Simms, Florence Mary. *Etoffe du pays, Lower St. Lawrence Sketches*, Toronto, The Musson Book Co. Ltd, 1913, 87 p.

1913 Wilson, Beckles. *Quebec: The Laurentian*

Province, London, Constable and Co., 1913, 271 p.

1917 Coyle, Donan. «The Mystery of the Ex-President, a Detective Story», *By-Water Magazine*, vol. 2 n° 7 (September 1917): 13–15, 17.

1917 Phalen, Robert F. «Quebec to the Saguenay», *By-Water Magazine*, vol. 2 n° 9 (November 1917): 20–23.

1920 Des Ormes, Renée. *Entre deux rives*, Québec, L'Action Sociale Ltée, 1920, 137 p.

1920 Potvin, Damase. *Le Tour du Saguenay, historique, légendaire et descriptif*, Québec, L'Éclaireur Ltée, 1920, 168 p.

1921: Agassiz, Garnault. ‹Canada's Unrivaled Summer Voyage› *The Canadian Illustrated Monthly*, vol. 6 n° 34 (May-June 1921): 5–22, 60.

1923: De Celles, Alfred jr. «Villégiature d'autrefois et d'aujourd'hui», *La Revue moderne*, vol. 4 n° 11 (1923): 20–22.

1923: Potvin, Damase. *The Saguenay Trip*, Montréal, Canada Steamship Lines [1939], 96 p.

1923 Todd, Irene. «The Newport of Canada: Murray Bay», *The Canadian Magazine*, vol. 61 n° 2 (June 1923): 143–149.

1924 Faris, John T. *Seeing Canada*, Philadelphia & London, J.B. Lippincott Co., 1924, 265 p.

Circa 1925 Hale, Katherine (pseud. of Amelia Beers Garvin). *Legends of the St. Lawrence*, Montréal, Canadian Pacific Railway, s. d., 47 p.

1926 Call, Frank Oliver. *The Spell of French Canada*, Boston, L.C. Page and Co., 1926, 372 p.

1926 Russell, John Fisher. *A Vacation at Manoir Richelieu*, Montréal, Canada Steamship Lines, 1926, 16 p.

1927 Potvin, Damase. *Sur la grand' route. Nouvelles, contes et croquis*, Québec, L'Auteur, 1927, 215 p.

1927 Anonymous. *Through the Land of the Voyageurs, Descriptive Notes and Illustrations of Old World Canada. The Route travelled by H.R.H. the prince of Wales on the S.S. St. Lawrence of the Canada Steamship Lines, Limited*, s. l., s. éd., [C.S.L.], 1927, 40 p.

1929 Roy, James A. «Cap-à-l'Aigle», *Queen's Quarterly*, vol. 36 n° 1 (winter 1929): 81–91.

1930 Davies, Blodwen. *Saguenay, «Sâginawa». The River of Deep Waters*, Toronto, McClelland and Stewart, 1930, 204 p.

Circa 1930 Tremblay, Jacques. *Neiges d'antan, mémoires d'enfance*, Chicoutimi, L'Auteur, 1983, 228 p.

Circa 1930 Tremblay, Jacques. *Supplément aux neiges d'antan*, Chicoutimi, L'Auteur, 1984, 38 p.

1931 Potvin, Damase. *Plaisant pays de Saguenay*. Québec, Tremblay [1931], 196 p.

1933 Gouin, Paul et Jean-Marie Gauvreau. «Un patriarcat d'artisans ruraux», *La Revue moderne*, 15ᵉ année n° 1 (novembre 1933): 5.

1937 Brinley, Gordon. *Away to Quebec, a gay journey to the Province*, Toronto, McClelland & Stewart Ltd., 1937, 286 p.

1938 Tweedsmuir, Lady. *Carnets canadiens*, Montréal, Les Éditions du Zodiaque, 1938, 162 p.

1939 Bugbee, Willis N. *Drifting Down the St. Lawrence, a Guide to «the Fairyland of America»*, New York, Fleming H. Revell Co., 1939, 220 p.

1939 Hogner, Dorothy Childs. *Summer Roads to Gaspe*, New York, E.P. Dutton and Co. Inc., 1939, 288 p.

1940 Donald, Jean Middleton. *Quebec Patchwork*, Toronto, The MacMillan Co., 1940, 368 p.

1942 Beston, Henry. *The St. Lawrence River of America*, Toronto, Rinehart and Co., 1942, 274 p.

1943 Skinner, Cornelia Otis and Emily Kimbrough. *Our Hearts were young and gay*, New York, Dodd, Mead & Company, 1943, 247 p.

1944 Lacoursière, Henri. «Voyage pittoresque dans Charlevoix-Saguenay», *Le Bulletin des agriculteurs*, vol. 40 n° 12 (1944): 24–27.

1944 Pacreau, Camille. *Un voyage au Saguenay*, Montmagny, Éd. Marquis, 1944, 156 p.

1945 Genevoix, Maurice. *Canada*, Paris, Flammarion, 1945, 253 p.

1945 Boivin, Léonce. *Dans nos montagnes (Charlevoix)*, Les Éboulements, s. éd., 1945 (3ᵉ éd.), 241 p.

1947 Oakley, Amy. *Kaleidoscopic Quebec*, New York, D. Appleton-Century Co., 1947, 278 p.

1948 Morgan, Patrick. «The Heifer», *The*

Atlantic, vol. 182 n° 1 (July 1948): 62–64.

1950 Sutton, Horace. *Footloose in Canada*, New York, Rinehart & Co. Inc., 1950, 291 p.

1950 Dean, Sidney W. et Marguerite Mooers Marshall. *We Fell in Love with Quebec*, Philadelphia, Macare Smith Co., 1950, 272 p.

1951 Davies, Blodwen. *Quebec, Portrait of a Province*, New York, Greenberg, 1951, 258 p.

1952 Mackenzie, John and Marjorie. *Quebec in your car*, Toronto, Clarke Irwin & Co. Ltd., 1952, 302 p.

1954 Dean, Sidney W. *All the Way by Water*, New York, Wilfred Funk Inc., 1954, 305 p.

1968 Cloutier, Eugène. *No Passport, a Discovery of Canada*, Toronto, Oxford University Press, 1968, 280 p.

1977 Born, David J. «Fondly Remembered. . . the Richelieu Cruise», *Telescope*, vol. 26 n°2 (March-April 1977): 31–35.

II. *Secondary Sources*

A. GENERAL

Alexander, James Edward (pseud. of William Agar Adamson). *Salmon-Fishing in Canada by a Resident*, London, Longman, Green, Longman and Robers, 1860, 350 p.

Audet, Francis-J. «Pierre-Édouard Leclère, 1798–1866», *Les Cahiers des Dix*, n° 8 (1943): 109–140.

Barbeau, Marius. *Au coeur du Québec*, Montréal, Les Éditions du Zodiaque, 1934, 200 p.

Barbeau, Marius. «Notre géographie en peinture», *Bulletin des Sociétés de géographie de Québec et de Montréal*, vol. 1 n° 5 (1942): 33–44.

Bayfield, H.W. *The St. Lawrence Pilot, comprising Sailing Directions for the Gulf and River St. Lawrence. . .* , London, Darling and Son, 1894, 708 p.

Bernatchez, Anne. «La calèche canadienne, éléments importants de la vie quotidienne de l'habitant de 1720 à 1850», *Culture et tradition*, vol. 4, (1979): 67–78.

Bertrand, Réal. *Thérèse Casgrain*, Montréal, Lidec, 1981, 63 p.

Blanchard, Raoul. *L'est du Canada français, «province de Québec»*, Montréal, Librairie Beauchemin Ltée, 1935, 2 vol.

Boardman, Mabel Thorp. *Under the Red Cross Flag at Home and Abroad*, Philadelphia & London, J.B. Lippincott Co., 1915, 333 p.

Bradley, Arthur G. *Le Canada. Empire des bois et des blés*, Paris, Pierre Roger et Cᶦᵉ, 1922, 278 p.

Brière, Roger. *Géographie du tourisme au Québec*, Montréal, Université de Montréal, thèse de doctorat (géopgraphie), 1967, 348 p.

Brière, Roger. «Les grands traits de l'évolution du tourisme au Québec», *Bulletin de l'Association des géographes de l'Amérique française*, n° 11 (septembre 1967): 83–95.

Brookes, Ivan S. *The Lower St. Lawrence: a pictorial history of shipping and industrial development*, Cleveland, Freshwater Press, 1974, 361 p.

Brooks, John. *Once in Golconda, a True Drama of Wall Street 1920–1938*, New York, Harper and Row, 1969, 307 p.

Brown, Alexander Crosby. «The Grand Saloons of Nineteenth-Century American Steamboats», *Antiques*, vol. 58 n° 2 (August 1950): 100–102.

Buchanan, A.W. Patrick. *The Buchanan Book. The Life of Alexander Buchanan, Q.C. of Montreal, Followed by an Account of the Family of Buchanan,* Montréal, Printed for private circulation, 1911, 475 p.

Buchanan, A.W. Patrick. *Later Leaves of the Buchanan Book*, Montréal, Printed for private circulation, 1929, 482 p.

Buchanan, A.W. Patrick. *The Bench and Bar of Lower Canada*, Montréal, Burton's Limited, 1925, 219 p.

Carrel, Frank. «The Modern Quebec», *By-Water Magazine*, vol. 2, n° 8 (1917): 25, 26.

Chambers, E.T.D. *The Ouananiche and its Canadian Environment*, New York, Harper and Brothers, 1896, 357 p.

Charlebois, Dr Peter. *Sternwheelers and Sidewheelers, The Romance of Steam Driven Paddleboats in Canada*, Toronto, N.C. Press Ltd., 1978, 142 p.

Cimon, Hector. *Un siècle de yachting sur le Saint-Laurent 1861–1964*, Québec, Librairie Garneau, 1966, 309 p.

Crane, Josephine Boardman *A Middle-West Child*, New York, L'Auteur, 1971, 31 p.

Croff, Mme E. *Nos ancêtres à l'œuvre à la Rivière-Ouelle*, Montréal, Lévesque, 1931, 212 p.

Croil, James. *Steam Navigation and its relation to the Commerce of Canada and the United States*, Toronto, William Briggs, 1898, 381 p.

De Larosière, Robert L. et Léo H. Thébaud. *History of The Thébaud Family Since its Founding in the United States in 1793*, New York, L'Auteur, 1962, 46 p.

Dempsey II, John B. «Canada Steamship Lines Limited: World's Largest Inland Water Transportation Company», *Inland Seas, Quarterly Journal of the Great Lakes Historical Society*, vol. 15 nº 1 (spring 1959): 4–14.

Dubuc, Alfred. «Montréal et les débuts de la navigation à vapeur sur le Saint-Laurent», *Revue d'histoire économique et sociale*, vol. 45 nº 1 (1967): 104–118.

Duff, sir Hector L. *The Sewells in the New World*, Exeter, W.M. Pollar and Co. Ltd., 1924, 122 p.

Duffy, Herbert S. *William Howard Taft*, New York, Minton, Balch & Company, 1930, 345 p.

Dutton, Diana et coll. *De la voile à la vapeur, la construction de navires dans les environs de Québec et Montréal*, Saint-Lambert, Le Musée Marsil, 1982, 64 p.

Ewan, John A. *Les hommes du jour, galerie de portraits contemporains «Troisième série: Edward Blake»*, Montréal, La Compagnie de Moulins à Papier de Montréal, 1891, p. 33–46.

Fleming, Sandford. *The Intercolonial, a Historical Sketch of the Inception, Location, Construction and Completion of the Line of Railway. . .*, Montréal, Dawson Brothers, 1876, 268 p.

Franck, Alain. *Le Saint-Laurent 1900–1960*, L'Islet, Musée maritime Bernier, 1980, 56 p.

Gibbon, John Murray. «The Canadian Guide», *The Nineteenth Century* (June 1922): 988–1001.

Girard, Alex. *La province de Québec*, Québec, Dussault et Proulx, 1905, 318 p.

Gregg, William. *History of the Presbyterian Church in the Dominion of Canada*, Toronto, Presbyterian Printing and Publishing Co., 1885, 646 p.

Guay, Donald. *La chasse au Québec, chronologie commentée (1603–1900)*, Québec, Temps Libre 3, 1982, 158 p.

Guernsey, Betty. *Gaby, the Life and Time of Gaby Bernier, couturière extraordinaire*, Toronto. The Marincourt Press, 1982, 200 p.

Guillet, Edwin C. *Pioneer Inns and Taverns*, Toronto, Ontario Publishing Co., 1954–1958, 4 vol.

Hallock, Charles. *The Fishing Tourist: Angler's Guide and Reference Book*, New York, Harper & Brothers, 1873, 239 p.

Hallock, Charles. *The Salmon Fisher*, New York, The Harris Publishing Company, 1890, 126 p.

Hicks, Frederick C. *William Howard Taft, Yale Professor of Law and New Haven Citizen*, New Haven, Yale University Press, 1945, 158 p.

Hudon, Paul-Henri. *Rivière-Ouelle de la Bouteillerie. Trois siècles de vie*, Comité du Tricentenaire, s. éd., 1972, 495 p.

Kavanagh, L.V. *History of Golf in Canada*, Toronto, Fitzhenry and Whiteside Ltd., 1973, 207 p.

King, major W. Ross. *The Sportsman and Naturalist in Canada or Notes on the Natural History of the Game, Game Birds and Fish of that Country*, London, Hurst and Blackett, 1866, 334 p.

Lefebvre, Jean-Jacques. «Présidents, Bourse de Montréal, 1874–1959», *B.R.H.*, vol. 67 nº 1 (1961): 57–61.

Legget, Robert F. *Railways of Canada*, Vancouver, Douglas and McIntyre, 1973, 255 p.

Lemoine, James Macpherson. *Chasse et pêche au Canada*, Québec, N.S. Hardy, 1887, 300 p.

Lemoine, James Macpherson. *The Explorations of Jonathan Oldbuck. Canadian History Legends, Scenery, Sport*, Québec, Demers, 1889, 265 p.

Lemoine, James Macpherson. *Les pêcheries du Canada*, Québec, Atelier Typographique du Canadien 1863, 146 p.

Limerick, Jeffrey et coll. *America's Grand Resort Hotels*, New York, Pantheon Books, 1979, 304 p.

Martin, Paul-Louis. *Histoire de la chasse au Québec*, Montréal, Boréal Express, 1980, 279 p.

McGinty, Brian. *The Palace Inns, A Connoisseur's Guide to Historic American Hotels*, Harrisburg (Penn.), Stackpole Books, 1978, 191 p.

Nettle, Richard. *The Salmon Fisheries of the*

St. Lawrence and its Tributaries, Montréal, John Lovell, 1857, 144 p.

O'Connor V.C. Scott. «Old France in Modern Canada», *National Geographic Magazine*, vol. 67 n° 2 (February 1935): 166–200.

Patterson, James T. *Mr Republican, a biography of Robert A. Taft*, Boston, Houghton Mifflin Co., 1972, 749 p.

Potvin, Damase. *Les oubliés*, Québec, Éditions Roch Poulin, s. d., 237 p.

Pringle, Henry F. *The Life and Time of William Howard Taft*, New York & Toronto, Farrar and Rinehart Inc., 1939, 2 vol.

Provencher, Jean. *C'était l'été. La vie rurale traditionnelle dans la vallée du Saint-Laurent*, Montréal, Boréal Express, 1982, 247 p.

Ross, Ishbel. *An American Family. The Tafts – 1678 to 1964*, Cleveland & New York, The World Publishing Company, 1964, 468 p.

Roy, J. Edmond. «La calèche canadienne», *B.R.H.*, vol. 2 n° 1 (1896): 10–13.

Roy, Pierre-Georges]. «Le docteur John Buchanan», *B.R.H.*, vol. 17 n° 4 (1911): 97–103.

Roy, Pierre-Georges. *La traverse entre Québec et Lévis*, Lévis, s. éd., 1942, 169 p.

Saint-Amour, Jean-Pierre. *La villégiature au Québec, problématique de l'aménagement du territoire*, Hull, Les Éditions Asticou, 1979, 178 p.

Schull, Joseph. *Edward Blake, The Man of the Other Way 1833–1881*, Toronto, MacMillan of Canada, 1975, 257 p.

Schull, Joseph. *Edward Blake, Leader and Exile 1881–1912*, Toronto, MacMillan of Canada, 1976, 266 p.

Smith, F. Percy. «History of Canada Steamship Lines Limited» *By-Water Magazine*, vol. 1 n° 1 (1916): 9, 18; vol. 1 n° 2 (1916): 11; vol. 1 n° 3 (1916): 25, 33; vol. 1 n° 4 (1916): 28, 30; vol. 1 n° 5 (1916): 24, 25; vol. 1 n° 6 (1916): 23, 27.

Stein, Jean. *Edie, An American Biography*, New York, Alfred A. Knopf, 1982, 455 p.

Stevens, G.R. *History of Canadian National Railways*, New York, The MacMillan Co., 1973, 538 p.

Sulte, Benjamin. «L'album du touriste, causerie à propos d'un livre nouveau», *L'Opinion publique*, vol. 3 n° 33 (15 août 1872): 386, 387.

Taft, Mrs William Howard. *Recollections of Full Years*, New York, Dodd, Mead & Co., 1914, 395 p.

Taylor, Griffith. «Two Patterns on the Gulf of St. Lawrence», *Canadian Geographical Journal*, vol. 30 n° 6 (1945): 254–275.

Tessier, abbé Albert. «Les voyages vers 1800», *Les Cahiers des Dix*, n° 6 (1941): 83–108.

Tremblay, Victor. «L'aventure du Carolina», *Saguenayensia*, vol. 10 n° 5 (septembre-octobre 1968): 116–121.

Trépanier, Léon. «Le docteur Warren, prince des clubmen, amant de la nature, analyse pour nous les diverses phases de sa vie», *La Patrie*, (27 février 1949): 56, 63, 86.

Trout, J.M. et Edward. *The Railways of Canada for 1870–71*, Toronto, Monetary Times, 1871, 213 p.

Tulchinsky, Gerald J.J. *The River Barons, Montreal Businessmen and the Growth of Industry and Transportation 1837–53*, Toronto, University of Toronto Press, 1977, 310 p.

Vieux-Rouge (pseud, de Pierre Arthur Joseph). *Les contemporains, série de biographies des hommes de nos jours*, Montréal. A. Filiatreault, édit., 1898–1899, 2 vol.

Wethered, H.N. et T. Simpson. *The Architectural Side of Golf*, New York, Longmans, Green and Co., 1929, 210 p.

Wilson, Ella Grant. *Famous Old Euclid Avenue of Cleveland. At one Time Called the Most Beautiful Street in the World*, s. 1., L'Auteur, 1932, 325 p.

Wilson, George H. *The Application of Steam to St. Lawrence Valley Navigation, 1809–1840*, Montréal, McGill University, Master's thesis, 1961, 287 p.

Anonymous. *Le club de golf Royal Québec*, Boischatel, privately published, 1974, 90 p.

Anonymous. «Le jeu de golf au Canada», *B.R.H.*, vol. 51 n° 6 (1945): 239.

Anonymous. «Nos premières places d'eau», *B.R.H.*, vol. 51 n° 6 (1945): 245.

Anonymous. «C.S.L. d'hier et d'aujourd'hui», *C.S.L. – Le Monde*, vol. 2 n° 1 (janvier 1976): 2; vol. 2 n° 2 (février 1976): 5; vol. 2 n° 3 (mars-avril 1976): 8; vol. 2 n° 4 (mai-juin 1976): 9, 10; vol. 2 n° 5 (juillet-août 1976): 7, 10, 11; vol. 2 n° 6 (septembre 1976): 7, 8; vol. 2 n° 7 (octobre-novembre 1976): 8, 9; vol. 2 n° 8 (décembre 1976): 7–9.

B. SPECIFIC

Arnold, Gustavus. «The Manoir Richelieu, An Historic Seigniory of Architectural Grandeur on the Ramparts of the St. Lawrence», *Michigan Society of Architects, Monthly Bulletin*, vol. 35 (April 1961): 22–27; vol. 35 (May 1961): 44–47.

Ayre, Robert. «The St. Lawrence North Shore, a Grand Country for Painters», *The Gazette* [Montréal] (21 August 1937): 5.

Baker, Victoria A. et coll. *Images de Charlevoix 1784–1950*, Montréal, Musée des beaux-arts de Montréal, 1981, 178 p.

Belleau, Pierre. «A-t-on oublié le petit train de La Malbaie?», *Le Soleil* (2 août 1978): C-7.

Bergeron, Marie-Paule et coll. *Le Manoir Richelieu, son histoire, sa région, ses gens*, s. l., s. éd., (Atelier de recherches du comité d'Action sociale de l'AFEAS de Clermont), 1978, 2 vol.

Bernier, Marcel. *Les voies de communication du comté de Charlevoix*, Québec, Université Laval, Mémoire de licence (géographie), 1979, 104 p.

Binsse, Harry Lorin. «Getting to Murray Bay in the Old Days», *The Manoir and the Colony Life Magazines*, vol. 6 n° 1 (summer 1957): 5, 17.

Blake, William Hume. «Chamard's», *The Murray Bay Habitant*, vol. 12 n° 3 (July 1918): 5.

Bouchard, Pierre-Paul. «Il était trois petits navires», *Revue Feu de Camp*, vol. 2 n° 3 (juillet 1966): 12, 13.

Bull, Harry A. «Down the St. Lawrence with Bow and Arrow», *Town and Country*, vol. 88 n° 4108 (July 1933): 46.

Cabot, Currie. «Snow-Scene, Murray Bay», *Vogue*, vol. 81 n° 2 (15 January 1933): 46, 47, 74, 78.

Carless, William. «The Murray Bay Festival», *Canadian Homes and Gardens*, vol. 6 n° 11 (1929): 82, 84, 86, 88.

Cimon, Henri. «Pointe-au-Pic», *B.R.H.*, vol. 2 n° 9 (1896): 137.

Cimon, Jean. «La côte de Charlevoix et le tourisme», *La Revue de l'Université Laval*, vol. 17 n° 2 (octobre 1962): 112–123.

Conseil Économique Régional de Charlevoix. *Charlevoix communautaire*, Beauceville, Éditions L'Éclaireur Ltée, 1975, 121 p.

Couturier, Jean-Marie. *La Malbaie économique*, Québec, Université Laval, thèse de maîtrise (commerce), 1951, 156 p.

Coverdale, William Hugh. *Tadoussac Then and Now—A History and Narrative of the Kingdom of the Saguenay*, New York, L'Auteur, 1942, 24 p.

Davies, Blodwen. «Manoir Richelieu—A Baronial Note on the Lower St. Lawrence», *The Canadian Passing Show*, vol. 3 n° 10 (July 1929): 29, 30.

Decelles, A.D. «À travers l'histoire, La Malbaie autrefois et aujourd'hui», *La Presse* (16 juin 1900): 14.

Desmeules, Jean. *Étude du tourisme dans les Laurentides au nord de la cité de Québec*, Québec, Ministère de l'Industrie et du Commerce, 1961, 57 p.

Des Ormes, Renée. *Célébrités*, Québec, Chez L'Auteur, 1927, 128 p.

Dubé, Philippe. «Faire l'histoire du pays visité: Charlevoix», *Loisir et société*, vol. 6 n° 1 (printemps 1983): 211–228.

Dufour, Lise Gratton. *Murray Bay Golf Club 1876–1976, Cent Ans!* [s.l., s. éd.], 1976, 16 p.

Dumais, Jacques. «Charlevoix: un comté gâté par la nature mais privé d'infrastructure touristique», *Le Soleil* (22 juillet 1972): 23.

En collaboration (Urbanex inc.). *Développement de la villégiature Charlevoix*, Québec, Éditeur officiel du Québec (Office de la planification et du développement du Québec), 1979, 293 p.

En collaboration. *Il était une fois... Cap-à-l'Aigle*, [La Malbaie], Imprimerie de Charlevoix, [1977] 46 p.

En collaboration. *La région de Charlevoix, travaux des étudiant(e)s de la maîtrise en Aménagement du territoire et développement régional dans le cadre du laboratoire d'aménagement 1983–1984*, Québec, Université Laval, 1984, 4 vol.

En collaboration. *Recueil historique Saint-Irénée*, La Malbaie, Imprimerie de Charlevoix, 1976, 59 p.

En collaboration. *1534 à 1984: 450 ans de navigation dans Charlevoix*, La Malbaie [Imprimerie de Charlevoix], 1984, 74 p.

Faessler, Carl. «Du cap Tourmente à Tadoussac», *Le Naturaliste canadien*, vol. 57 n° 6–7 (1930): 143–147; vol. 57 n° 8–9 (1930): 172–177.

Faessler, Carl. «La Côte Nord», *Le Naturaliste canadien*, vol. 59 n° 4 (1932): 81–107.

Frazier, George. «North Woods Newport», *Holiday*, vol. 12 n° 3 (September 1952): 98–103, 120.

Gouin, Olivier Mercier. «Quand les petits bateaux blancs voguaient au fil de l'eau du Saint-Laurent et du Saguenay», *Perspectives Dimanche*, vol. 10 n° 34 (27 août 1978): 8, 9.

Grenier, Jacques. «J'ai retrouvé mon bateau du Saguenay à Copenhague», *Perspectives Dimanche*, vol. 6 n° 32 (4 août 1974): 3, 4.

Hale, Richard W. jr. «A History of Canada's Second Oldest Golf Course», *The Manoir and Colony Life Magazine*, vol. 10 n° 1 (1961): 6, 7, 14, 20, 21, 23, 28, 29.

Herridge, Dr W.T. «Murray Bay: a Distinguished Paradox», *The Canadian Magazine*, vol. 64 n° 8 (September 1925): 228–230, 235, 250.

Hogue, Marthe B. *Un trésor dans les montagnes*, Québec, Les Éditions Caritas, 1954, 279 p.

Johnstone, Ken. «The Hotel with the Elegant Air», *Maclean's* vol. 65 n° 8 (15 April 1952): 12, 13, 30–33.

Kerry, Esther W. *Church of St. Peter-on-the-Rock, What the Records Tell Us, 1872–1972*, Montréal, s. éd., 1972, 28 p.

K.K.B. «W.H. Blake», *The Canadian Bookman*, vol. 5 n° 11 (1923): 297.

Laflamme, Joseph Clovis K. «Le comté de Charlevoix, *Commission de géologie du Canada, Rapport annuel (nouvelle série)*, vol. 5 (1890–1891): 51–53.

Leblanc, Maurice. *Golf, Manoir Richelieu, études photographiques*, Trois-Rivières, J.C. Blouin & Fils Inc., s. d., [36 p.].

Legendre, J.-Thérèse. «Vers le milieu du 19ᵉ siècle Murray Bay devint le rendez-vous d'été de nombreuses familles anglaises», *Le Plein-Jour sur Charlevoix* (28 septembre 1977): 4.

Lessard, Michel. «Dans le comté de Charlevoix au début du siècle. . . Un millionnaire», *Photo Sélection*, vol. 4 n° 6 (janvier-février 1985): 14–17.

Masten, C.A. «William Hume Blake, K.C.», *The Canadian Bar Review*, vol. 2 n° 4 (1924): 229–231.

Morgan, Patrick. *La Malbaie, Province of Quebec, Once a Village with an Old Church and Old Customs*, New York, L'Auteur, 1962, [5 p.].

O'Neill, George. «The Fascinating Charlevoix Country», *Canadian Geographical Journal*, vol. 25 n° 1 (July 1942): 40–46.

Pépin, Gaston. *Essai de monographie du comté de Charlevoix*, Québec, Université Laval, Mémoire de licence (commerce), 1945, 49 p.

Petit-Martinon, Charles. «Les Hudon vivent en vrais châtelains...», *Le Petit Journal* (semaine du 25 août 1963): A-45.

Pope, Maud M. *The Church of St. Peter-on-the-Rock, Cap-à-l'Aigle, Que.*, Montréal, s. éd., 1950, 17 p.

Potvin, Damase. *Thomas, le dernier de nos coureurs de bois. Le parc des Laurentides*, Québec, Les Éditions Garneau, 1945, 272 p.

Selnar, Peter. *The Construction and Planning of the Manoir Richelieu*, Montréal, McGill University, (technical paper), 1967, 33p.

Spencer, Arthur. «The Magnificent Manoir at Murray Bay», *Mayfair*, vol. 26 n° 5 (May 1952): 40, 41, 97–101.

Stow, Charles Messer. «Finest Collection of Canadiana», *Canada Steamship Lines Chart*, vol. 17 n° 5, (s.d.): 3–6.

Tibbits, Sarah B. *The Murray Bay Protestant Church for Fifty Years 1867–1917*, s. i., s. éd., [1917], 18 p.

Toler, Henry Pennington. «The Land of the Singing Ski», *The Canadian Passing Show*, vol. 5 n° 4 (1931): 19.

Tremblay, François. *William Hugh Coverdale, collectionneur*, La Malbaie, Musée régional Laure-Conan, 1979, 63 p.

Tremblay, Raynald. *Un pays à bâtir, Saint-Urbain-en-Charlevoix*, Québec, Les Éditions La Liberté, 1977, 308 p.

Tremblay, Réjean. «La grange Bhérer retrouve sa toiture de chaume», *Le Confident*, (20 juin 1979): 10.

Uzzell, Thomas H. *Golf in the World's Oldest Mountains*, s. i., Canada Steamship Lines, s. d., [50 p.].

Vézina, Raymond. «L'art documentaire au service des sciences humaines: le cas du comté de Charlevoix au Québec», *Cahiers de géographie de Québec*, vol. 21 n° 53–54 (septembre-décembre 1977): 293–308.

Viau, René. *La plus vieille église de Charlevoix: Ste-Agnès*, La Malbaie, Imprimerie de Charlevoix, [1979], [4 p.].

Wade, F.C. «William Hume Blake», *The University of Toronto Monthly*, vol. 24 n° 9 (June 1924): 412–415.

Anonymous. «Burned Manoir to be replaced by next season», *The Gazette* [Montréal], (13 September 1928): 1, 7.

Anonymous. «Jours de vrai sport, Murray Bay, Québec», *La vie forestière*, vol. 16 n° 1 (1931): 305.

Anonymous. «Le rassemblement de la famille Mackay à Cap-à-l'Aigle», *Le Confident de la rive nord* (15 août 1979): 18.

Anonymous. «Le trou de La Malbaie» *L'Opinion publique*, vol. 3 n° 26 (27 juin 1872): 305, 309.

Anonymous. «Summer Homes are Calling», *The Canadian Passing Show*, vol. 6 n° 5 (1932): 14.

Anonymous. «The Passing of the Manoir», *The Canadian Passing Show*, vol. 3 n° 1 (1928): 26, 39.

Anonymous. «The World on Holiday», *The Canadian Passing Show*, vol. 6 n° 6 (1932): 10.

Anonymous. «Vue des chutes Fraser», *L'Opinion publique*, vol. 3 n° 29 (18 juillet 1872): 342, 346.

Anonymous. «William Howard Taft», *La Presse* (1er mars 1930): 13.

VILLAS ON THE CLIFF

The reader should note that this bibliography is not exhaustive of material on resort architecture. I have, however, taken care to include under primary sources all the manuscripts which make reference to villas in Charlevoix and their builders. This led me to pay to particular attention to maps, architectural drawings and plans, and designs and sketches. The importance of the information provided by such documents which I have consulted in both public and private collections, should not be underestimated. The material included in secondary sources begins with a list of general works on the history and theory of architecture, which provide a wider context in which to understand resort architecture. The first part of the section on more specific works deals with regional architectural traits, which provide a background to a better understanding of the architectural countryside of Charlevoix. I have then provided biographical information on architects and information on the firms where they worked in an attempt to describe more precisely the contribution of professionals to the region. A list of articles where villas are mentioned completes the bibliography.

I. *Primary Sources*

A. MANUSCRIPTS
1. Public Archives

Olmsted Associates 342. Manuscript Division. 1888–1899. The Library of Congress (Washington).
J.-Charles Warren Frère Éloi Gérard (Talbot), «Famille Warren», La Malbaie, 29 janvier 1927, 17 p. Coll. Musée régional Laure-Conan (La Malbaie).
Stanford White «Stanford White Correspondence», Copy Books, nᵒˢ: 18, 20, 22, 23, 24, 25, 26. Coll. Columbia University (New York).

2. Private Archives

Sir Lomer Gouin «Verte feuille», Livre des visiteurs (1918–1950), 57 p. Coll. Mme Thérèse Gouin-Décarie.
J.-Charles Warren «Lettre manuscrite de J.-Charles Warren au Dr James Warren», Cleveland (Ohio), 3 août 1893, 4 p. Coll. Piller-Tahy.
Du notaire J. Roland Warren 6947. «Déclaration de décès et immeubles: succession de M. Charles Warren», 19 octobre 1929, 5 p. Coll. Warren et Thibeault, notaires. 4137. «Testament de Charles Warren», 15 avril 1925, 1 p. Coll. Warren et Thibeault, notaires.

B. MAPS AND PLANS

1. Maps

Drouyn, Maurice (Tremblay & Drouyn). *Plan of Harlan Subdidivision, :Part of Lot 747 of the Official Cadastre of the Parish of St. Etienne de la Malbaie, County of Charlevoix P.Q. Québec*, s. éd. 30 octobre 1933. 1 pl. Échelle: 1″ = 100′-0″. Coll. Musée régional Laure-Conan (La Malbaie).

Goad, Charles E. *Murray Bay including Pointe A Pic, Quebec*. Montréal et Toronto. s. éd., août 1906. 5 pl. Échelle: 1″ = 100′-0″. Coll. M. et Mme William G. Yonkers.

Pouliot, Émilien (Joncas & Malouin). *Plan du village de Pointe-au-Pic, comté de Charlevoix*, Québec, s. éd., 17 juin 1929. 1 pl. Échelle: 1″ = 200′ = 0″. Coll. Municipalité de Pointe-au-Pic (Charlevoix).

Vincent, H. *Plan des lots appartenant à Mme A.B. Buchanan, Pointe-au-Pic*, La Malbaie, s. éd., 30 août 1917. 1 pl. Échelle: 1 arpent au pouce. Coll. M. Guy Van Duyse.

Warren, Charles. *Map of Pointe a Pic Village, Malbaie Village & Malbaie Parish*, s. 1., s. éd., janvier 1924. 1 pl. Échelle: 10 chaînes au pouce [10 chaînes = ¹/₈ mille]. Coll. Musée régional Laure-Conan (La Malbaie), gift of Mme Charlotte Brisson.

Anonymous. *Plan of Property Belonging to Dr Elzéar Pelletier at Cap-à-l'Aigle, Que. Being Lot No 68 and part of Lot 69, Range Cap-à-l'Aigle Seigneury of Mount Murray (La Malbaie), Charlevoix County*, s. 1. s. éd., octobre 1925. 1 pl. Échelle: 1″ = 20′-0″. Coll. M. et Mme Louis R. Pelletier.

2. Architectural Plans

Fetherstonhaugh, Durnford, Bolton & Chadwick. *House for F. Peter Ryan Pointe, au Pic*, Montréal, 12 mars 1947. 4 pl. Échelle: $^1/_4'' = 1'\text{-}0''$. Coll. Musée régional Laure-Conan (La Malbaie), gift of M. Patrick Séguin.

Howells & Stokes. *Cottage for Mrs. R.B. Minturn, Murray Bay, Canada*, New York, 10 juillet 1907. 6 pl. Échelle: $^1/_4'' = 1'\text{-}0''$. Coll. Mrs Ruth Mitchell Cogan.

Howells & Stokes. [*The Murray Bay Protestant Church*], New York, 12 August 1909. 1 pl., n° 1. S. éch. Coll. University of Toronto (Toronto), G.M. Wrong Papers, Thomas Fisher Rare Book Library, n° 36, box 9.

Humphrey & Séguin. *Salle à déshabillage prop. Mme J.G. Bourne, La Malbaie, Qué.*, Montréal, 21 mai 1963. 2 pl. Échelle: $^3/_8'' = 1'\text{-}0''$. Coll. Musée régional Laure-Conan (La Malbaie), gift of M. Patrick Séguin.

Humphrey & Séguin. *Résidence d'été pour M. et Mme Mark Donohue*, Montréal, 1967. 9 pl. N° 6702. Échelle $^1/_4'' = 1'\text{-}0''$. Coll. Musée régional Laure-Conan (La Malbaie), gift of M. Patrick Séguin.

Janin, Georges. [*Cap-à-l'Aigle, Première maison de mon père le docteur Elzéar Pelletier*.], s. 1., s. d. 1 pl. Échelle: $^1/_4'' = 1'\text{-}0''$. Coll. M. et Mme Louis R. Pelletier.

King, Frederic R. *Residence for Mrs F.H. Cabot*, New York, 1er novembre 1956. 6 pl. Échelle: $^1/_8'' = 1'\text{-}0''$. Coll. Mr and Mrs Francis H. Cabot.

Lamontagne, Gravel & Brassard. *Esquisse préliminaire d'une addition au château Murray, Pointe-au-Pic, Murray Bay*, Chicoutimi, octobre 1930. 1 pl. Échelle: $^1/_8'' = 1'\text{-}0''$. Coll. privée, Québec.

Little, Robert A. *A Summer House for Charles P. Taft*, Cleveland (Ohio), [1957]. 9 pl. Échelle: $^1/_4'' = 1'\text{-}0''$. Coll. M. and Mme Walter Warren.

Mackenzie, Philip. *A.R. Gillespie, Cap-à-l'Aigle, Existing Conditions*, Montréal, 3 mai 1967. 5 pl. Échelle: $^1/_4'' = $ Coll. privée, Montréal.

Olmsted Brothers. *Mrs T.D. McCagg, Pointe à Pic, Murray Bay, P.Q.*, Brookline (Mass.), 3 août 1899. 1 pl. N° 4. Échelle: $^1/_4'' = 1'\text{-}0''$. Coll. Frederick Law Olmsted National Historic Site, n° 348.

Shennan, David. *Alterations to Cottage at Cap-à-l'Aigle for Dr E. Pelletier*, s. 1., s. d. 6 pl. Échelle: $^1/_4'' = 1'\text{-}0''$. Coll. M. et Mme Louis R. Pelletier.

Shennan, David. *Bungalow at Cap-à-l'Aigle, Murray Bay for Dr E Pelletier*, Montréal, 16 avril 1913. 6 pl. Échelle: $^1/_4'' = 1'\text{-}0''$. Coll. M. et Mme Louis R. Pelletier.

Shennan, David. *Manoir Richelieu Golf Club, Murray Bay, Quebec. The New Club House*, Montréal, 3 novembre 1937. 15 pl. Échelle: $^1/_8'' = 1'\text{-}0''$. Coll. privée, Québec.

Todd, Frederick G. *Subdivision Plan of Pointe a Gaz Being Part of the Seigniory of Mount Murray, Cap-à-l'Aigle, P.Q.*, Montréal, 20 juillet 1903. 1 pl. Échelle: $1'' = 200'\text{-}0''$. Coll. Musée régional Laure-Conan (La Malbaie).

3. Architectural Surveys

Delisle, Pierre. *Darly Fields, Cap-à-l'Aigle* (arch. Charles Warren, 1914), Québec, septembre 1981. 1 pl. Échelle: 2 cm = 1 m. Coll. Musée régional Laure-Conan (La Malbaie).

Delisle, Pierre. *Penteaves, Pointe-au-Pic* (arch. Charles Warren, 1923), Québec, septembre 1981. 1 pl. Échelle: 2 cm = 1 m. Coll. Musée régional Laure-Conan (La Malbaie).

Drolet, Simon. *Blairvocky 'T Vlaams Hof, Pointe-au-Pic, 1893*, Québec, septembre 1983. 1 pl. Échelle: 1 cm = 1 m. Coll. Musée régional Laure-Conan (La Malbaie).

Mackenzie, M.B. *Torwood, Cap-à-l'Aigle*, Montréal, 1972. 4 pl. Échelle: $1'' = 5'\text{-}0''$. Coll. privée, Montréal.

Morgan, Alexis. *Bas de l'Anse*, Cap-à-l'Aigle, 1983. 5 pl. Échelle: $^1/_4'' = 1'\text{-}0''$. Coll. privée, Boston.

Anonymous. *Blairvocky, Diagram of First Floor, Pointe à Pic, Que.*, s. 1., octobre 1893. 1 pl. s. éch. Coll. M. Guy Van Duyse.

4. Sketches and Drawings

Janin, Georges. *Mont Plaisant*, s. 1., 1899. 1 pl. Échelle: $1'' = 10'\text{-}0''$. Coll. M. et Mme Louis R. Pelletier.

Mackenzie, Philip. [*Résidence de Sybil Kennedy*], Magog, août 1984. 2 pl. Échelle: $1'' = 8'\text{-}0''$. Coll. Musée régional Laure-Conan (La Malbaie).

Warren, J.-Charles. *Summer Residence for a Seashore-Place*, s. 1., s. d. 1 pl. S. éch. Coll. Mme Doreen Warren Doucet.

C. VISUAL MATERIALS

1. Photographs

a) Public Collections

Archives photographiques de la Canada Steamship Lines Ltd.
Coll. Le Groupe C.S.L. Inc. (Montréal).
Archives photographiques Notman
Coll. Musée McCord (Montréal).
Collection de cartes postales
Coll. Bibliothèque publique de Westmount (Montréal).
Inventaire des bâtiments historiques du Canada
Coll. Ministère de l'Environnement, Parcs-Canada (Hull).
Inventaire des biens culturels du Québec
Coll. Ministère des Affaires culturelles (Québec).

b) Private Collections

Coll. Mrs. C.H.A. Armstrong
Coll. Mrs. Ruth Mitchell Cogan
Coll. Mme Doreen Warren Doucet
Coll. M. et Mme Georges Fournier
Coll. Mr and Mrs. F.R.L. Osborne
Coll. M. et Mme Louis R. Pelletier

Coll. Mr and Mrs Horace Taft
Coll. Mme Angéline T. Tremblay
Coll. Dr et Mme Georges William Tremblay
Coll. Mme Henriette Warren
Coll. M. et Mme Jean De Roussel Warren
Coll. M. et Mme Roger Warren

D. PUBLISHED MATERIALS

1. Reference

Cameron, Christina. *Index of Houses Featured in «Canadian Homes and Gardens» from 1925 to 1944*, Ottawa, Canadian Inventory of Historic Buildings, Parks-Canada, 1980, 162 p.

En collaboration. *Inventaire des marchés de construction des archives civiles de Québec 1800–1870*, Ottawa, Direction des parcs et lieux historiques nationaux (Parcs-Canada), 1975, 3 vol.

En collaboration. *Inventaire des dessins architecturaux à l'Université Laval*, Ottawa, Direction des parcs et lieux historiques nationaux (Parcs-Canada), 1980, 392 p.

Richardson, A.J.H. «Guide to the Architecturally and Historically Most Significant Buildings in the Old City of Quebec with a Biographical Dictionary of Architects and Builders», *Bulletin of the Association for Preservation Technology*, vol. 2 no 3–4 (1970): 1–144.

Richardson, A.J.H. *Quebec City: Architects, Artisans and Builders*, Ottawa, National Museum of Man, Parks-Canada, 1984, 583 p.

Withey, Henry F. et Elsie Rathburn Withey. *Biographical Dictionary of American Architects (deceased)*, Los Angeles, New Age Publishing, 1956, 678 p.

Anonymous. *Montréal fin de siècle. Histoire de la métropole du Canada au dix-neuvième siècle*, Montréal, The Gazette Printing Company, 1899, 216 p.

II. Secondary Sources

A. GENERAL

Amos, Louis A. «Architecture of Quebec Province», *Québec* [London, G.B.], vol. 9 no 4 (May 1934): 54, 55.

Andrews, Robert. «The Changing Styles of Country Houses», *The Architectural Review*, vol. 11 (1904): 1–4.

Andrews, Wayne. *Architecture, Ambition and Americans, a Social History of American Architecture*. 1964. New York, The Free Press, 1978 (revised edition), 332 p.

Bing, Samuel. *La culture artistique en Amérique*, Paris, s. éd., 1896, 119 p.

Bottomley, William Lawrence. «A Selection from the Works of Delano & Aldrich», *The Architectural Record*, vol. 54 no 1 (July 1923): 2–71.

Carless, William. «The Architecture of French Canada», *The Journal, Royal Architectural Institute of Canada*, vol. 2 n° 4 (July-August 1925): 141–145.

Charney, Melvin. «Pour une définition de l'architecture au Québec», *Architecture et urbanisme au Québec*, Montréal, Presses de l'Université de Montréal, 1971, p. 11–42.

Coffin, Lewis A. et coll. *Small French Buildings*, New York, Charles Scribner's Sons, 1926, 275 p.

Cortissoz, Royal. *Portraits of ten Country Houses Designed by Delano & Aldrich*, New York, Doubleday, Page and Company, 1924, 16 p., 60 pl.

Dow, Joy Wheeler. *American Renaissance, a Review of Domestic Architecture*, New York, William T. Comstock, 1904, 182 p.

Downing, Andrew Jackson. *The Architecture of Country Houses: Including Designs for Cottages, Farm Houses and Villas ...*, New York, D. Appleton & Co., 1850, 484 p.

Downing, Andrew Jackson. *A Treatise on the Theory and Practice of Landscape Gardening*, New York, Funk & Wagnalls, 1967 (reprint), 576 p.

Downing, Andrew Jackson. *Victorian Cottage Residences*, New York, Dover Publications, 1981 (reprint), 261 p.

Downing, Antoinette, F. et Vincent J. Scully. *The Architectural Heritage of Newport Rhode Island 1640–1915*. 1952. New York, American Legacy Press, 1982, (revised edition) 526 p.

Dupont, Jean-Claude et coll. *Habitation rurale au Québec*, Montréal, Hurtubise HMH, 1978, 268 p.

Edgell, G.H. *The American Architecture of To-Day*, New York, Charles Scribner's Sons, 1928, 401 p.

Gagnon-Pratte, France. *L'architecture et la nature à Québec au dix-neuvième siècle: les villas*, Québec, Ministère des Affaires culturelles (Musée du Québec), 1980, 334 p.

Gardner, Eugene Clarence. *Illustrated Homes: A Series of Papers Describing Real Houses and Real People*, Boston, James R. Osgood and Co., 1875, 287 p.

Garvin, James L. «Mail-Order House Plans and American Victorian Architecture», *Winterthur Port-Folio*, vol. 16 n° 4 (Winter 1981): 309–334.

Gauthier-Larouche, Georges. *Évolution de la maison rurale traditionnelle dans la région de Québec*, (Les Archives de Folklore n° 15), Québec, Les Presses de l'Université Laval, 1974, 321 p.

Gauvreau, Jean-Marie. *Artisans du Québec*, Trois-Rivières, Éditions du Bien Public, 1940, 224 p.

Gauvreau, Jean-Marie. «Évolution et tradition des meubles canadiens», *Mémoires de la Société royale du Canada*, 3ᵉ série, tome 38, section 1 (mai 1944): 121–128, 4 pl.

Gowans, Alan. *Looking at Architecture in Canada*, Toronto, Oxford University Press, 1958, 232 p.

Hamlin, Talbot Faulkner. *The American Spirit in Architecture*, New Haven, Yale University Press, 1926, 339 p.

Hamlin, Talbot Faulkner. *Architecture Through the Ages*, New York, P. Putnam's Sons, 1940, 684 p.

Hitchcock, Henry-Russell. *Architecture: Nineteenth and Twentieth Centuries*, Baltimore, Penguin Books, 1958, 510 p.

Hooper, Charles-Edw. *The Country House, a Practical Manual of the Planning and Construction of the American Country Home and its Surroundings*, New York, Doubleday, Page and Co., 1906, 330 p.

Huxley, Anthony. *An Illustrated History of Gardening*, New York & London, Paddington Press, 1978, 352 p.

Kalman, Harold D. *The Railway Hotels and the Development of the Château Style in Canada*, Victoria (B.C.), University of Victoria (Maltwood Museum), 1968, 47 p.

Kane, Patricia E. *300 Years of American Seating Furniture*, Boston, New York Graphic Society, 1976, 319 p.

Kidney, Walter C. *The Architecture of Choice: Eclecticism in America 1880–1930*, New York, George Braziller, 1974, 178 p.

Lessard, Michel et Gilles Vilandré. *La maison traditionnelle au Québec*, Montréal, Éditions de l'Homme, 1974, 493 p.

Lessard, Michel et Huguette Marquis. *Encyclopédie de la maison québécoise*, Montréal, Les Éditions de l'Homme, 1972, 728 p.

Loup de Viane, T. *Mon jardin au Canada*, Paris, Bibliothèque Pratique de la Famille, 1969, 29 p.

Lyle, John M. «The Allied Arts at the Recent Toronto Chapter Exhibition», *The Journal, Royal Architectural Institute of Canada*, vol. 4 (May 1927): 164–169.

Lyon, Irving W. *The Colonial Furniture of New England*. 1891. New York, E.P. Dutton, 1977, 285 p.

Massicotte, Édouard-Z. «Les maisons de bois d'autrefois», *B.R.H.*, vol. 40 n° 6 (1934): 447, 448.

Massicotte, Édouard-Z. «En quoi couvrait-on les maisons?», *B.R.H.*, vol. 44 n° 1 (1938): 13–16.

McMordie, Michael. «The Cottage Idea», *RACAR*, vol. 6 n° 1 (1979): 17–27.

Morisset, Gérard. *L'architecture en Nouvelle-France*, Québec, Éditions du Pélican, 1980 (réédition de 1949), 150 p., planches-photos.

Mumford, Lewis. *Roots of Contemporary American Architecture*, New York, Dover Publications, 1972, 452 p.

Murray, A.L. «Frederick Law Olmsted and the Design of Mount Royal Park, Montreal», *Journal of the Society of Architectural Historians*, (October 1967): 163–171.

Newton, Roger Hale. «Our Summer Resort Architecture — an American Phenomenon and Social Document», *The Art Quarterly*, vol. 4 n° 1 (Winter 1941): 297–321.

Noppen, Luc. «La maison québécoise : un sujet à redécouvrir», dans «Architectures: la culture dans l'espace», *Questions de culture*, n° 4 (1983): 69–101.

Olmsted, Frederick L. «Terrace and Veranda — Back and Front», *Garden and Forest*, vol. 1 (6 June 1888): 170, 171.

Post, Emily (Mrs Price Post). *The Personality of a House*, New York, Funk & Wagnalls Co., 1930, 521 p.

Price, Bruce. «The Suburban House», *Scribner's Magazine*, vol. 8 n° 1 (July 1890): 3–19.

Price, C. Matlack. *The Practical Book of Architecture*, Philadelphia & London, J.B. Lippincott Co., 1916, 348 p.

Roth, Leland M. *A Concise History of American Architecture*, New York, Harper and Row, 1980, 381 p.

Rouillard, Dominique. *Le site balnéaire*, Bruxelles, Pierre Mardaga éditeur, 1984, 357 p.

Roy, Pierre-Georges. *Vieux manoirs, vieilles maisons*, Québec, Commission des monuments historiques de la province de Québec (Proulx), 1927, 376 p.

Rusk, William Sener. «The Influence of Norman Architecture in French Canada», *Bulletin de l'Institut Français de Washington*, n° 13 (décembre 1940): 1–10.

Saylor, Henry M. *Bungalows, their Design, Construction and Furnishing, with Suggestions also for Camps, Summer Homes and Cottages of Similar Character*, New York, McBride, Nast and Co., 1913, 206 p.

Scully, Vincent J. «Romantic Rationalism and the Expression of Structure in Wood: Downing, Wheeler, Gardner and the «Stick Style» 1840–1876», *The Art Bulletin*, vol. 35 n° 2 (June 1953): 121–142.

Scully, Vincent J. «American Villas», *The Architectural Review*, vol. 115 n° 687 (March 1954): 169–179.

Scully, Vincent J. *The Single Style and the Stick Style, Architectural Theory and Design from Downing to the Origins of Wright*. 1955. New Haven & London, Yale University Press, 1971, 184 p.

Scully, Vincent J. *The Shingle Style Today or the Historian's Revenge*, New York, George Braziller, 1974, 118 p.

Scully, Vincent J. *Modern Architecture, The Architecture of Democracy*, New York, George Braziller, 1982 (10th edition), 158 p.

Séguin, Robert-Lionel. «La grange octogonale», *B.R.H.*, vol. 67 n° 1 (1961): 93–97.

Sheldon, George William. *Artistic Country-Seats, Types of Recent American Villa and Cottage Architecture ...*, New York, Da Capo Press, 1979 (reprint 1887), 2 vol.

Tallmadge, Thomas E. *Story of Architecture in America*, New York, W.W. Norton & Company Inc., 1936, 332 p.

Thomas, George E. and Carl Doebley. *Cape May, Queen of the Seaside Resorts, its History and Architecture*, Philadelphia, The Art Alliance Press, 1976, 202 p.

Thompson, Deborah et al. *Maine Forms of American Architecture*, Camden (Maine), Downeast Magazine, 1976, 362 p.

Turcot, Henri. *The French-Canadian Homespun Industry*, Ottawa, Department of Trade and Commerce, 1928, 19 p.

Traquair, Ramsay. *The Cottages of Quebec*, Montréal, McGill University Publications, Series 8 (Art and Architecture), n° 5, 1926, 14 p.

Traquair, Ramsay. *The Old Architecture of Quebec, a Study of the Buildings Erected of New France from the Earliest Explorers to the Middle of the Nineteenth Century*, Toronto, The Mac-Millan Company, 1947, 324 p.

Upjohn, Richard. «The Colonial Architecture of New York and the New England States», *Proceedings of the American Institute of Architects Annual Convention*, vol. 3 (17 November 1869): 47–51.

Van Brunt, Henry. «On the Present Condition and Prospects of Architecture», *Atlantic Monthly*, vol. 57 n° 341 (March 1886): 374–384.

Wheeler, Gervase. *Homes for the People, in Suburb and Country; the Villa, the Mansion and the Cottage*, New York, Charles Scribner, 1855, 443 p.

Wheeler, Gervase. *Rural Homes; or Sketches of Houses Suited to American Country Life ...*, Auburn & Rochester, Alden & Beardsley, 1855, 298 p.

Whiffen, Marcus. *American Architecture since 1780, a Guide to the Styles,* Cambridge (Mass.), The M.I.T. Press, 1969, 313 p.

Wright, Janet. *L'architecture pittoresque au Canada*, Ottawa, Parcs Canada, 1984, 184 p.

Anonymous. «Archeology and American Architecture», *The American Architect and Building News*, vol. 4 n° 145 (5 October 1878): 114, 115.

B. SPECIFIC

1. Regional Architecture

En collaboration. *Analyse du paysage architectural de la municipalité de Pointe-au-Pic*, Québec, Ministère des Affaires municipales (Municipalité régionale de comté de Charlevoix-Est, schéma d'aménagement), 1984, 37 p.

En collaboration. *Corpus de faits ethnographiques québécois: région de Charlevoix*, Québec, Université Laval, Travaux du CÉLAT, 1978, 2. vol.

Gauthier, Raymonde et Luc Noppen. *Le paysage architectural de Charlevoix,* Québec, Université Laval, Groupe de recherche PAISAGE (vol. 4), 1976, 87 p.

Léonidoff, Georges-Pierre. *L'architecture domestique de Charlevoix: le contexte évolutif et les granges-étables*, Québec, Université Laval, thèse de maîtrise (histoire), 1979, 283 p.

Léonidoff, Georges-Pierre. *Origine et évolution des principaux types d'architecture rurale au Québec et le cas de la région de Charlevoix*, Québec, Université Laval, thèse de doctorat (histoire), 1980, 55 pages liminaires, 860 p.

Raveneau, Jean. «Analyse morphologique, classification et protection des paysages: le cas de Charlevoix», *Cahiers de géographie de Québec*, vol. 21 n° 53–54 (septembre-décembre 1977): 135–186.

2. Architects

Baldwin, Charles C. *Stanford White.* 1931. New York, Da Capo, 1976, 399 p.

Delano, William A. *Random Rhymes*, New York, Private Publication, 1952, 67 p.

Dufresne, Henri. «Les faits et dits de la vie estivale à Pointe-au-Pic», *La Patrie*, (7 août 1955): 7.

Granger, Alfred Hoyt. *Charles Follen McKim, a Study of his Life and Work.* 1913. New York, Benjamin Blom Inc., 1972, 146 p.

Harrison, Wallace K. «Edward J. Mathews 1913–1980», *The Century Year-Book*, [New York, The Century Association] (1981): 260, 261.

Hewlett, J. Monroe et coll. «Stanford White as Those Trained in his Office Knew Him», *The Brickbuilder*, vol. 15 n° 12 (1906): 245–247.

Jacobs, Peter. «Frederick G. Todd and the Creation of Canada's Urban Landscape», *Bulletin The Association for Preservation Technology*, vol. 15 n° 4 (1983): 27–34.

Lavine, Sigmund A. *Famous American Architects*, New York, Dodd, Mead and Company, 1967, 158 p.

Moses, Lionel. «McKim, Mead & White — A History», *The American Architect*, vol. 121 n° 2394 (23 May 1922): 412–424.

Noppen, Luc et Marc Grignon. *L'Art de l'architecte, trois siècles de dessin d'architecture à Québec*, Québec, Musée du Québec/Université Laval, 1983, 293 p.

Reilly, C.H. *McKim, Mead & White*, New York, Benjamin Blom Inc., 1972, 24 p. planches.

Ridley, H.M. «Canada's Architectural Movement — The «Diet Kitchen» School and its

Propaganda for the Art», *Saturday Night* (12 March 1927): 1, 2.

Roth, Leland M. *The Architecture of McKim, Mead & White 1870–1920, A Building List*, New York & London, Garland Publishing Inc., 1978, 213 p. planches.

Smith, Eugenia B. *Rhode Island Resort Architecture by McKim, Mead and White*, University of Wisconsin, Master's thesis, 1964, 180 p., 67 planches-photos.

Walker, C. Howard. «Stanford White — His Work», *The Brickbuilder*, vol. 15 n° 12 (1906): 243, 244.

Wiggs, H. Ross. «Louis A. Amos», *Journal, Royal Architectural Institute of Canada*, vol. 25 n° 10 (1948): 394.

Anonymous. «Charles Follen McKim», *Architects' and Builders' Magazine*, vol. 42 n° 2 (November 1909): 41–44.

Anonymous. «The Talk of the Town, Architect», *The New Yorker*, vol. 34 (5 April 1958): 23, 24.

Anonymous. «William Delano, Architect, Dead», *New York Times* (13 January 1960): 48.

Anonymous. «Classicist in Architectural Tradition», *American Institute of Architects Journal*, vol. 57 (May 1972): 54.

3. Villas

Cabot, Francis H. ««Les Quatre Vents», a Far-Northern Garden», *Arnoldia*, vol. 45 n° 4 (Autumn 1985): 19–31.

Carroll, Campbell. «Canadiana ... Tadoussac's unique collection», *Canadian Homes and Gardens*, vol. 19 n° 5 (1942): 22, 23, 49.

Gill, Brendan et Dudley Witney. *Summer Places*, New York, Methuen, 1978, 223 p.

Jones, Cranston. *Homes of the American Presidents*, New York, McGraw-Hill Book Co., 1962, 232 p.

Knott, Leonard L. «English Summers in French Canada», *Canadian Homes and Gardens*, vol. 12 n°ˢ 6–7 (1935): 28, 29, 46.

Legendre, J.-Thérèse. «Les grands domaines de Charlevoix», *Le Soleil* (11 septembre 1978): B-3; (12 septembre 1978): A-8.

Maloney, Elizabeth McElroy. «Picturesque Murray Bay», *Arts and Decorations*, vol. 46 (May 1937): 16-18.

Moholy-Nagy, Sibyl. *Native Genius in Anonymous Architecture in North America*. 1957. New York, Schocken Books, 1976, 190 p.

Moonan, Wendy Lyon. «Canadian Classics», *Town and Country*, vol. 137 n° 5042 (November 1983): 293–304.

Shennan, David. «Hotel Tadoussac, Tadoussac, Quebec», *Journal, Royal Architectural Institute of Canada*, vol. 21 n° 7 (1944): 152–156.

Stokes, Isaac Newton Phelps. *Random Recollections of a Happy Life*, New York, Private Publication (44 copies), 1941, 314 p.

Vaughan, Marilou. «Gardens: Les Quatre-Vents in the French Canadian Province of Quebec», *Architectural Digest*, vol. 36 n° 5 (June 1979): 124–130.

Waters, Mackenzie. «Round a Court — A Unique Plan for a Summer Residence», *Canadian Homes and Gardens*, vol. 14 n° 7–8 (1937): 14, 15.

Anonymous. «A Clapboard Cottage at Cap-à-l'Aigle», *Canadian Homes and Gardens*, vol. 5 n° 5 (1928): 48.

Anonymous. «Hon. William Taft's Summer Home at Murray Bay», *Canadian Homes and Gardens*, vol. 5 n° 10 (1928): 32.

Anonymous. «Thatching and Sentinal Populars at Pointe-au-Pic», *Canadian Homes and Gardens*, vol. 5 n° 5 (1928): 25, 28.

Anonymous. «A Working Farm in Murray Bay», *Town and Country*, vol. 97 n° 4237 (June 1942): 26–29.

Anonymous. «Cottage for Rent», *Colony Life* (Summer 1966): 7–11.

Illustration Credits

The illustrations in this book have been borrowed from various collections, public and private. I wish to express my thanks to the organizations listed below and to the individuals who kindly lent me their valuable documents.

PUBLIC COLLECTIONS

Archives de l'Université Laval (Québec)
Archives du Séminaire de Québec (Québec)
Archives nationales du Canada (Ottawa)
Archives nationales du Québec (Québec)
Art Gallery of Ontario (Toronto)
Bibliothèque de la législature (Québec)
Bibliothèque nationale du Québec (Montréal)
Boston Public Library (Boston)
Canadien National (Montréal)
Frederick Law Olmsted National Historic Site (Brookline, Mass.)
Groupe CSL Inc. [Canada Steamship Lines] (Montréal)
Inventaire des biens culturels du Québec (Québec)
Library of Congress (Washington)
Mariners Museum (Newport News, Virg.)
Massachusetts Historical Society (Boston)
Metropolitan Museum of Art (New York)
Municipalité de Pointe-au-Pic (Charlevoix)
Musée du Québec (Québec)
Musée McCord (Montréal)
Musée régional Laure-Conan (La Malbaie)
Musées nationaux du Canada (Ottawa)
New York Historical Society (New York)
New York Public Library (New York)
Ontario Archives (Toronto)
Queen's University Archives (Kingston)
Royal Ontario Museum (Toronto)
Société canadienne du microfilm (Montréal)
Société historique du lac Saint-Louis (Montréal)
University of Toronto (Toronto)
Vancouver Art Gallery (Vancouver)
Westmount Public Library (Montréal)

PRIVATE COLLECTIONS

Mrs A.S. Adair
Mrs C.H.A. Armstrong
Mrs Elizabeth Bacque
Mme Lisa Binsse
Mr A. Brian Buchanan
Mr Erskine B. Buchanan
Mr Ian E. Buchanan
Mr and Mrs Francis H. Cabot
Mrs Ruth Mitchell Cogan
M. Paul Couturier
Miss Louise Crane
Mrs Katharine G. Currier
Mme Thérèse Gouin Décarie
Mr and Mrs John B. Dempsey II
M. and Mme Paul Desmeules
Mme Doreen Warren Doucet
M. Michel Doyon
M. Jean Duberger
Mr and Mrs F. Victor Elkin
Mlle Lucie Forget
Mr and Mme Georges Fournier
Mr and Mme Roland Gagné

Miss Frances H. Gault
Mme Madeleine Sévigny Giguère
Mme Lorenzo Gilbert
Mr and Mrs A.R. Gillespie
Mr and Mrs Thomas C. Hoopes
Mr Frank J. Humphrey
Mr Colin W. Kerry
Mme Thérèse Fraser Lizotte
Rev and Mrs Donald B. Mackay
Mrs Margery Mackenzie
Mrs Helen Taft Manning
Mr and Mrs John McGreevy
Mrs Robert B. Minturn
Mrs Maud Morgan

Mr Patrick Morgan
Mrs Mary B. Naylor
Mrs Diana Thébaud Nicholson
M. and Mme. Burroughs Pelletier
M. and Mme Louis R. Pelletier
Mme Louise Piller-Tahy
Mme Pierre Sévigny
Dr and Mrs Hervey I. Sloane
Mr and Mrs Horace Taft
Mme Aline Vachon
M. Guy Van Duyse
Mme Henriette Warren
M. and Mme Pierre Warren
M. and Mme Roger Warren

ILLUSTRATIONS

1 *The Old Bread Oven, Murray Bay, lower St Lawrence.* M and Mme Pierre Warren.

2 *Philippe Gaultier de Comporté at Malbaie, New France, 1672* National Archives of Canada, C-40597. This drawing, enhanced in water-colour, by the well-known historical painter C.W. Jefferys, was used in 1929 as the sketch for a large painting that now hangs in a room at Manoir Richelieu in Pointe-au-Pic.

3 *Map of The Estate in Canada, dedicated to the dauphin* National Archives of Canada, PH 900, 1731. The original is at Service Historique de La Marine, Vincennes, France.

4 *Colonel Fraser, master of Lovat* Photograph taken from J.R. Harper, *The Fraser Highlanders*, 1979 edition, cover.

5 *View of the taking of Quebec*, 13 September 1759 Print after a drawing by Captain Harvey Smyth. A photoengraving appears as the frontispiece in *The Conspiracy of Pontiac and the Indian War after the Conquest of Canada* (Boston: Little Brown 1907) vol. 1.

6 *A View of the cathedral, Jesuits College, and Recollect Friars Church, taken from the gate of the governor's House* National Archives of Canada, C-361. This drawing by Richard Short, engraved by P. Canot and published in London in 1761, forms part of a series of twelve prints of the city of Quebec after the Conquest.

7 *Detail from a print by Richard Short, published in London in 1761* National Archives of Canada, C-361.

8 *Captain John Nairne at Murray Bay, 1761* National Archives of Canada, C-40592. This water-colour by C.W. Jefferys, enhanced in crayon, was used as a sketch for a large canvas now hanging at the entrance to the St Lawrence Room in Manoir Richelieu at Pointe-au-Pic.

9 *Sergeant James Thompson (1732–1831)* Photograph taken from J.R. Harper, *The Fraser Highlanders*, 1979 edition, opposite p. 114.

10 *John Nairne (1731–1802)* Private collection, New York. Portrait painted in Scotland by Sir Henry Raeburn about 1795, photographed in New York by Paul Hunter in 1983.

11 *Christine Nairne (1774–1817)* Private collection, Québec. Miniature on ivory painted about 1805 by an artist in Edinburgh, name unknown.

12 *Thomas Nairne (1787–1813)* Private collection, Québec. Miniature on ivory painted about 1805 by an artist in Edinburgh, name unknown.

13 *Imports from Scotland* Marius Barbeau, National Museums of Canada, 80055.

14 *Imports from Scotland* Marius Barbeau, National Museums of Canada, 80306.

15 *Nairne's seigneurial property, about 1925* Archives nationales du Québec, GH 870-82.

16 *Nairne's seigneurial property about 1925* Archives nationales du Québec, 874-327.

17 *Plan for cultivating the farm at Murray Bay* National Archives of Canada, C-60319 (Collection Nairne, MG 23 G III 23, vol. 5).

18 *Simon Fraser (1769–1844)* Musée régional Laure-Conan, gift of Mme Thérèse Fraser Lizotte. This portrait is attributed to the Canadian painter Jean-Baptiste Roy-Audy, although Fraser family tradition has it that the portrait was painted in Scotland.

19   *Fraser Manor at Mount Murray* Notman Photographic Archives, McCord Museum, 8809.

20   *Murray Bay and Mount Murray* Bibliothèque nationale du Québec. Detail from William Vondenvelden's *A New Topographical Map of the Province of Lower Canada ...* (London 1803).

21   *The valley of St. Étienne* National Archives of Canada, C-11701. Engraving by John J. Bigsby, taken from his work *The Shoe and Canoe* (London 1850), vol. 1, facing p. 228.

22   *Mal Bay or Murray Bay* Bibliothèque nationale du Québec. Detail from Joseph Bouchette's *Topographical Map of the Province of Lower Canada ...* (London 1815).

23   *A view of Mal Bay, bearing north-north-west for three leagues, taken 17 November 1784* National Archives of Canada, C-2013. Watercolour by James Peachey.

24   *Colonel Nairne's settlement at Mal Bay* Vancouver Art Gallery 71.8. Water-colour painted by George Heriot in 1798. Until recently it belonged to the owners of Nairne Manor at La Malbaie.

25   *Mal Bay* National Archives of Canada, C-11700. Drawing by John J. Bigsby, taken from his work *The Shoe and Canoe* (London 1850), vol. 1, facing p. 226.

26   *The Valley of St. Étienne* National Archives of Canada, C-103600. Map by John J. Bigsby, taken from *The Shoe and Canoe*, facing p. 228.

27   *John McNicol Nairne (1808–61)* Vancouver Art Gallery, 80.16. Oil on canvas by Antoine Plamondon, painted around 1830. It hung in Nairne Manor until the latter was demolished in 1960.

28   *Steamboat wharf, Montréal* National Archives of Canada, C-80319. The man who made this lithograph, James Duncan, came over with the British army about 1825. He settled in Montréal and earned a great reputation for his landscapes.

29   *Murray Bay* National Archives of Canada, C-3963.

30   *Lord and Lady Minto* Private collection, Québec. Piece of embroidered fabric, 8cm × 5.5cm.

31   *The village of La Malbaie, 11–12 July 1840* National Archives of Canada, C-58168. Taken from H.J. Warre's sketchbook "Fishing tour on board the schooner *Fanny* below the Saguenay on River St. Lawrence, July 1840," collection Henry James Warre, MG 24, F 71, vols. 5–6: 38–39.

32   *The Saguenay tour* Queen's University Archives, box 183. Taken from the advertising folder *The Beauty Spots of Canada* (1895).

33   *For Murray Bay and Rivière-du-Loup* Taken from the daily *Le Canadien* (23 July 1849), 3.

34   *Loading a schooner at low tide* National Archives of Canada, C-82785. Taken from *Picturesque Canada* (Toronto 1882), 63.

35   *Murray Bay* Taken from Henry M. Burt, *Guide through the Connecticut Valley to the White Mountains and the River Saguenay* (Springfield Mass. 1874), facing p. 287.

36   *"Excursions to Murray Bay, River Du Loup, Kakouna, and the Far-Famed River Saguenay"* Taken from the cover page (recto) of J.M.G.'s travel guide, published in 1856.

37   *"Excursions to Murray Bay, River Du Loup, Kakouna, and the Far-Famed River Saguenay"* Taken from the cover page (verso) of J.M.G.'s travel guide.

38   *On the route to Saguenay* "Map of the Lower St. Lawrence and Saguenay Rivers Showing the Route of the Steamer *Saguenay* 1856." Facing the frontispiece of *Excursions to Murray Bay, River Du Loup, Kakouna, and the Far-Famed River Saguenay* (Quebec 1856).

39   *On the route to Saguenay* Taken from "The *Saguenay*," *Harper's New Monthly Magazine* (July 1859): 145.

40   *The Steamer Magnet* National Archives of Canada, C-4854. This photograph was taken around 1867 by Alexander Henderson of Montreal.

41   *Indians making bark canoe* Notman Photographic Archives, McCord Museum, MP 260. This photograph by Alexander Henderson was obviously taken when he arrived at Pointe-au-Pic in the *Magnet* (see fig. 40).

42   *The Richelieu Company's steamer Québec leaving the wharf at Montréal for Québec* National Archives of Canada, C-50342. From *Canadian Illustrated News* (30 July 1870): 72, 73.

43   *Passengers transferring from one steamer to another in Québec* National Archives of Canada, C-58740. From *L'Opinion publique* (15 August 1872): 390. After a sketch by Edward Jump.

44 *Disembarking at La Malbaie* National Archives of Canada, C-58762. From *L'Opinion Publique* (29 August 1872): 416. After a sketch by Edward Jump.

45 *Arrival at La Malbaie from Québec* National Archives of Canada, C-59257. From *L'Opinion Publique* (31 July 1873): 368. After a sketch by Edward Jump.

46 *Map of the Saguenay River* Taken from M.F. Sweetser's *The Maritime Provinces: A Handbook for Travellers* (1875), facing p. 336.

47 *The steamer* Saguenay The Mariners Museum, QO 848. Oil painting by G. Beaulieu, Québec (48cm × 33cm).

48 *An Indian village of twenty to thirty hearths, near the quay at Pointe-au-Pic* Archives nationales du Québec, N 174-41. Photograph by J.E. Livernois around 1890. In Québec, the name Livernois has been linked to photography since 1854, the year in which Jules Isaîe Benoît, called Livernois, opened his studio. However, it was his son, Jules-Ernest (1851–1933), who made the reputation of the Livernoises in this sphere from 1874 until the beginning of the 1930s.

49 *The menu aboard the steamer* Saguenay Mr and Mrs F. Victor Elkin.

50 *The steamer* St Lawrence The Mariners Museum, QO 847. Oil painting by G. Beaulieu, Quebec (48cm × 33cm).

51 *An excursion in 1875* Advertisement in *Le Canadien* (22 July 1875), 2.

52 *A first-class cruise ship* M. and Mme Roland Gagné.

53 *The prestigious décor of the steamer* Richelieu M and Mme Roland Gagné.

54 *The steamer* Montreal Royal Ontario Museum, 977-177–3.

55 *The Richelieu and Ontario Navigation Company* The Mariners Museum, LP 2767.

56 *From Niagara to the sea* Musée régional Laure-Conan. Taken from the cover of the official guide of the Richelieu and Ontario Navigation Company (1900).

57 *The Québec Central Railway* Taken from *All-Round Route and Panoramic Guide of the St. Lawrence ...* (Montreal 1896), p. ii.

58 *The Intercolonial Railway* Taken from the frontispiece of Kilby W. Reynold's travel guide, *Intercolonial Railway: the Fast Line of Canada* (New Brunswick, May 1893).

59 *The ferry* Eureka Notman Photographic Archives, McCord Museum, 3887.

60 *The wharf at Pointe-au-Pic* Notman Photographic Archives, McCord Museum, 3888.

61 *Flying the R & O flag* Boston Public Library. Photograph taken from the Richelieu and Ontario Navigation Company's brochure, *Hotels and Steamers of Canada* (1906).

62 *The steamer* Canada *alongside Cap-à-l'Aigle quay around 1900* Notman Photographic Archives, McCord Museum, 3189.

63 *Destination Murray Bay* Notman Photographic Archives, McCord Museum 4914.

64 *Captain H.W. Gagné (1873–1961)* Mme Aline Vachon.

65 *The steamer* Richelieu Coll. The Mariners Museum (Newport News, Virginia) ref. Eldridge Call, under the title "Richelieu off Murray Bay," 18 July 1950.

66 *For a real holiday, take a cruise!* Canada Steamship Lines, *Saguenay Cruise*, vol. 1.

67 *Central House* National Archives of Canada, L-10134. Taken from *L'Opinion publique* (25 August 1881): 399.

68 *The hotelier Geroges Duberger standing between his parents* Jean Duberger. Daguerreotype, photographer unknown, dated around 1865.

69 *Arthur Buies, a regular resident at The Hotel Duberger* Musée du Québec, uncatalogued. Oil painting on canvas by Edmond Lemoyne, 56.5cm × 71.5cm.

70 *Pier at Murray Bay on the St. Lawrence River* Library of Congress, 39144-D4. Detroit Photographic Company, 12775.

71 *The Canadian calash* Photogravure from Burt's *Guide through the Connecticut Valley to the White Mountains and the River Saguenay*, 287.

72 *Xavier Warren's house about 1890* Mme Henriette Warren.

73 *Riverside House, Murray Bay* Notman Photographic Archives, McCord Museum 323, 661 II.

74 *Jessie and William Chamard around 1880* Notman Photographic Archives, McCord Museum, 329, 795 II.

75 *Chamard's Lorne House (1878–98)* Inventaire des biens culturels du Québec, 79–485 (45).

76 *The new Chamard's* Metropolitan Toronto Library Board.

77 *To let at Cap-à-l'Aigle!* Taken from *Le Touriste* (3 July 1885). The only existing copy is in the National Archives of Canada.

78 *Thomas Bhérer's farm at Cap-à-l'Aigle, 1896* Mr Colin W. Kerry. Copy available in Notman Photographic Archives, McCord Museum, MP 051–77.

79 *The Bhérer Barn, Cap-à-l'Aigle* Notman Photographic Archives, McCord Museum, 3191, "Thatched Barn, Cape-à-l'Aigle."

80 *The convalescent home, Murray Bay* New York Historical Society, 59187. This illustration appeared in an unidentified periodical.

81 *At the village of Pointe-au-Pic* National Archives of Canada, C-7945, "Murray Bay Village from Point a Pique, P.Q."

82 *Between fresh water and the sea* Archives nationales du Québec, N 1075-58, "48: Pointe à Pic (Murray Bay)." Photograph taken by Jules-E. Livernois about 1895.

83 *Hotèl at Murray Bay* Notman Photographic Archives, McCord Museum, 3259. Sketch by the architects Maxwell and Shattuck.

84 *A daring construction* "Floor Plans of the Manoir Richelieu," in *The Lower St. Lawrence and the Saguenay* (circa 1905), 9. New York Public Library.

85 *A daring construction* M. and Mme Roland Gagné.

86 *Richelieu Manoir* Notman Photographic Archives, McCord Museum, 5310, "Manoir Richelieu, Murray Bay, Que."

87 *A salt-water pool* Notman Photographic Archives, McCord Museum, 5317, "Manoir Richelieu, Swimming Pool, Murray Bay, Que."

88 *Quite a sight!* Notman Photographic Archives, McCord Museum, 4918, "View from Manoir Richelieu, Murray Bay, Que."

89 *Château Murray (1904–78)* Canadien National, 16858.

90 *The new Richelieu Manoir* Canada Steamship Lines. A print of the photograph by S.J. Hayward of Montréal, 34007.

91 *A peaceful interior* National Canadian, 32224. Photograph by Associated Screen News (Montréal), 4449-9.

92 *Triumphant ostentation* Canada Steamship Lines. Photograph by Associated Screen News (Montréal), 4449-4, "Main Lobby."

93 *Elegance is all* Canada Steamship Lines. Photograph by Hayward Studios (Montréal), 16920.

94 *Winter sports* Mr and Mrs John B. Dempsey II. "Map of the Bobsleigh Run and Principal Ski Trails in the Vicinity of Manoir Richelieu, Murray Bay."

95 *Music!* Canada Steamship Lines. Photograph by Arnott and Rogers (Montréal), 10776-13.

96 *The magic of the setting* Canada Steamship Lines. Copy available in the National Archives of Canada, PA 803012, "Des clients se promenant sur une terrasse du Manoir Richelieu sur le fleuve Saint-Laurent à Murray Bay, Québec, 1937."

97 *A life-style unique in America* Cover page of the travelogue written and illustrated by Frank H. Taylor, *Glimpses of St. Lawrence Summer Life* (New York 1884).

98 *Pointe-au-Pic, La Malbaie, St. Irénée* Cover page of the supplement to *Le Soleil* (4 August 1923). Original stored in the Bibliothéque de la législature.

99 *Fishing by torchlight* National Archives of Canada, C-41915. This water-colour, "Torch Light Fishing in North America," was done by John Heariside Clark.

100 *Prohibition against fishing by torchlight, 27 April 1793* National Archives of Canada, C-103404, Coll. John Nairne, MG 23 G III 23, vol. 5, "Prohibition against fishing by torchlight by John Nairne and Malcolm Fraser."

101 *A typically Canadian scene* Royal Ontario Museum, 954.188.2. This oil painting, "Officers Trophy Room," was done by Cornelius Krieghoff, in 1840.

102 *The benefits of rustic life* Mr and Mrs Philip Mackenzie. Photograph taken from one of William Hume Blake's albums, "Dark of House," around 1900.

103 *The benefits of rustic life* Mr and Mrs Philip Mackenzie. Photograph taken from one of William Hume Blake's albums, "Petit Lac Carré from Cliffs," around 1900.

104 *Lawyers on holiday* Mr and Mrs Philip Mackenzie. Photograph taken from one of William Hume Blake's albums, "Landing Place, Lac Carré," around 1900.

105 *Lawyers on holiday* Mr and Mrs Philip Mackenzie. Photograph taken from one of William Hume Blake's albums, "Nous autres," around 1900.

106 *Local guides* Mr and Mrs Philip Mackenzie. Photograph of Thomas Fortin and his son, taken from one of William Hume Blake's albums, no title.

107 *Local guides* Mr and Mrs Philip Mackenzie. Taken from one of the Blake family's albums, "The Broken Canoe."

108 *To sportsmen, fishermen, and tourists* National Archives of Canada, L 9612. Announcement from *Le Touriste* (3 July 1885): 3.

109 *Les Grands Jardins, in the heart of the Laurentides Park* Archives nationales du Québec, D 310. This map was drawn in 1902 by W.C.J. Hall, superintendent of the Park of the Laurentians from the time of its foundation.

110 *The camp of Club la Roche* Mme Lorenzo Gilbert (Thomas Fortin's youngest daughter).

111 *Thomas Fortin (1858–1941)* Mme Lorenzo Gilbert. Charcoal sketch by the Montréal artist André Morency in 1930.

112 *Camp Ronevsorg on Lake Chaudière, St-Placide* Mme Pierre Sévigny (née Corinne Kernan). Photograph by the American photographer Stewart (Wellsville, New York).

113 *The game of golf* National Archives of Canada, C 76887. Illustration from "The Game of Golf: Some Impressions of Our Special Artist," *Canadian Illustrated News* (12 November 1881): 309.

114 *Murray Bay Golf Club* circa *1900* Mr Erskine B. Buchanan.

115 *The start of eighteen holes* Canadien National, 25651.

116 *The Manoir Richelieu golf-course* M. and Mme Louis R. Pelletier. Plan drawn in Pointe-au-Pic in 1923 by Hector Warren.

117 *A lady golfer around 1930* Canadien National, 4682.

118 *The inauguration of golf at Manoir Richelieu* M. and Mme Roland Gagné.

119 *Pocket money for the kids* Canadien National, 25653.

120 *A semi-aerial sport* Canada Steamship Lines.

121 *Lawn tennis at Manoir Richelieu in 1902* Notman Photographic Archives, McCord Museum, 3372, "Manoir Richelieu, Murray Bay."

122 *Tennis on clay courts* Musée régional Laure-Conan, gift of M. and Mme Georges Fournier. Print by photographer Donat Girard of Pointe-au-Pic, from a negative on glass plate.

123 *The Beach at Murray Bay* National Archives of Canada, C 56410. Drawing attributed to Edward Jump, from *Canadian Illustrated News* (12 August 1871): 97.

124 *Bathing, a public event* M. and Mme Roland Gagné.

125 *A quick dip in the sea* Mme Madeleine Sévigny Giguère.

126 *The Trou* M. and Mme Roland Gagné. "The Trou (Murray Bay)," attributed to Livernois, and taken around 1900.

127 Lunch *al fresco* Mrs Maud Morgan.

128 *Giddyup!* National Archives of Canada, C 58778. Illustration from *Canadian Illustrated News* (7 September 1872): 148. This sketch by Edward Jump was entitled "Murray Bay: A Hay-Cart Ride to the Lake."

129 *A ride in the cart* Archives du Séminaire de Québec. This photograph, taken about 1890, is attributed to Livernois of Québec.

130 *A habitant's house around 1890* Mr Erskine B. Buchanan. Print from one of the Buchanan family's albums, "Old Habitant House (1890)."

131 *Through the meadows* National Archives of Canada, PA 9732, "Through the Meadows, Cap-à-l'Aigle, P.Q." around 1900. This photograph is by William James Topley, who in 1868 opened a branch in Ottawa of the William Notman Studio; he became the owner four years later. Until he retired in 1923, he enjoyed an enviable reputation as a photographer of portraits, landscapes, architectural monuments, and everyday life.

132 *Afloat and ashore at Murray Bay* National Archives of Canada, C 124430. Illustrations from *Canadian Illustrated News* (2 September 1871): 160.

133 *Enjoying the river* From *Picturesque Canada* (Toronto 1882), 709. The American sketcher Frederick B. Schell worked as an illustrator for different magazines before being employed by *Harper's Magazine* in New York.

134 *Makeshift marina* Canadien National, 17315.

135 *The first Protestant church at Pointe-au-Pic* Notman Photographic Archives, McCord Museum 3283, "Murray Bay Church."

136 *The Murray Bay Protestant Church* Musée régional Laure-Conan. Photograph by Jacques Blouin.

137 *On the steps of Maison Rouge in 1892* Private collection (Toronto). Photograph by Alexandre Roy.

138 *In front of Mille Roches* Mrs Elizabeth Bacque.

139 *George MacKinnon Wrong (1860–1948)* University of Toronto. Portrait in oils painted about 1908 by Emma Mann Swan in her villa at Pointe-au-Pic, The Studio.

140 *William Hume Blake (1861–1924)* M. and Mme Paul Desmeules. Photograph signed Notman and Sons.

141 *On the terrace of Le Caprice* Mrs Elizabeth Bacque. Photograph taken about 1910.

142 *St. Anne-in-the-Field, Point-au-Pic* Notman Photographic Archives, McCord Museum, 3281, "St.-Anne-in-the-Field."

143 *Alexander Brock Buchanan (1832–1917)* Mr A. Brian Buchanan. Photograph reproduced by Notman and Sons from a daguerreotype.

144 *Then and now* From the work of R.R. McIam and James Logan, *The Clans of the Scottish Highlands* (London 1980), 25. Imaginary sketch of the chieftain of the Buchanan clan, done by R.R. McIan about 1845.

145 *Then and now* Mr Ian E. Buchanan. Photograph of Erskine B. Buchanan taken 31 July 1950. Print from one of the Buchanan family's albums.

146 *George Thomas Bonner (1837–1924)* Mr and Mrs Francis H. Cabot.

147 *The Cabot family going to church* Mrs Maud Morgan. This photograph, taken about 1910, comes from one of the Cabot family's albums.

148 *Maud B. Cabot* Mrs Maud Morgan. This photograph appears in *Holiday* (September 1952): 99.

149/150 *An invitation to Cabot Manor* Mrs Maud Morgan.

151 *The Morgans* Mr Patrick Morgan.

152 *The grandmother at the centre of everything* Mr and Mrs F.R.L. Osborne. Photograph taken about 1910.

153 *The young Taft family around 1895* Mrs Helen Taft Manning.

154 *Summer 1924* Musée régional Laure-Conan, gift of M. and Mme Georges Fournier. Photograph by Donat Girard of Pointe-au-Pic, from a negative on glass plate.

155 *The president and his descendants* Mrs Helen Taft Manning.

156 *The Taft family song* Mrs Helen Taft Manning.

157 *Ex-President Taft at Pointe-au-Pic* Musée régional Laure-Conan. (La Malbaie). Postcard in circulation about 1920.

158 *At the Monument to the Braves, Cap-à-l'Aigle* Mrs Mary B. Naylor.

159 *Sir Charles Fitzpatrick (1853–1942)* Mme Pierre Sévigny (née Corinne Kernan).

160 *Mabel Thorp Boardman (1861–1946)* Miss Louise Crane. Photograph by Clenedinst Studio (Washington).

161 *Elizabeth Hewlett Scudder Thébaud Binsse (1863–1957)* Mme Lisa Binsse.

162 *Harry Lorin Binsse de St-Victor (1905–71)* Musée régional Laure-Conan. Photograph by Peter F. Ryan at the quayside in Pointe-au-Pic, 1951.

163 *At Pointe-au-Pic, an ideal spot* Société canadienne du microfilm. Cover page of *La Patrie* (19 August 1922).

164 *Sir Rodolphe Forget (1861–1919)* Musée régional Laure-Conan. This photograph was taken from the album "Gil'Mont St-Irénée-les-Bains," 1906, put out by the Quéry Frères Studio of Montréal. William and Adélard Quéry had worked at Notman's from 1864 to 1881 before opening their own studio, which they kept going till 1910.

165 *Gil'Mont, sonnet to Lady Forget* Mlle Lucie Forget. Taken from the visitor's book at Gil'mont. It had once belonged to Lady Forget.

166 *Gil'Mont, St-Irénée-les-Bains, 1906* Musée régional Laure-Conan. Cover page of the album "Gil'Mont."

167 *Gil'-Mont, St Irénée-les-Bains, 1906*

Musée régional Laure-Conan. Photograph taken from the album "Gil'Mont." "The Outside Staircase."

168   *Gil'Mont, St Irénée-les-Bains, 1906* Musée régional Laure-Conan. Photograph taken from the album "Gil'Mont," "The Living-Room."

169   *Gil'Mont, St Irénée-les-Bains, 1906* Photograph taken from the album "Gil-Mont," "The Greenhouse."

170   *The Spinney, Pointe-au-Pic, 1906* Dr and Mrs Hervey I. Sloane. Cover page of the album "The Spinney."

171   *The Spinney, Pointe-au-Pic, 1906* Dr and Mrs Hervey I. Sloane. Photograph taken from the album "The Spinney," "House from Lawn."

172   *The Spinney, Pointe-au-Pic, 1906* Dr and Mrs Hervey I. Sloane. Photograph taken from the album "The Spinney," "Drawing Room."

173   *The Spinney, Pointe-au-Pic, 1906* Dr and Mrs Hervey I. Sloane. Photograph taken from the album "The Spinney," "Miss Neff and Foxgloves."

174   *The Reverend Alexander B. Mackay (1842–1901)* Rev. and Mrs Donald B. Mackay.

175   *The Cap-à-l'Aigle church (1889–1962)* Ontario Archives.

176   *Malbaie, 1885* M. and Mme Louis R. Pelletier. Reproduction of a daguerreotype.

177   *The young grow up ...* Mrs A.S. Adair (née Roslyn Kyle.)

178   *St Peter-on-the-Rock, Cap-à-l'Aigle* Musée régional Laure-Conan. Photograph by Jacques Blouin, 1982.

179   *I dreamed I went to Murray Bay ...* Mr Thomas C. Hoopes. This home-made postcard was sent to Marcia Hoopes in 1955 (19cm × 14cm).

180   *Unity amid diversity* Boston Public Library. Photograph taken from a brochure of the Richelieu and Ontario Navigation Company, *Hotels and Steamers of Canada* (1906).

181   *Young Charles and his brother Edouard* Mme Louise Piller-Tahy. Reproduction of a daguerreotype dating from around 1875.

182   *Jean-Charles Warren (1868–1929)* Musée régional Laure-Conan, gift of Mme Henriette Warren. Photograph by Livernois, taken in Québec around 1915.

183   *Château Murray, Pointe-au-Pic* M. and Mme Louis R. Pelletier.

184   *Plans of the Minturn house* Mr and Mrs F.R.L. Osborne. This drawing was done on tracing cloth in 1894.

185   *Plans of the Minturn house* Mr and Mrs F.R.L. Osborne. This drawing was done on tracing cloth in 1894.

186   *Susanna Shaw Minturn's house* Mr and Mrs F.R.L. Osborne.

187   *The best place to enjoy the view* Mr and Mrs Horace Taft. Photograph from a family album, "Deciding on Position of House, 1903."

188   *Building a villa* Mr and Mrs Horace Taft. Photograph from a family album, "Building of the Charles Warren's House (1st week)."

189   *Building a villa* Mr and Mrs Horace Taft. Photograph from "Building of the Charles Warren's House (3rd week)."

190   *Building a villa* Mr and Mrs Horace Taft. Photograph from "Building of the Charles Warren's House (6th week)."

191   *Building a villa* Société canadienne du Microfilm. Photograph from the cover page of *La Patrie* (19 August 1922).

192   *For a Seashore Place* Mme Dorren Warren Doucet. Drawing in ink on cardboard by the architect Jean-Charles Warren about 1915, for a house on the edge of the St Lawrence for the Donohue family.

193   *The Donohue house* Musée régional Laure-Conan. Photograph by Jacques Blouin, 1982.

194   *Rayon d'Or* Musée régional Laure-Conan. Photograph by Jacques Blouin, 1982.

195   *A simple and spontaneous construction* Musée régional Laure-Conan. Photograph by Jacques Blouin, 1982.

196/197   *Le Barachois* Musée régional Laure-Conan. Photograph by Jacques Blouin, 1982.

198   *Interpretation of the traditional style* Musée régional Laure-Conan. Photograph by Jacques Blouin, 1982.

199   *Darly Fields* Musée régional Laure-Conan. Plan drawn by Pierre Delisle. Print taken in September 1981.

200   *One of Charles Warren's characteristic interiors* Musée régional Laure-Conan. Photograph by Jacques Blouin, 1982.

201   *Comfort with a country accent* Musée régional Laure-Conan. Photograph by Jacques Blouin, 1982.

202   *True to life* Musée régional Laure-Conan. Photograph by Jacques Blouin, 1982.

203   *Bel Adon* Photograph from *Canadian Homes and Gardens* (May 1928): 48.

204   *Bel Adon* Musée régional Laure-Conan. Photograph by Jacques Blouin, 1984.

205   *Penteaves, with its Norman charm* Musée régional Laure-Conan. Photograph by Jacques Blouin, 1984.

206   *Penteaves* Musée régional Laure-Conan. Plan drawn by Pierre Delisle in September 1981.

207   *Skilled techniques* Musée régional Laure-Conan. Photograph by Jacques Blouin, 1984.

208   *Les Hirondelles* Musée régional Laure-Conan. Photograph by Jacques Blouin, 1982.

209   *The nobility of simplicity* Musée régional Laure-Conan. Photograph by Jacques Blouin, 1982.

210   *A plan of development* Musée régional Laure-Conan, gift of Mme Charlotte Brisson. Map drawn by Charles Warren, "Map of Pointe à Pic Village, Malbaie Village and Malbaie Parish," 1924.

211   *Les Pins Rouges* Inventaire des biens culturels du Québec, C.80-072-8 (35). Photograph by Pierre Lahoud and Pierre Bureau.

212   *A choice location* Notman Photographic Archives, McCord Museum, 3893, "Murray Bay from the Hillside."

213   *Harry Staveley (1848–1925)* Archives of Laval University. Taken from a photomontage by Jos. Beaudry (1890).

214   *La Maison Rouge* Musée régional Laure-Conan, gift of Mrs C.H.A. Armstrong. Photograph by Samuel H.N. Kennedy (Québec) around 1890.

215   *The firm McKim, Mead and White in 1906* Photograph from Charles C. Baldwin, *Stanford White* (New York: Da Capo Press 1976), facing p. 114.

216   *A building designed by Charles F. McKim* Mr and Mrs F.R.L. Osborne.

217   *Georges Janin (1853–1917)* Photograph from *Montréal fin de siècle, histoire de la métropole du Canada au Dix-Neuvième siècle* (Montreal: The Gazette Printing 1899), 107.

218   *Mont Plaisant* M. and Mme Louis R. Pelletier. "Perspective (before construction) of the summer residence for Doctor Elzéar Pelletier by Georges Janin, I.C. 1899."

219   *Mont Plaisant* M. and Mme Louis R. Pelletier. Photograph from a family album of M. and Mme Burroughs Pelletier.

220   *Ground plan of Mont Plaisant* M. and Mme Louis R. Pelletier. This plan was drawn by Georges Janin in 1899 (unsigned).

221   *Beau Jardin* Musée régional Laure-Conan. Photograph by Jacques Blouin, 1982.

222   *Stanford White (1853–1906)* Photograph taken from Charles C. Baldwin, *Stanford White*, facing p. 362.

223   *Bord de l'eau* Municipality of Pointe-au-Pic. Photograph by Jules Blouin, about 1960.

224   *View over the river* Municipality of Pointe-au-Pic. Photograph by Jules Blouin, about 1960.

225   *A refreshing interior* Municipality of Pointe-au-Pic. Photograph by Jules Blouin, about 1960.

226   *Mr and Mrs I.N. Phelps Stokes, 1897* Metropolitan Museum of Art, 38–104. Oil on canvas by John Singer Sargent (214cm × 101cm).

227   *Isaac Newton Phelps Stokes (1864–1944)* New York Historical society, 7243. Oil on canvas by DeWith M. Lockman, 1930 (126cm × 101cm).

228   *The second Minturn house* Mrs Robert B. Minturn. Photograph taken about 1915.

229   *The second Minturn house* Musée régional Laure-Conan. Photograph by Jacques Blouin, 1984.

230   *Ground plan of the Minturn house* Mrs Ruth Mitchell Cogan. Plan by the firm of Howells and Stokes, April 1907. Photographic reproduction by Donald D. Breza.

231   *Elevation of the Minturn house* Mrs Ruth Mitchell Cogan. Plan by the firm of Howells and Stokes, April 1907. Photographic reproduction by Donald D. Breza.

232   *The Murray Bay Protestant Church* University of Toronto, Thomas Fisher Rare

Book Library, G.M. Wrong Papers 36, box 9. Sketch by the firm of Howells and Stokes, 12 August 1909.

233 *The Murray Bay Protestant Church* Musée régional Laure-Conan, gift of Mrs C.H.A. Armstrong.

234 *The Murray Bay Protestant Church* Laure-Conan Musée régional. Photograph by Jacques Blouin, 1982.

235 *Plan of Doctor Elzéar Pelletier's property* M. and Mme Louis R. Pelletier. "Plan of Property Belonging to Dr. Elzéar Pelletier at Cap-à-l'Aigle," October 1925.

236 *Le Sorbier* M. and Mme Burroughs Pelletier.

237 *Front elevation* M. and Mme Louis R. Pelletier. Plan no. 4 by David Shennan, no date, unsigned.

238 *Le Sorbier after renovation* Musée régional Laure-Conan. Photograph by Jacques Blouin, 1982.

239 *Le Gîte* M. and Mme Louis R. Pelletier. Sketch by David Shennan, 1913, and photograph of the house after construction, 1914.

240 *Panorama over the St. Lawrence* M. and Mme Louis R. Pelletier. Reproduction of a photograph by Burroughs Pelletier, about 1925.

241 *William Adams Delano (1874–1960)* New York Historical Society, 32138. Plaster bust signed Malvina Hoffman, 1941.

242 *Mur Blanc* Musée régional Laure-Conan. Photograph by Jacques Blouin, 1982.

243 *Designed for the site* Musée régional Laure-Conan. Photograph by Jacques Blouin, 1982.

244 *Summer Mansion on Ocean Drive, Newport, Rhode Island* Photograph from "House at Newport, Rhode Island: Delano & Aldrich, Architects," *The Architectural Record* (July 1923): 5.

245 *Projecting dormer windows* Photograph from "House at Newport, Rhode Island: Delano & Aldrich, Architects," *The Architectural Record* (July 1923): 6.

246 *Projecting dormer windows* Musée régional Laure-Conan. Photograph by Jacques Blouin, 1982.

247 *Louis-Auguste Amos (1869–1948)* Photograph from *The Montreal Daily Star* (21 August 1948), 18.

248 *Verte Feuille* Mme Thérèse Gouin Décarie.

249 *James Hampden Robb (1898–1988)* Private collection (Québec). Photograph by Philippe Dubé, 1982).

250 *Les Falaises* Musée régional Laure-Conan. Photograph by Jacques Blouin, 1984.

251 *Les Falaises* Musée régional Laure-Conan. Photograph by Jacques Blouin, 1982.

252 *Les Quatre Vents* Musée régional Laure-Conan. Photograph by Jacques Blouin, 1984.

253 *Elevation of Les Quatre Vents* Mr and Mrs Francis H. Cabot. Plan no. 4 by Frederic R. King, architect, 1 November 1956.

254 *Noblesse oblige* Musée régional Laure-Conan. Photograph by Jacques Blouin, 1983.

255 *A project by Edward J. Mathews (1903–80)* Mr and Mrs Francis H. Cabot. Sketch by Edward J. Mathews.

256 *A small model farm at the entrance to Les Quatre Vents* Mr and Mrs Francis H. Cabot.

257 *A certain view of space* Musée régional Laure-Conan. Photograph by Jacques Blouin, 1982.

258 *The New Manoir Richelieu* National Archives of Canada, C-40338. Sketch by the Montréal architect John S. Archibald.

259 *Donald Mackenzie Waters (1894–1968)* Art Gallery of Ontario, N-1886. Photograph from "The Diet Kitchen Group," *Saturday Night* (12 March 1927): 1.

260 *High Acres* Inventaire des biens culturels du Québec, C-80-072-33 (35). Photograph by Pierre Lahoud and Pierre Bureau.

261 *A unique plan for a summer residence* National Archives of Canada, L-11951. From an article by Mackenzie Waters, "Round a Court: Unique Plan for Summer Residence," *Canadian Homes and Gardens* (July–August 1937): 14.

262 *An interior courtyard* Musée régional Laure-Conan. Photograph by Jacques Blouin, 1982.

263 *An interior kept deliberately sparse* Musée régional Laure-Conan. Photograph by Jacques Blouin, 1982.

264 *Robert Walker Humphrey (1916–72)* Mr

Frank J. Humphrey. Photograph taken about 1940.

265 *Sunnybrae Farm* Musée régional Laure-Conan. Photograph by Jacques Blouin, 1982.

266 *Ciel sur Mer* Musée régional Laure-Conan. Photograph by Jacques Blouin, 1982.

267 *A exotic interior* Mr Frank J. Humphrey.

268 *A fine example of traditional architecture* Inventaire des biens culturels du Québec, Gariépy B-5.

269 *Elevation of Défense de Passer* Musée régional Laure-Conan, gift of Patrick Séguin.

270 *Défense de Passer* Inventaire des biens culturels du Québec, 80–141–16A (35). Photograph by Pierre Lahoud and Pierre Bureau.

271 *The nicely curved profile of the Fraser manor* Mrs Maud Morgan.

272 *The predominant roof* Musée régional Laure-Conan. Photograph by Jacques Blouin, 1982.

273 *Rotunda designed by Humphrey and Séguin* Musée régional Laure-Conan, gift of Patrick Séguin. Sectional elevation no. 2.02 for a changing-room for Mme J.G. Bourne, La Malbaie, by the firm of Humphrey and Séguin, 21 May 1963.

274 *Rotunda designed by Humphrey and Seguin* Musée régional Laure-Conan. Photograph by Jacques Blouin, 1982.

275 *Recycled materials* Musée régional Laure-Conan. Photograph by Jacques Blouin, 1984.

276 *A plan by Guy Mongenais* Mme Pierre Sévigny. From "Old Materials Used Again," *Book of Homes* (1952).

277/278/279 *An industrial building* Musée régional Laure-Conan, gift of Mr Philip Mackenzie.

280 *Architect's sketch* Musée régional Laure-Conan, gift of Mr Philip Mackenzie. Sketch down in 1984 by Philip Mackenzie, who had built Sybil Kennedy's cottage in 1960.

281 *A bungalow on the cliff* Musée régional Laure-Conan.

282 *A constant search for the essential* Musée régional Laure-Conan, photograph by Jacques Blouir.

283 *An austere house* M. Michel Doyon. Stereoscopic print, around 1860.

284 *Glen Cottage at Murray Bay, around 1860* Notman Photographic Archives, McCord Museum, MP-030/82, "Glen Cottage, Murray Bay, 1860s."

285/286 *From rustic house to ornate cottage* Mr Erskine B. Buchanan. Photograph taken from one of the Buchanan family's albums.

287 *The Aviary* Mr and Mrs A.R. Gillespie. Drawing by A. Josey, August 1917.

288 *Front and side elevations* Mr and Mrs A.R. Gillespie. Plan drawn in 1967 by the architect Philip Mackenzie, no. E-5.

289 *Ground plan* Mr and Mrs A.R. Gillespie. Plan drawn in 1967 by the architect Philip Mackenzie, no. E-1.

290 *The Collard house* Musée régional Laure-Conan. Photograph by Jacques Blouin, 1983.

291 *Romantic traditionalism* Musée régional Laure-Conan. Photograph by Jacques Blouin, 1982.

292 *Chouette* Mrs Maud Morgan. Snapshot taken in 1932, from one of the Morgan family's albums.

293/294 *Chouette* Musée régional Laure-Conan. Photograph by Jacques Blouin, 1984.

295 *Terrebonne* Mrs Diana Thébaud Nicholson.

296 *Clos des Lupins* Musée régional Laure-Conan. Photograph by Jacques Blouin, 1982.

297 *Murray Village* Notman Photographic Archives, McCord Museum, 3286, "Murray Bay Village, around 1900."

298 *Les Cerceaux* Mr and Mrs Thomas C. Hoopes. Photograph taken around 1930.

299 *La Folie Rose* Musée régional Laure-Conan. Photograph by Jacques Blouin, 1982.

300 *Duncairn* Miss Frances H. Gault. Photograph taken around 1925.

301 *The suburban phenomenon in the country* Musée régional Laure-Conan. Map drawn by C.C. Duberger, *Murray Bay Atlas and Maps of Its Environs* (Murray Bay 1895), plate 2.

302 *Blairvocky* Mr Erskine B. Buchanan. Photograph from one of the Buchanan family's albums.

303 *Regency style* Musée régional Laure-Conan. Photograph by Jacques Blouin, 1983.

304 *A logical arrangement of interior space*

M. Guy Van Duyse. "Diagram of First floor, Pointe-à-Pic, Que., Oct. 1893."

305   *A Flemish villa* Musée régional Laure-Conan. Photograph by Jacques Blouin, 1983.

306   *A more functional layout* Musée régional Laure-Conan. Plan drawn by Simon Drolet. Revised in 1983.

307   *A small entrance hall* Musée régional Laure-Conan. Photograph by Jacques Blouin, 1983.

308   *A visitor from Moscow at Villa mon Repos* Musée régional Laure-Conan. Photograph by Jacques Blouin, 1982.

309   *A wooden château* M. Paul Couturier.

310   *Villa Bellevue* Mme Aline Vachon.

311   *Worthy of a smart neighbourhood* Musée régional Laure-Conan. Photograph by Jacques Blouin, 1983.

312   *The Spinney* Musée régional Laure-Conan. Photograph by Jacques Blouin, 1982.

313   *Comfort by the fire* Musée régional Laure-Conan. Photograph by Jacques Blouin, 1982.

314   *Jardin Joyeux* Musée régional Laure-Conan. Photograph by Jacques Blouin, 1982.

315   *An inviting entrance* Musée régional Laure-Conan. Photograph by Jacques Blouin, 1984.

316   *A later model* Musée régional Laure-Conan. Photograph by Jacques Blouin, 1982.

317   *Torwood* Musée régional Laure-Conan. Photograph by Jacques Blouin, 1983.

318   *Ground plan* Mrs Margery Mackenzie. Revised by Malcolm B. Mackenzie in 1972.

319   *The imposing profile of Porte-Bonheur* Musée régional Laure-Conan. Photograph by Jacques Blouin, 1982.

320   *Le Cran* Musée régional Laure-Conan. Photograph by Jacques Blouin, 1982.

321   *Suburban planning* Municipality of Pointe-au-Pic. Map by Émilien Pouliot, *Plan of the village of Pointe-au-Pic, County of Charlevoix* (Québec 17 June 1929).

322   *Northern Lights* Inventaire des biens culturels du Québec, C-80-072-31 (35). Photograph by Pierre Lahoud and Pierre Bureau.

323   *Bringing the outside in* Mme Louise Crane. Photograph by Associated Screen News (Montréal), CSL 170-2.

324   *Rochegrise* Musée régional Laure-Conan. Photograph by Jacques Blouin, 1983.

325   *Sur la Côte* Westmount Public Library. Coloured postcard entitled "View from Murray Bay Hill, Murray Bay, Lower St. Lawrence River."

326   *A shaggy façade* Musée régional Laure-Conan. Photograph by Jacques Blouin, 1982.

327   *The Tibbits' house* Musée régional Laure-Conan, gift of M. and Mme Georges Fournier. Print of photograph by Donat Girard of Pointe-au-Pic, from a glass plate negative, around 1920.

328   *Composite materials* Musée régional Laure-Conan. Photograph by Jacques Blouin, 1982.

329   *A summer drawing-room* Musée régional Laure-Conan. Photograph by Jacques Blouin, 1982.

330   *Ça Nous Va* Musée régional Laure-Conan. Photograph by Jacques Blouin, 1982.

331   *Canaan Cottage* Musée régional Laure-Conan. Photograph by Jacques Blouin, 1982.

332   *St. Antoine Cottage* Musée régional Laure-Conan. Photograph by Jacques Blouin, 1982.

333   *A suite of furniture signed Charles Warren* Musée régional Laure-Conan. Photograph by Jacques Blouin, 1982.

334   *Furniture in Style* Musée régional Laure-Conan. Drawing by Jean-Claude Carbonneau. Revised in September 1982.

335   *American inspired* Musée régional Laure-Conan. Photograph by Jacques Blouin, 1982.

336   *British inspired* Musée régional Laure-Conan. Photograph by Jacques Blouin, 1982.

337   *Joseph Bouchard* Musée régional Laure-Conan, gift of M. Clément-Joseph Bouchard. Reproduced from an old print touched up with water-colours, around 1920.

338   *The refined line of modern art* Musée régional Laure-Conan. Photograph by François Tremblay, 1982.

339   *Cache-Cache* Musée régional Laure-Conan. Photograph by Jacques Blouin, 1982.

340   *Front and side elevations* Private collection (Boston). Revised in 1983 by Alexis Morgan.

341 *Ground plan* Private collection (Boston). Revised in 1983 by Alexis Morgan.

342 *At the edge of the sea* M. and Mme Roger Warren. Photograph by Claire Dagenais, around 1980.

343 *Patrick Morgan (1904–82)* Private collection (New York). Reproduced from a colour transparency (35mm), taken by Francis H. Cabot in October 1981 at Bas de l'Anse.

344 *An English-style park for Quatre Vents* Mr and Mrs Francis H. Cabot. Colour sketch drawn by Patrick Morgan around 1960.

345 *Lake Libellule* Musée régional Laure-Conan. Photograph by Jacques Blouin, 1982.

346 *A French-style garden* Mr and Mrs Francis H. Cabot. Colour sketch drawn by Patrick Morgan around 1960.

347 *Towards the French-style garden* Musée régional Laure-Conan. Photograph by Jacques Blouin, 1984.

348 *Rope bridge* Musée régional Laure-Conan. Photograph by Jacques Blouin, 1984.

349 *Flowers at Les Falaises* Musée régional Laure-Conan. Photograph by Jacques Blouin, 1982.

350 *Nature tamed* Musée régional Laure-Conan. Photograph by Jacques Blouin, 1982.

351 *A mixed garden* Musée régional Laure-Conan. Photograph by Jacques Blouin, 1984.

352 *A garden on the sea* Musée régional Laure-Conan. Photograph by Jacques Blouin, 1982.

353 *Twin Poplars* Musée régional Laure-Conan. Photograph by Jacques Blouin, 1982.

354 *Angels in our lands* Musée régional Laure-Conan. Photograph by Jacques Blouin, 1982.

355 *Water scenery at Tamarack Top* Musée régional Laure-Conan. Photograph by Jacques Blouin, 1982.

356 *A garden-city in Charlevoix* Musée régional Laure-Conan. Plan prepared by the Montréal landscapist Frederick G. Todd under the title "Subdivision Plan of Pointe A Gaz being part of the seigneury of Mount Murray, Cap à l'Aigle, P.Q.," 20 July 1903.

357 *Mrs T.D. McCagg, Pointe-au-Pic, Murray Bay* Frederick Law Olmsted National Historic Site. Job 348, plan no. 3, E.B. McCagg, Pointe-au-Pic.

358/359 *At the edge of the wood* Dr and Mrs Hervey L. Sloane. Photographs taken from the album "The Spinney," 1906.

360 *One of the attractions at The Spinney* Musée régional Laure-Conan. Photograph by Jacques Blouin, 1982.

361 *Henry Dwight Sedgwick (1861–1957)* Mr and Mrs F.R.L. Osborne. Photograph by Helen Brewer, around 1940.

362 *At Robert B. Minturn's* Mr and Mrs. Robert B. Minturn. Photograph taken about 1915.

363 *The garden as an oasis* Private collection (Pointe-au-Pic).

364 *The Giberts' vast kitchen-garden* Musée régional Laure-Conan, gift of Mr. A. Brian Buchanan. Photograph taken about 1925, attributed to Donat Girard of Pointe-au-Pic.

365 *A belvedere* Musée régional Laure-Conan, gift of M. and Mme Georges Fournier. Print taken by the photographer Donat Girard of Pointe-au-Pic, from a negative on glass plate, about 1920.

366 *The force of panorama* Louise Crane. Photograph by Associated Screen News (Montréal), CSL 175-1, CSL 175-2.